STEMathematics: EXPLORATIONS IN APPLIED COMPUTATION AND MODELING
(Volume 1)

Elliott Ostler

© Elliott Ostler 2015

First printing 2015

All rights reserved. No part of this publication may be reproduced, stored in a retrieval system, transmitted or utilized in any form or by any means, electronic, mechanical, photocopying, recording or otherwise without permission in writing from the publisher.

>Cycloid Publications
>PO Box 572
>Elkhorn, Nebraska
>USA

Ostler, Elliott
STEMathematics: Explorations in Applied Computation and Modeling (Volume 1)

ISBN: 978-0-9966741-0-2

First Edition. Printed in the United States of America

STEMathematics: EXPLORATIONS IN APPLIED COMPUTATION AND MODELING

PREFACE

For a number of years now, mathematics teaching and learning has conformed to a relatively unimaginative series of routines and exercises that have been described by a number of mathematics education reformists as trivial, meaningless, uninspiring, and even as one mathematician put it, "soul crushing." What a way to justify the need for a book, right? Mathematics certainly does not have to be experienced that way, but it is a bit odd that a subject considered so important within the recent national STEM efforts and so fundamental in explaining the technologies we use every day, can be so poorly represented in schools. Assumptions aside, we surely recognize that mathematics is poorly represented in schools. There is a mountain of evidence that tells us we have a lot to improve. We have worked for decades to understand why the American education system has produced fewer and fewer students who are prepared to tackle math-intensive college degrees and careers, and in the wake of declining interest and falling university mathematics enrollments, we have labored like zealots to create Standards that should better define how we need to proceed, but with little success.

As frustrating as the problems seem to be, the causes are not really what most of us who are in the field would consider a mystery. The problems in teaching mathematics at the secondary level are actually quite well understood by mathematics education professionals. Many educators can point to specific, realistic solutions to the problems we currently face but the culture of today's public schooling system and the differing perceptions about what determines "successful mathematics education" has slowed worthwhile reform efforts to a virtual standstill. The result is a system of education where teachers, lawmakers, and educational reformers have a difficult time agreeing on what kinds of mathematics should be valued and how a conceptual understanding of mathematics can actually be measured. What most of us do agree on, however, is that the majority of American secondary students find their mathematics curriculum and instruction to be trivial, meaningless, uninspiring, and quite possibly soul crushing. As harsh as that assessment may sound, the discouraging reality is that there is simply too much compelling, research-based evidence published every year to suggest otherwise. Something clearly needs to change because a lot appears to be wrong, but there is a silver lining. Teachers can still inspire students if they choose to be knowledgeable enough in their field to show how mathematics can be interesting and useful, both within and beyond the concepts they are required to teach. It should never be the case that a teacher of mathematics does not see the intellectual merit or application of what they are teaching, but far too often, it is.

So what mathematics is important to learn? Certainly those who are in charge of drafting documents like the Common Core State Standards are sure they know. Other groups who would embrace a completely different set of skills are as equally confident. Who is right, and why? Admittedly these sound like complex questions, and indeed we have debated this issue nonstop, but the answer is actually very simple. All math is important... depending on your perspective. But for some reason, we have convinced ourselves that we all have to know the same things and that we have to learn those things in the same way. What could be more uninspiring than that? I recently visited a small used-book store and in the mathematics section, which contained a pretty meager selection (in my opinion), there were 37 different titles represented. Not 37 books where five were geometry, seven were algebra, etcetera. No, I mean books on 37 different kinds of mathematics. Most of these were fat books too; the kinds of books that intimidate you just by looking at the table of contents. I sometimes feel like my degree programs in mathematics failed me because there is so much I do not understand. I think this until I remember how much there is to know about the world. And yet to be quite honest, I am not really interested in understanding the entire world. You could not coerce me to be interested in some of those mathematical topics no matter how hard you tried, and most mathematicians probably would feel the same way. Certainly many school students feel this way.

We have a finite amount of time in which to learn things, and for all intents and purposes, an infinite number of things to learn. Given this fact, does it not make sense to be thoughtful about what we choose to spend our time learning? So why then do we go to such lengths to apply a one size fits all curriculum to a diverse group of young learners that we know have different backgrounds, needs, interests, abilities, and goals? It is especially perplexing for me to reflect on the nature of the Standards documents in mathematics and observe how many of them proclaim, with great confidence, what students should know, but never broach the subject of how the knowledge should be learned or applied, nor indeed, why what has been selected on behalf of the students is important in the first place. I have never witnessed a single reasonable justification about *how* students should learn within a standards document, other than the popular catch phrases and campaign slogans about how important it is to be able to think and solve problems in the 21st century, but those are not really what I am talking about. By the way, most of those 37 titles of math books I mentioned were targeting some specific application of mathematics and discussed at length why the content was necessary. Most made a very compelling case about why what they were sharing was important. The mathematics standards should be at least equally compelling. If we dare to think beyond the standards, what would help students become more excited about learning mathematics?

One emerging educational trend that may help to provide context and engagement for 21st century mathematics teaching and learning is the meta-disciplinary view of Science, Technology, Engineering, and Mathematics (STEM). Of course the idea of integrating mathematics with other content disciplines is not as novel as many STEM reformists would have you believe but the popularity of the STEM movement does help pave the way for motivating new possibilities. STEM is not important simply because STEM reformists tell us it is important, mind you. STEM can help define what mathematics is important from different points of view. It is important because it can help broaden our perceptions of how math is used in different environments. It is important because *how* individuals are *engaged* in learning is much more important than *what* they are learning, and this is a point that cannot be emphasized enough. The response... more Standards documents that have been eagerly provided by nearly every professional STEM related organization, state boards of education; and now of course we are blessed with Common Core State Standards. Does it strike you as curious that these documents dedicate much less time describing what mathematical learning experiences should look like, and so much on what math content should look like? Further, the mathematical content that the framers of these documents have determined to be necessary fills every minute of the school year, effectively eliminating the possibility of looking at anything in depth. But what if something is interesting to students and they want to know more about it? Too bad, no time.

Integrated STEM, on the other hand, can provide meaningful contexts, challenges, excitement, and motivation in a math classroom in ways that the mathematics curriculum on its own cannot promise. Engaging, unique looks at STEM integrated content is critical for motivating students because learners will not invest themselves in content they consider tedious. They will invest themselves even less if the way in which the content is presented is not engaging. And this is not something that we should blame on the hubris of youth. No one, given a choice, would select a boring topic over an interesting one. So, the most profound impact of the STEM movement is that it may help motivate mathematics teachers to bring new resources, perspectives, and *methods* into their classrooms. In fact, it is because of my own research in STEM that I asked myself some simple questions that led to the decision to write this book.

Is it possible that mathematics teachers struggle to inspire their students because they themselves find the math they are teaching trivial, meaningless, uninspiring, or... soul crushing? Some probably do. Is it because they view successful mathematics learning within the very narrow parameters of textbook problems and believe that only a few gifted students are really able to learn math? Some probably do. Or perhaps because they hold the perception that all you need to do mathematics is paper, pencil, and maybe a calculator, and there is no other way to learn it than to buckle down and practice hundreds upon hundreds of problems. Some probably do. I know of many teachers (a large number holding Masters Degrees in mathematics) who consider themselves competent mathematicians because they can do textbook problems. Yet, when asked to adapt their knowledge to other settings they often have difficulties seeing what others who are not well versed in math might call *obvious*. They are often even very slow at solving simple textbook problems taken out of context, and yet they often embrace timed testing. This observation is not meant as a criticism, but rather as a way to justify why we need to teach mathematics differently. If mathematicians have difficulties applying what they know, what hope do the unconverted masses have?

The reasons the mathematicians I was describing have difficulty solving relatively simple problems is more than likely because they typically operate within narrowly defined ways of thinking despite the fact that they really do have lots of mathematical knowledge. They have not had the right *experiences* to recognize innovative ways to use their mathematical tools. The mathematics texts from which they learn do not provide mathematical perspectives, only proofs, demonstration exercises, and practice problems; and so we have produced generations of mathematics teachers who are great at doing textbook problems but are reticent to try looking at other perspectives, even in subjects as closely related as physics. Mathematicians need to see mathematics in much broader terms so they can help their students see mathematics in much broader terms. They need to see how and why certain types of maths emerged the way they did. They need to understand the historical influences of mathematics on society. To do this, they must actively seek new perspectives and learn new applications. Most of all, they need to find interactive ways to share these ideas with their students.

PURPOSE AND SCOPE

STEMathematics is a book written primarily for secondary level math teachers but other curious learners may find the topics interesting as well. The book you are reading is written as a series of articles designed to help teachers generate new ideas for their students by presenting unique mathematical connections and phenomena. Some of the articles are long and focus on math such as calculus and parametric equations. Some are as short as a few pages and focus on very simple but unique applications of arithmetic. All of the content falls within the scope of the contemporary, Standards-based, secondary level mathematics curriculum, but it explores the topics from unique and interconnected STEM-based perspectives, and in a way that is designed to help teachers become better applied mathematicians. It is the kind of book I wish I had when I was learning math the first time. There are no proofs, practice exercises, lesson plans, timed tests, or worksheets for students. The book is simply a series of mathematical explorations that describe how parts of our world work. They can be read for general information or researched deeply for conceptual understandings. The reader does, however, need to keep in mind that the resource is designed for math teachers and not for scientists or engineers. For that reason, the articles are limited in scope to ideas that, with some imagination, can be adapted to the secondary mathematics classroom.

Twenty articles are generally themed around integrated STEM perspectives and focus on applications that describe the physical world. The first section, in which the articles are more traditional math, emphasizes thinking in terms of coordinate geometry and other applied mathematical perspectives. In some sense this was inspired by Newton's *Mathematical Principles of Natural Philosophy*; not in content, but in its efforts to explain the world around us through the language of mathematics. Section Two begins to provide tangible applications of algebra and geometry by describing a number of mathematical *devices*. These devices are essentially *machines* that have no moving parts, and which rely on the interplay of geometric relationships to function. Further, the section re-purposes the term *Mathematical Engineering*. Section

Three extends the idea of applied geometric devices by introducing the concept of engineering more formally. This is accomplished by describing physical models of the geometric structures presented in the first two chapters by presenting a number of mechanical devices. Section Four provides a number of unique, integrated mathematical principles from physics, mechanical engineering, and product design.

As I close, one quick disclaimer is probably appropriate. Mathematics describes, in one form or another, virtually every aspect of our world so it is impossible to provide a resource that will interest everyone or honor all the important mathematics there is to know. There is simply too much to learn, and therefore, too much to include. The main difficulty I had in writing STEMathematics (*Volume One*) was not selecting topics or completing the articles, but rather, deciding what to omit. I have no doubt that some readers will decide that I have selected all the wrong topics. To them I would happily suggest that they submit ideas for *Volume Two*. The articles contained herein really just represent jumping off points for investigating other areas of STEM. It is my hope that after reading one, some, or all of the articles in this book, you will have discovered something that you might like to explore in more detail; and if you teach math, I hope that you find something new to share with your students. Enjoy.

Contents

PREFACE 3

SECTION 1: SIGNIFICANT EQUATIONS AND APPLIED GEOMETRY 12

    ARTICLE 1: SEGMENTS AND CIRCLES 13

    ARTICLE 2: ELLIPSE CONSTRUCTIONS 31

    USING A STRAIGHT EDGE 31

    ARTICLE 3: THE BRACHISTOCHRONE PROBLEM 46

    ARTICLE 4: GUILLOCHE PATTERNS AND APPLIED PARAMETRIC EQUATIONS 62

    ARTICLE 5: PI 78

    ARTICLE 6: THE PYTHAGOREAN THEOREM 92

SECTION 2: MATHEMATICAL "DEVICES" 110

    ARTICLE 7: NOMOGRAPHS: AN INTRODUCTION TO MATHEMATICAL ENGINEERING 111

    ARTICLE 8: THE SOLUTION SHARK: A NEW RULER TECHNOLOGY 127

    ARTICLE 9: NAPIER'S BONES AND LATTICE COMPUTATION 152

    ARTICLE 10: CONSUL THE EDUCATED MONKEY AND NUMBER PYRAMIDS 170

    ARTICLE 11: BASIC SUNDIALS AND THE MEASUREMENT OF TIME 179

SECTION 3: MECHANICAL 201

DEVICES 201

    ARTICLE 12: SEXTANTS, ASTROLABES, AND STEREOGRAPHIC PROJECTION 202

ARTICLE 13: REULEAUX POLYGONS AND DRILLING SQUARE HOLES 222

ARTICLE 14: STRAIGHT LINE LINKAGES 239
AND THE RATIO GAUGE 239

ARTICLE 15: PENDULUMS, GEARS, AND 261
GRANDFATHER CLOCKS 261

ARTICLE 16: CONSTRUCTING 282
ROBOTIC LEGS 282

SECTION 4: PHYSICS 306
AND MATH 306

ARTICLE 17: USING A MULTI-METER FOR 307
ELECTRICAL MEASUREMENTS 307

ARTICLE 18: OPTICS AND THE 336
GEOMETRY OF LIGHT 336

ARTICLE 19: ENGINEERING MECHANICS (EXPLORATIONS IN STATICS) 359

ARTICLE 20: USING CALCULUS IN PRODUCT DESIGN 371

INDEX OF ARTICLE TERMS AND AUTHORITIES....................383

SECTION 1: SIGNIFICANT EQUATIONS AND APPLIED GEOMETRY

For many of us, simply hearing the word *mathematics* conjures images of endless lists of practice exercises and formulas to memorize from some mathematics textbook. If this is true, it is enormously unfortunate, but you can consider yourself to be in good company. Over the past 50 years, the United States has been producing high school graduates that feel unprepared to take on challenging mathematics coursework in college. Much of the hopelessness they feel is due to the fact that they are never really exposed to interesting concepts that show the natural relationship between different kinds of mathematics. In general Algebra, Geometry, Advanced Algebra, Pre-Calculus, Trigonometry, and Calculus are still divided into individual *courses*, each with their own unique topics and accompanying textbook. Nothing could misrepresent the nature of mathematics more than how we have structured it in American secondary schools. Yet, the truth of the matter is that different areas of mathematics almost always relate in some ways. The integrated mathematical topics presented here in *Section One* will begin to illustrate how much there still is to know about familiar topics. The mathematical concepts presented in *Section One* are as follows:

Article 1: Segments and the Circle
Article 2: Ellipse Construction Methods Using a Straight Edge
Article 3: The Brachistochrone Problem
Article 4: Guilloche Patterns and Parametric Equations
Article 5: Pi
Article 6: Pythagorean Theorem

ARTICLE 1: SEGMENTS AND CIRCLES

ABSTRACT: The Segments and Circles manuscript overviews some of the lesser known relationships that can be applied within intersections and segments associated with circular regions. Specifically, measurements and constructions related to the Vesica Piscis, geometric applications of the chord-chord power theorem, trigonometric measurements, and segment-chord calculations are presented.

INTRODUCTION

The circle has sometimes been referred to as the *anchor* of geometry. Indeed this is quite a statement considering that the circle is really just a uniformly curving line in a plane that meets itself where it starts. In some ways, exploring geometry can really be thought of as an evolution of our understandings of a circle because it is one of the few mathematical ideas we learn as very young children and continue to explore as we progress through school. Even now applications of the circle continue to provide opportunities for new scientific and engineering advancements, which is what connects it nicely with emerging national STEM efforts.

Let us suppose for a moment that we wanted to summarize ideas about circles, and about segments related to circles. What should we include? *Pi* for sure because it is arguably the most familiar number in the world. *Radius* would probably be included because without it we cannot really even tactically define a circle. *Diameter*, *Circumference*, and *Chord* all make sense too. But how about the Vesica Piscis? Or maybe the Sagitta? Many of us are not familiar with these terms, but even if we are, that does not necessarily mean we know about circles and circle relationships from a tactical STEM standpoint. What I mean is that we may not know about how circles can be used as tools. Although a circle is not typically thought of as a device for performing tasks such as measuring line segments and angles, calculating roots, constructing polygons, determining trigonometric ratios, or even completing more complex tasks like mapping stereographic projections, those are actually just a few of the engineering applications associated with this deceptively simple figure. The *Segments and Circles* article will not present topics such as stereographic projections but it will describe various constructions of circle segments, geometrically define trigonometric ratios, and examine special intersections that can be used for making physical measurements.

INVESTIGATION AND NOTES

We will begin this section by demonstrating the predictability of various segment measurements, which can be shown to have incremental square roots within the two overlapping circles as seen in Figure 1.1. The football shaped region created in the intersection is most commonly recognized as a *Venn diagram*, which originated with the writings of a 19th century English logician named John Venn. The Venn diagram is most commonly used in Set Theory and probability but has many other applications as well. Much earlier this overlapping region was referred to as the *Vesica Piscis* and routinely appeared in forms of sacred geometry. The term Vesica Piscis can be roughly interpreted as "fish container."

The Vesica Piscis can be found in the intersection of two circles having equal radii and overlapping such that each circle passes through the center point of the other. For our purposes we will assume that circles A and B (Figure 1.1) each have a radius of 1 unit. The line segment AB of length 1 unit connects the center points of the two circles. Perpendiculars are then constructed through points A and B such that they create parallel diameters identified by intersections at points C, D, E, and F.

Figure 1.1: Vesica Piscis and root segments

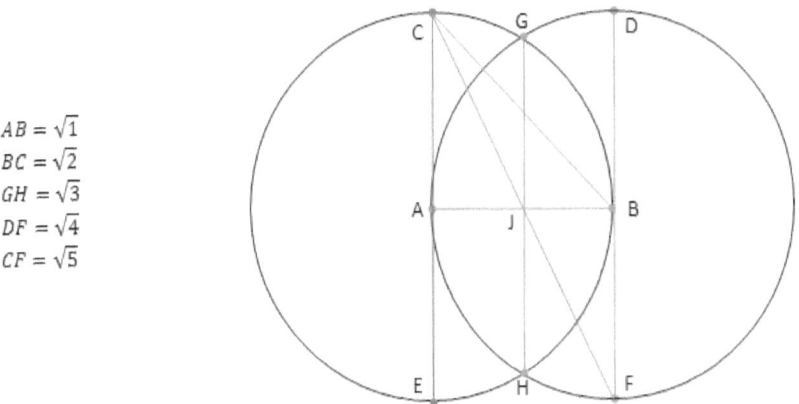

$AB = \sqrt{1}$
$BC = \sqrt{2}$
$GH = \sqrt{3}$
$DF = \sqrt{4}$
$CF = \sqrt{5}$

The circles intersect at points G and H. The center of the entire figure is located at point J. Given the arrangement of segments related to the Vesica Piscis, the segments noted in Figure 1.1 can be approximately verified (by measurement) as the square roots of the first five natural numbers.

The ratios found within the Vesica Piscis also set the stage for the constructions of regular polygons. Connecting the segments from the top of the Vesica to each circle's center point creates an equilateral triangle having unit length sides. Further, if we extend segment AB to create diameters for each large circle, connecting the top and bottom of the Vesica to the outer end of either diameter creates an equilateral triangle inscribed perfectly in the circle and thus verifying the measurements associated with the central angle theorem and the *inscribed angle theorem* (see Figure 1.2).

Figure 1.2: Vesica Piscis and triangles

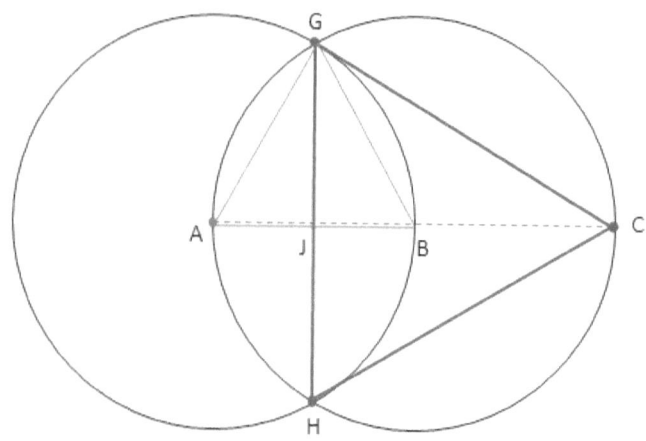

By observing the various intersections of two circles, we have been able to generate line segments of predictable length as well as creating some of the first mathematically precise regular polygons. Because we also know that the simplest regular polygons generally have interior angles that are factors of 360 degrees, we can easily construct regular polygons having sides of 3, 4, 5, 6, and 8 sides using three intersecting circles and their resulting Vesica regions. The most amazing part of these constructions is that no measurements or calculations are necessary. The polygons shown immediately hereafter are not inscribed polygons, but note how the angles needed for the development of each of these regular polygons is defined by the intersections of the three circles (Figures 1.3 and 1.4). All of the polygons use the segment AB as a base, and then use points A and B as vertices for each polygon. Note also that point F represents the center of arc AB. The construction of the triangle and square are apparent based on previous illustrations. The pentagon is constructed by using segment AB as a base and connecting points A and B to where the dashed segments defined by EF and CF intersect the circles.

Figure 1.3: Three-Circle Vesica for Creating Triangle, Square, and Pentagon

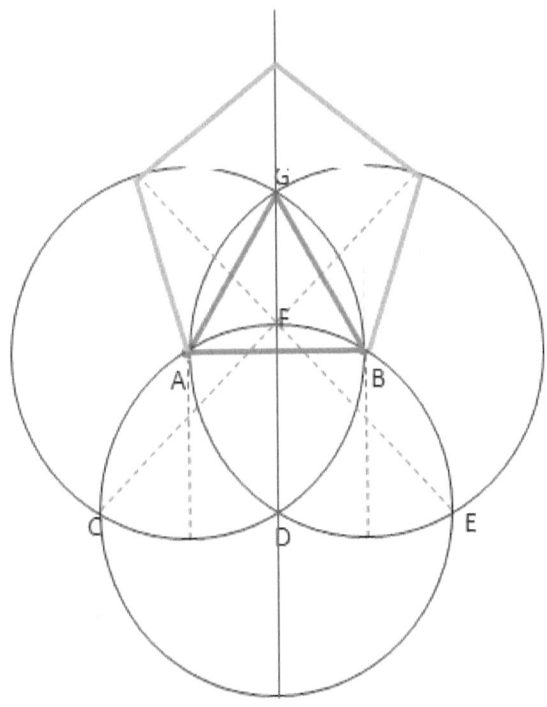

Figure 1.4: Three-Circle Vesica for Creating Hexagon and Octagon

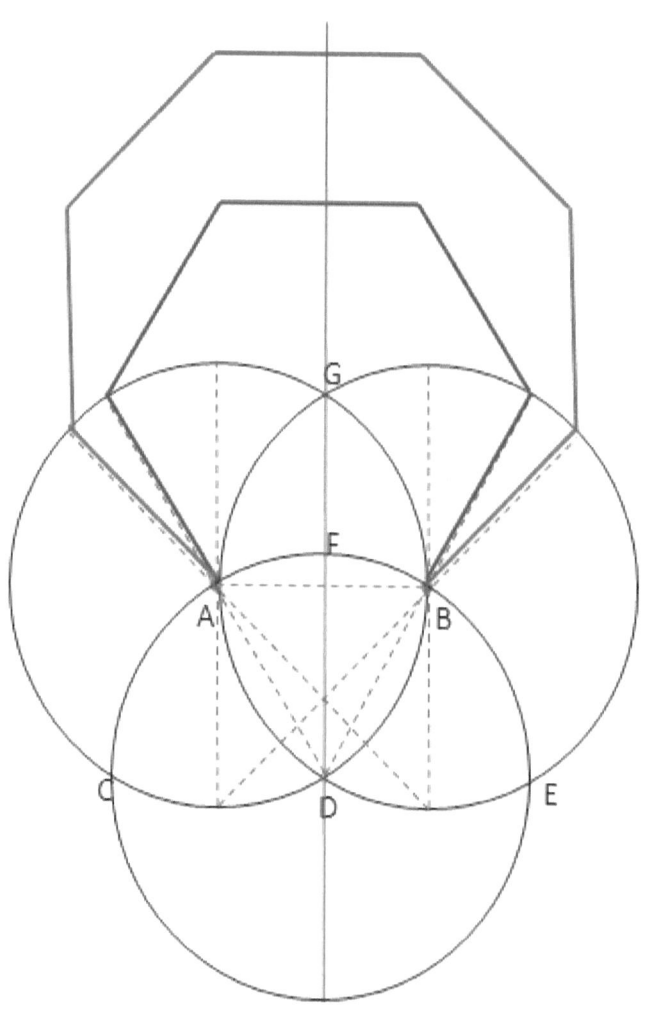

The intersections within the Vesica arrangements establish angle measurements of 60, 90, 108, 120, and 135 degrees respectively. The 108 degree angle in particular is valuable because of the ability to combine it with other angles to create other less common angle sums and differences. The proofs or *verifications* of these angle sums and differences have not been included in this section, but the realization of the methods allowed early mathematicians to create angle measurement tools that were accurate to the degree. It should be noted, as well, that the polygons created above can all be *inscribed* within a single circle using similar techniques for finding the intersections and relationships in the interior segments.

From here we will continue by generating relationships for random chords within the circle that will ultimately allow us to use the circle as a tool for "squaring" rectangles. We will proceed with a general and familiar set of developmental verifications for *inscribed angle* measures versus *central angle* measures. This will help us develop the triangle similarities needed for verifying the *Chord-Chord Power Theorem*. Once done, we will have a circular tool for measuring and calculating square roots other than those illustrated in Figure 1.1.

Figure 1.5 illustrates that the ratio between a *central angle* and an *inscribed angle* is 2:1. That is to say that a central angle measures twice an inscribed angle subtending the same arc. Assume we subtend the arc AC with a randomly inscribed angle ABC and a central angle ADC. To verify the relationship, we will extend a diametric segment BE and use the resulting triangles to establish the ratio. Because all segments extending from the center point D must be a radius and therefore congruent, we have created two isosceles triangles, ABD and DBC. Angle DAB is congruent to angle ABD; likewise, angle DBC is congruent to angle BCD.

Figure 1.5: Central-Inscribed Angle Verification

Given: $\triangle ABD = 180$
$\triangle DBC = 180$
$\angle BDE = 180$ (by def. of straight angle)

Verify: $2(\angle ABC) = \angle ADC$

$\angle DAB = \angle ABD$
$\angle DAB + \angle ABD + \angle ADB = \angle ADB + \angle ADE$
$\angle DAB + \angle ABD = \angle ADE$
$2(\angle ABD) = \angle ADE$
$2(\angle DBE) = \angle EDC$ (by same method)
$2(\angle ABD) + 2(\angle DBE) = \angle ADE + \angle EDC$
$2(\angle ABD + \angle DBC) = \angle ADC$
Q.E.D. $2(\angle ABC) = \angle ADC$

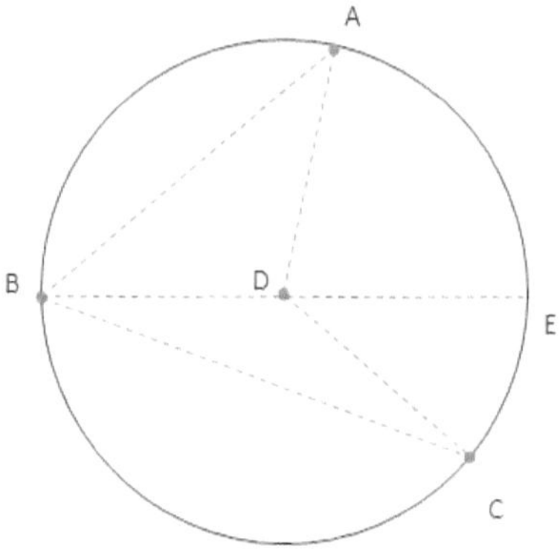

Because we have now verified that an inscribed angle measures half of the central angle intersecting the same points on the circle, and by definition, half of the arc it subtends, we can now use the circle to create perfect right angles simply by inscribing an angle that subtends any diametric arc. This is one of the most powerful properties of a circle because, once verified, it is no longer necessary to assume that perpendicular intersections exist. From a practical standpoint, a circle can be used to create measurements associated with Pythagorean triples and trigonometric ratios.

So far there have been no surprises. We will continue with one more verification so as not to make assumptions about reliability of using our circle as a measurement tool. It will be helpful to establish a relationship between intersecting chords in a circle. The verification to be presented is commonly referred to as the *Chord-Chord Power Theorem* or the Intersecting Chords Power Theorem. There are various other names as well that appear in contemporary math books such as the Crossing Chords Product rule, but they all mean the same thing. Suppose that two randomly placed chords AB and CD intersect in a circle at point P. Verify that the product of the segments of chord AB is equal to the product of the segments of chord CD (Figure 1.6). We will first connect the end points of the chords creating segments AC and BD. This is done so that we may use properties of similar triangles and thus, create proportions using the segments of each triangle.

We can easily verify that triangles ACP and PBD are similar to one another by demonstrating congruence between of pairs of angles. We know, for instance, that angles ACD and ABD are congruent because they subtend the same arc AD. The same is true for angles CAB and CDB. They must be congruent because they both subtend the arc CB. The angles opposite one another at point P are congruent because they are vertical angles. Therefore with paired angles having equal measures, we have identified triangles ACP and PBD as similar. Because we also know that matching parts of similar triangles must be similar, we can establish proportions using the segments shown in Figure 1.6. The verification is extremely simple in that it only requires us to set up the proportions and then cross multiply to verify the Chord-Chord Power Theorem.

(Diagram can be found on the following page)

Figure 1.6: Chord-Chord Power Theorem Verification

Given: △ACP ~ △DBP

Verify: AP·PB = CP·PD

       AP/PD = CP/PB
Q.E.D. AP·PB = CP·PD

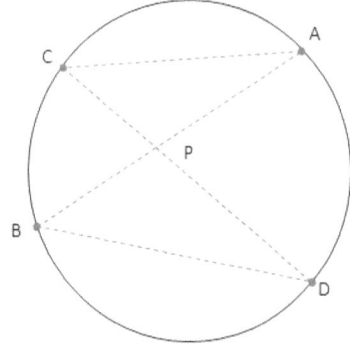

    We have now arrived at the point where we can start using the circle as a measurement tool. The Chord-Chord Power Theorem provides a nice tool for calculating square roots by *measuring*. If the crossing chords consist of a diameter and a perpendicular segment, then the segment perpendicular to the diameter must be split into two even segments, which can be written as a numeric square (Figure 1.7). Suppose the vertical segment represents a diameter and the horizontal segment intersects the diameter at a right angle. By moving the horizontal segment to a point where it divides the vertical segment into some desired proportion, say for example 1 inch and 3 inches, which have a product of 3, then the horizontal segments must also have a product of 3. The horizontal segments, having the same product, means that one of the segments, measuring from the point of intersection to the edge of the circle, must measure the square root of 3, or about 1.73 inches. We can actually verify this by measuring with a ruler, and thus we have discovered a way to use a circle as a tool for literally measuring the value of square roots.

Figure 1.7: Circle used for measuring square roots

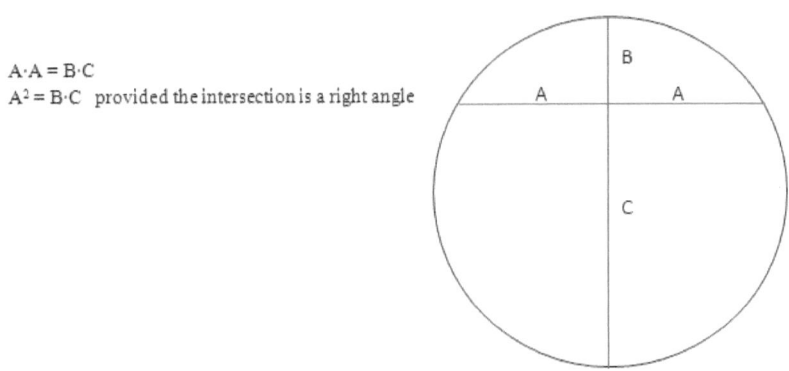

A·A = B·C
A² = B·C provided the intersection is a right angle

Given the nature of this discovery, it must now be possible to use the circle as a tool for other constructions and measurements. One such construction is the process of *squaring* a rectangle. This process can generally be thought of as an "engineering" procedure whereby we design, using geometric tools, a method for completing some ostensibly unrelated task. Suppose we have a rectangle measuring 9 units on the base and 4 units in height. The area of this rectangle can obviously be calculated at 36 square units. The Chord-Chord Power Theorem is then used as a way to construct the *Geometric Mean* of the rectangle, which is essentially the process of finding the square root of the product of the sides representing the area. A square with an area of 36 square units and a side length of 6 units is the result. We will demonstrate the general case of the process geometrically (Figure 1.8).

Figure 1.8: Squaring a rectangle

Step 1: Begin with a rectangle
Step 2: Extend the top segment of the rectangle by H.
Step 3: Bisect the new top segment (point M)
Step 4: Using point M as the center, construct a circle using half the sum of the length and width of the rectangle as the radius
Step 5: Construct the segment S as an extension of rectangle side H to the point on the circle
Step 6: Construct the square using the magnitude of S.

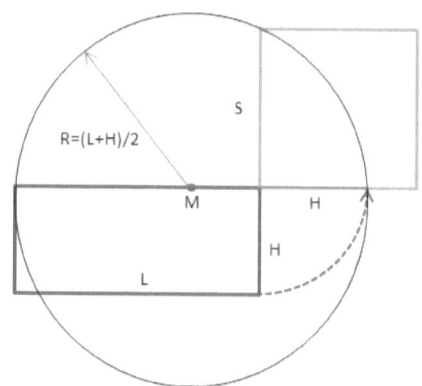

Note that the construction process for squaring a rectangle uses nothing more than the Chord-Chord Power Theorem. That is to say, based on the verification provided back in Figure 1.7, we can say that $M \cdot H = S^2$ but also represent the product geometrically. We have then *engineered* a geometric method for illustrating the geometric mean. By extension, this method gives us tools to transform any right triangle into a right isosceles triangle, which, in turn, gives us new tools for verifying triangle theorems. Additionally, we can use what we now know about chords to derive formulas for calculating various irregularly shaped regions within the circle. The *segment* is one such shape, but all calculations such as that used for the segment presume that the radius of the circle is a known value.

Now, what if we want to continue by calculating the area of a circular region and are only able to measure the length of a chord and the *versine* of a given angle? A common question at this point is, "what is the versine?" The versine is a rarely used trigonometric function. It is a perpendicular bisecting segment for a chord that connects the chord to the middle of the arc it subtends (Figure 1.9). The versine is also sometimes referred to as the *Sagitta*. Another way to visualize the versine is as the difference between the radius of a circle and the *apothem* of regular figure inscribed in the circle (i.e. apothem + versine = radius). Note that using this method in a practical way does require us to be able to measure both the chord and the versine. There are a number of other ways to obtain the radius as well. A general case using the chord relationships given in Figure 1.7 is presented.

In this example, V represents the versine, C is the chord length, and the diameter of the circle is represented in terms of twice the radius. Once again relying on the Chord-Chord Power Theorem, the product can be represented by the diameter segments $V \cdot (2r - V) = (C/2)^2$. Keep in mind that we are solving for the radius so that other circular regions can be calculated as well as the area associated with the segment between the chord and its corresponding arc.

(Diagram can be found on the following page)

Figure 1.9: *Calculating radius using the Chord-Versine relationship*

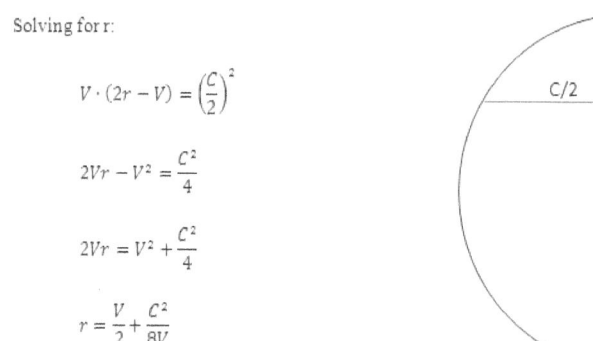

Solving for r:

$$V \cdot (2r - V) = \left(\frac{C}{2}\right)^2$$

$$2Vr - V^2 = \frac{C^2}{4}$$

$$2Vr = V^2 + \frac{C^2}{4}$$

$$r = \frac{V}{2} + \frac{C^2}{8V}$$

Before we conclude with a final look at some additional segments associated with a circle, two other things are probably worth mentioning. First, this article is brief. There is clearly much more to know about the mathematics of the circle than could possibly be presented here. The proofs and verifications for the relationships presented in most academic resources are abundant, and are generally designed for the sake of mathematical discovery and not necessarily for their potential in applied settings. Nevertheless, they are worth exploring because *mental engineering* often comes from theory transforming into some seemingly obscure application.

Some other topics related to circles have been passed over deliberately because they will surface in subsequent articles. Others still are beyond the scope of this manuscript. At any rate, the current article will conclude with a number of bibliographic citations that provide additional insights into the mathematics of the circle for those who may be interested in knowing more. Secondly, the discoveries and verifications presented thus far have been focused on the *measurement* of segments and angles within and around the circle, this to better allow the reader to adapt the topics to the applied nature of STEM. We will carry this theme into the last presentation as well; however, we will finally place the circle on the Cartesian plane so we can explore the measurement aspects more concretely.

In more formal mathematics, the circle has a number of representations. It can be represented in Cartesian form: $(x - h)^2 + (y - k)^2 = r^2$, or in polar form: $x = a + \cos t; y = b + \sin t$. But so far we have not concerned ourselves with the specific position of our circle. This is because we have not needed to know a specific location to complete our verifications. Occasionally, though, it can be helpful to identify graphical points on a circle because they simultaneously give us a frame of reference for locations and distances. Such is the case with a standard unit circle, which is seen so routinely in trigonometry. In fact, trigonometry is the focus of our last verification. By positioning a unit circle on a coordinate plane with a center point of (0,0) we are able to *measure* various segments simply by looking at their positions graphically. For example, in the first quadrant of a unit circle, the x and y coordinate points on the circle are defined by ($\cos \theta$, $\sin \theta$) but those trigonometric ratios are actually horizontal and vertical distances that can be measured by counting on a graph, or more accurately by using a ruler. The sine and cosine functions of course are obvious because they actually define the coordinate values of the points on the circle itself. The graphs of the other trigonometric ratios are typically presented as functions in terms of radians and so it is a bit unusual to see how the segments they represent connect to the unit circle. Figure 1.10 illustrates versions of all six trigonometric functions placed in reference to the unit circle. Note that these are ratios that can all be measured with a standard ruler, and which also correspond to distances on a graph.

Figure 1.10: Trigonometric functions on the unit circle

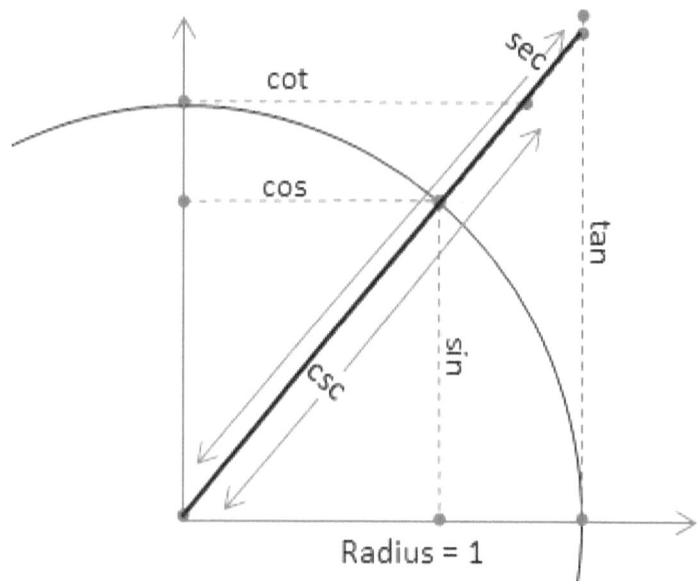

Note how easily the Pythagorean identities can be verified within this arrangement of the segments in a circle. The right triangle arrangements of the segments illustrate this concept extremely well. Also, the ratio identities can be demonstrated quite nicely. For example the quotient of $\sin\theta/\cos\theta$ being equivalent to $\tan\theta/1$ is apparent when we examine the proportion of the triangles containing the sin and cos segments next to the tan and the radius. There are a few other arrangements of segments which demonstrate trigonometric ratios as well. All of them can be verified by measurement and so they can easily be justified as mental engineering applications.

SUMMARY

The circle is certainly a figure that is both simple and complex. Many more circle applications and relationships will be demonstrated in a number of articles throughout the book. The potential to *measure* the trigonometric segments using a ruler represents some great examples for applied engineering based projects, and this fashion of *mental engineering* is one of the goals of the book. For the most part, the idea of using a circle as a tool is a bit foreign to mathematicians because the circle is worthy of study on its intellectual merits alone. Yet in the context of STEM, knowing some common circle applications may be helpful in understanding the overall properties of design. In fact, we will revisit the idea of a circle in Article 20.

The current article worked systematically through verifying the measurements of both angles and segments simply by overlapping circles in a predictable way. Methods for relating segments within circles were then presented and ultimately applied to the task of *squaring* a rectangle. The same Chord-Chord relationship was then used to determine the radius of a circle and ultimately, we evolved the chord relationships into the idea of comparing the triangle segments that are most commonly used for trigonometry. The fact that many of these geometric investigations can be experienced in a tangible way lends a great deal of credence to the idea of STEM itself. The best learning is often interactive and found lurking in many of the concepts we already know.

ADDITIONAL READINGS

Beckman, P. (1971). *A History of Pi*. Macmillian: New York. ISBN - 9780312381851

Lawlor, R. (1982). Sacred Geometry: Philosophy and Practice (Art and Imagination). Thames & Hudson. ISBN: 978-0500810309

Schneider, M.S. (1995). A Beginner's Guide to Constructing the Universe: Mathematical Archetypes of Nature, Art, and Science. ISBN – 978-0060926717

ARTICLE 2: ELLIPSE CONSTRUCTIONS USING A STRAIGHT EDGE

ABSTRACT: This article describes several methods and algebraic verifications for defining and sketching elliptical paths using a partitioned straight edge. Specifically, the Trammel method, the Parallelogram method, and two circle methods will be presented. Applications of the ellipse in physics and engineering will also be described.

INTRODUCTION

Though the *ellipse* is very similar in shape and Cartesian formula to the popular circle (in fact, the circle is a special form of the ellipse), it is probably one of the most underrepresented figures in computational forms of geometry and pre-calculus algebra. The ellipse is typically studied in the context of conic sections and is simply the result of the intersection of a right circular cone and a plane in such a way that a closed curve is produced. In analytic geometry the ellipse is described as the locus of all points in a plane such that the sum of the distances to two focal points is a constant value. Just as is the case with circles, the ellipse can be represented using a number of different formulas including Cartesian and polar forms. But the functional study of ellipses is typically fairly limited in scope and rarely includes a description of applications outside of traditional analytic geometry. For example, many people can recite the formula used to calculate the area of a circle. Some of these people may even have seen various methods for deriving that area formula. But the same is not true for an ellipse even though the area formula is very similar. Further, very few people have seen or even understand the derivation of the formula for calculating the area of an ellipse.

Applications of elliptical forms are numerous and have greatly influenced advancements in science, engineering and technology through the *enlightened* ages, which is why the topic is being presented in this book. For example, in science both Kepler and Newton used data from elliptical orbits for deriving the First Law of Planetary Motion and the Law of Universal Gravitation. Elliptical sections are also used in physics as reflectors for capturing and emitting sound and light waves. Further, they are used in mechanics for devices like gears to improve efficiency in angular speed and torque for bicycles. As a side note, elliptical paths and graphs are even used to describe phenomenon in statistics and finance, but that is a step back toward theoretical application and those ideas are generally not explored herein.

Unlike traditional presentations of ellipses as formula-based conic sections however, this article will focus on the physical construction of ellipses using a straight edge. The methods are presented as a way to build an understanding of how elliptical points are distributed and how the methods used for constructing ellipses may be used to influence the development of new mathematical and engineering devices, so let us begin.

INVESTIGATION AND NOTES

This section will begin with a short description of how the most familiar and common method for drawing an ellipse leads naturally to a number of applications. The method is commonly referred to as the "pin and string" method, and takes advantage of the definition of an ellipse, so let us revisit that definition. An ellipse is a closed figure where the sum of the distances from the ellipse to two fixed interior points is a constant value.

In Figure 2.1, we can observe the two points, labeled f_1 and f_2 as the focal points. From each of these points a string is pulled taught and used to define the locus of points enclosing the foci by drawing around them. It would make sense how acoustic devices, for instance, could leverage this idea into a usable tool since all sound waves generated at one focal point and going toward the other would travel the exact same distance and therefore arrive at the opposite focus at the same time. The same would be true for many devices omitting or collecting any kind of electromagnetic radiation such as radio waves or even light.

Figure 2.1: The Pin and String Method

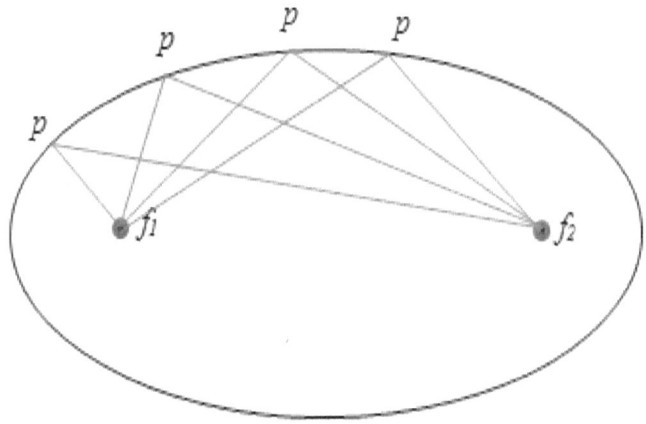

Two focal points are defined in the diagram by the two points f_1 and f_2. The string is then pulled tight and the ellipse is drawn around the foci. The pin and string method does not require a straight edge for construction but it does provide some clues about the definition of an ellipse and how it is connected to the idea of geometric constructions. A question that may emerge is do *straight edge* methods exist for constructing an ellipse? And why do we need them if the pin and string method is so simple? The truth is that the pin and string method is simply not that practical in some instances despite the fact that it illustrates the very definition of the ellipse. Figure 2.2 illustrates a lesser known method called the *trammel method*, which provides some additional value in constructing an ellipse.

This method uses a marked straight edge such as a ruler and allows us to have complete control over the shape of the ellipse. The lengths of the major and minor axes can be selected by marking points on the straight edge. For the ellipse in Figure 2.2, a defined length a is selected as the *semi-major axis* and is the distance from the arrow at the point marked on the ruler to the right end of the ruler. Another value b is used for the *semi-minor axis* and is the distance from the arrow at point b to the right end of the ruler. Once points a and b are marked on the ruler, we can draw any number of points outlining the elliptical path by rotating the ruler by small increments, being sure to always keep point b on the x-axis and point a on the y-axis. We do this by using the arrow at each of the points. The points of the ellipse are then drawn at the end of the ruler. Typically the ruler will be moved in small increments. The following figure illustrates that no matter how a trammel is moved, as long as point a stays on the y-axis and point b stays on the x-axis, the end of the ruler will outline the elliptical path.

Figure 2.2: Ellipse Construction Using the Trammel Method

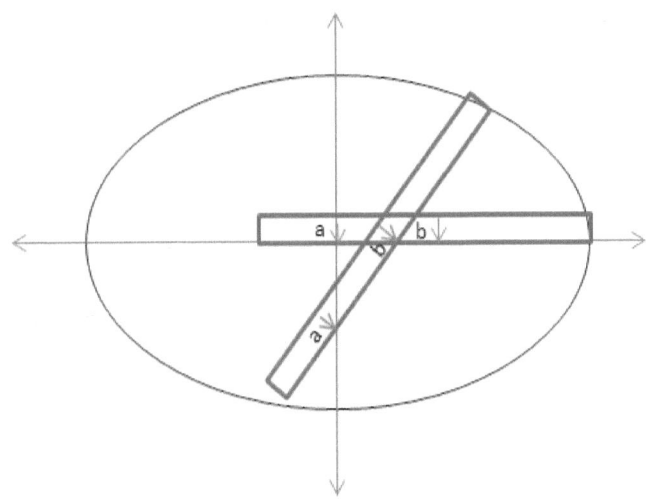

How do we know this method works? Rather than trying to guess how it was originally conceived, let us verify that the ruler segments create mathematical distances that are consistent with the way an ellipse is analytically represented. We will do this by using similar triangles and the Pythagorean Theorem. The goal will be to derive the formula for an ellipse written in standard form. The verification is presented in Figure 2.3 using points in the first quadrant.

Figure 2.3: Verification of Trammel Method

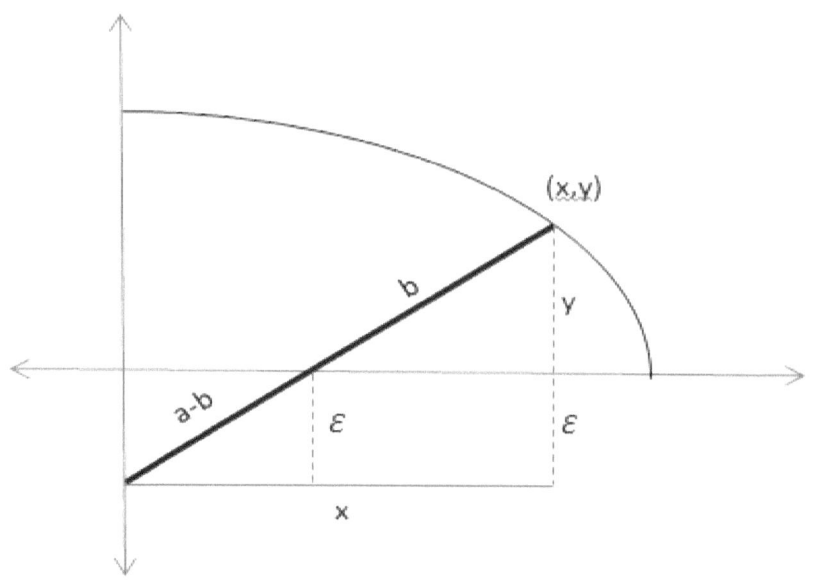

Assume that the length of the darkened trammel is *a*, which is also the length of half of the major axis. As previously described, segment *b* remains constant and extends from the *x*-axis to the point on the ellipse. For a given point (*x,y*), a set of triangles is defined. Using the Pythagorean Theorem we see the following:

$$x^2 + (y + \varepsilon)^2 = a^2$$

Using similar triangles we can represent ε as a proportion in terms of *y*, *a*, and *b*. We will use the two small triangles and solve for ε using proportions.

$$\frac{\varepsilon}{a-b} = \frac{y}{b} \quad \therefore \quad \varepsilon = \frac{y(a-b)}{b}$$

We now substitute our expression for ε into the original Pythagorean equation and simplify the result. In Step 2, we simplify inside the parentheses to a single rational expression.

$$x^2 + \left(y + \frac{y(a-b)}{b}\right)^2 = a^2$$

$$x^2 + \left(\frac{yb}{b} + \frac{ya - yb}{b}\right)^2 = a^2$$

$$x^2 + \left(\frac{yb + ya - yb}{b}\right)^2 = a^2$$

Squaring the second term to remove the parentheses and dividing through by the a squared term verifies our method. Note that we have derived the equation for the standard form of an ellipse.

$$x^2 + \left(\frac{ya}{b}\right)^2 = a^2$$

$$x^2 + \frac{y^2 a^2}{b^2} = a^2$$

$$\frac{x^2}{a^2} + \frac{y^2 a^2}{b^2 a^2} = \frac{a^2}{a^2}$$

$$\frac{x^2}{a^2} + \frac{y^2}{b^2} = 1$$

We have now demonstrated that the outer ends of the hypotenuses of the right triangular segments representing the trammel define the elliptical path by the analytic ellipse equation. Although this method is not a rigorous proof-based formula derivation, it does provide some nice insights into how algebra and Cartesian geometry connect in applied contexts. The trammel method has a history dating all the way back to Archimedes. The "trammel of Archimedes" was one of the earliest known tools for physically tracing out the path of an ellipse. Some mathematical historians refer to this tool as an ellipsograph. There are a number of other "segment" methods (that is to say, methods using segments for verification) for creating elliptical paths, and most of them rely on the same kinds of algebraic derivations as presented in the trammel method, but they are still worth examining even if the algebraic proofs become routine.

Another *segment method* used for tracing elliptical paths is the *Parallelogram method*. This method relies on a matrix of rectangular coordinates, which, when connected create a series of intersections that fall in an elliptical pattern. Suppose for example that we want to produce an ellipse that has a major axis twice that of the minor axis. We begin by outlining a rectangular pattern of points in a ratio that is the same as the ratio of the major to minor axes. Figure 2.4 presents the process. Note how the increments around the edge of the rectangle are at a ratio of 2:1 when comparing the major axis to the minor axis. We use straight segments that start at each end of the major axis and extend incrementally counter clockwise from each end of the major axis. The intersections of each pair of segments with matching numbers trace out the path of the ellipse.

Figure 2.4: Parallelogram method

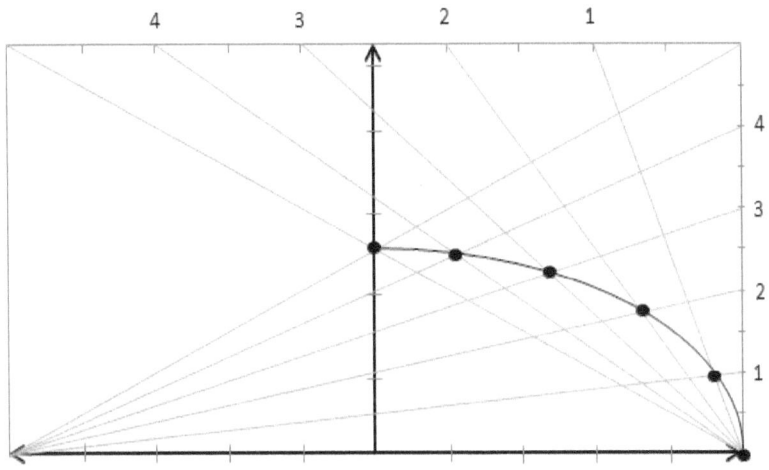

The Parallelogram method can be verified in a number of ways, again using similar triangles and other trigonometric or polar methods. For now, however, I will leave those verifications to the reader so additional methods using circles can be presented.

A fourth construction method for the ellipse takes us back to ideas about the utility of circles. Elliptical paths can be traced out very accurately by using concentric circles. The concentric circles method is also sometimes called the *draftsman's method* because it can easily be produced with a T-square or other similar device. As seen in Figure 2.5, the concentric circles method divides two concentric circles into any number of proportional sectors, which are basically pie shaped regions within a circle. By extending horizontal and vertical segments from the points where each radius intersects the circles, we see a pattern of segments intersecting at right angles that, once again, form an elliptical path through a discrete set of coordinates. Note that the semi-major axis is defined by the radius of the outer circle and the semi-minor axis is defined by the radius of the inner circle.

(Diagram can be found on the following page)

Figure 2.5: The Concentric Circles Method

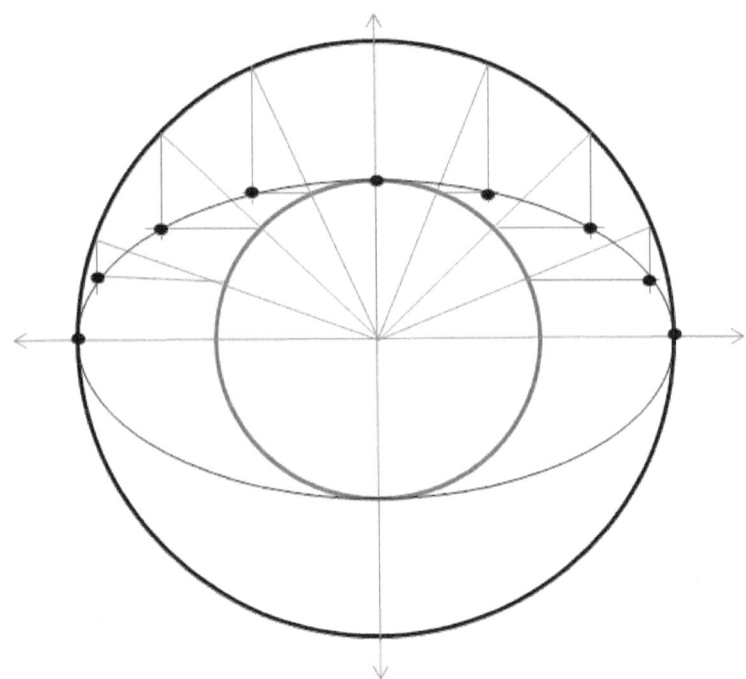

The final method presented in Figure 2.7 also uses a circle, but rather than the right angle intersections appearing from parallel and perpendicular segments coming off of the edges of the circles, as was done in Figure 2.5, we will use right angle segments created from a series of segments that originate from the elliptical foci and *glance* off of the edge of the outer circle at right angles. This method is sometimes referred to as the envelop method.

Once the focal points of the ellipse have been established, the envelop method can be used to create an elliptical path very quickly using something akin to a carpenter's triangle or even the corner of a piece of paper. Right angle segments can be drawn using any right triangle. We will begin by using a circle to define the value for the length of the major axis. The major axis of the ellipse will be equal to the diameter of the circle and the minor axis can be chosen as any value less than the diameter. The focus points can then be located geometrically by extending a segment of length *a* from the vertex of the top or bottom of the semi-minor axis to a point along the semi-major axis. The process is illustrate in Figure 2.6

Figure 2.6: Locating the Focal Points

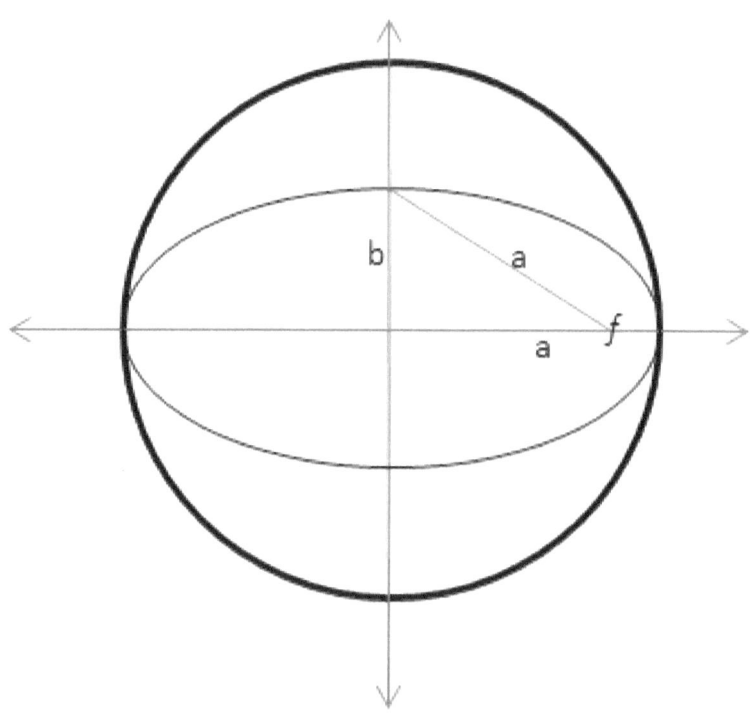

Notice that the diagonal segment *a* in Figure 2.6 can be constructed from the focus point *f* to the end of the semi-minor axis. Both focal points can be located geometrically using this method. Once the focal points have been located, we can sketch our ellipse as shown in Figure 2.7.

Figure 2.7: Constructing the Ellipse with the Envelop Method

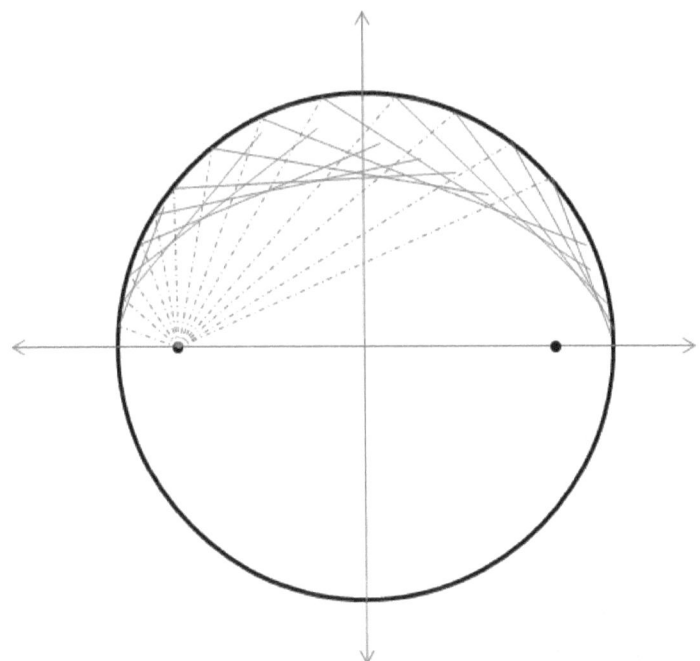

Note specifically how the orthogonal segments to those originating from the left side focus point create what are essentially a set of tangent lines to the ellipse. An infinite number of tangent lines would define the elliptical path. One other idea that is noteworthy about this method is that only one focus point is needed to sketch the entire ellipse. This was an idea that helped lend credence to Kepler's First Law of Planetary Motion. Although the envelop method was not used in its exact form, the observation and recording of heavenly bodies typically happened by tracking motion of an object around a single focus point rather than around two specifically plotted foci. The focus point was normally an object, like a planet or star. Other applications of ellipses are available for the keen observer.

SUMMARY

Many other interesting examples of ellipses can be found in engineering and science. For example, the cross sections of many fluid transport vehicles, such as tanker trucks, appear to be circular but are actually elliptical. The reason is that an elliptical tank can hold a high volume of fluid and have a lower center of gravity, and would therefore be more stable. Tanker trucks also have a lower elevation, due to their elliptical form, allowing them to more easily pass under low bridges and other obstructions.

Elliptical figures are commonly used in optics, specifically in the development of certain kinds of lenses as a way to manipulate light waves. They can also be found in architecture, art, mechanical engineering, and a host of other areas, but at this point, additional applications will be left to the reader. At any rate, the lack of functionality that most teachers and students associate with conic sections is more an issue of not being exposed to the many geometric representations of this very common shape. But with a little exploration, we can discover a number of ways to apply the concepts of ellipses and even other conic forms as well.

ADDITIONAL READINGS
Akopyan, A.V., & Zaslavsky, A.A. (2007). *Geometry of Conics*. American Mathematical Society. ISBN 9780821843239

Downs, J.W. (2003). *Practical Conic Sections: The Geometric Properties of Ellipses, Parabolas, and Hyperbolas*. Dover Publications. ISBN 9780486428765

Milne, J.S. (2006). *Elliptic Curves*. BookSurge Publishers. ISBN 1419652575

ARTICLE 3: THE BRACHISTOCHRONE PROBLEM

ABSTRACT: The *Brachistochrone* problem (also known as the *tautochrone* problem) is one of the earliest and most challenging problems in the calculus of variation. The presentation contained herein is a mathematical demonstration of the shortest time it takes for a particle of constant mass to move between two points as influenced by gravity but not friction. A discrete example originally posed by Archimedes is provided demonstrating how the shortest path does not always result in the shortest time. A presentation of the general case using calculus is offered as well.

INTRODUCTION

In the late 1600's calculus was still in its infancy but a number of brilliant mathematicians of the time were making groundbreaking discoveries almost daily. During this intellectually competitive era, one of the greatest problems posed to the founders of the calculus was the Brachistochrone Problem. The word *brachistochrone* is reportedly of Greek origin and is a joining of the word *brachistos* roughly meaning "shortest" or "least in magnitude" and *chronos* which is "time passage" or simply "time." The problem seeks to resolve the age old question of determining the shortest distance/time between two points. We have all been taught that the path in question is a straight line, and indeed, the actual shortest distance between two points in Euclidean 2-space is a straight line.

Archimedes posed this problem but incorrectly concluded that the resulting path was the arc of a circle connecting the two points. But the question posed in the brachistochrone problem is a better question from an engineering dynamics standpoint, and that is, what is the most *efficient* path. For example, a short path for a road may take a long time, or be economically unfeasible because of certain variables such as mountains or water. In engineering, a number of different constraints, such as cost or production time, could require us to consider the question of efficiency from different viewpoints and so problems like that posed in the brachistochrone are excellent ways to illustrate just how complex and also how elegant some non-intuitive solutions can be. The question here is to find the shape of a path that a particle, influenced only by gravitational force and discounting friction, would be if the primary constraint is the "shortest time" or *brachistochrone*. There are of course many stories associated with the solution to this problem. It was so famous, in fact, that it is even referenced in classic literature, including Melville's *Moby Dick* and Tolstoy's *War and Peace*.

As the classic story is told, the problem was first posed as a calculus of variations problem in 1696 by Johann Bernoulli in a letter to "…the most brilliant mathematicians in the world." The problem was posed as follows: Given two points A and B in a vertical plane, what is the curve traced out by a point acted on only by gravity, which starts at A and reaches B in the shortest time? The problem sounds simple but it took the founders of calculus substantial effort to solve it.

INVESTIGATION AND NOTES

Let us begin with a geometric representation of the question. If we represent points A and B on a graph where A is the point (1,1) and B is the point (0,0), the shortest path would intuitively be the line $y = x$

from 0 to 1. That intuitively obvious result however, is incorrect. Figure 3.1 illustrates the position, velocity, and acceleration equations based on the paths of falling objects. The difference in acceleration (force) of an object falling unencumbered toward a sibling gravitational point (for instance an apple falling directly toward the earth) and one encumbered by a path such as that outlined between points A and B would be that the magnitude of acceleration for a diagonal path would be the force of gravity multiplied by the sine of the angle created by the path. Using this model, the force of gravitational acceleration for the given line $y = x$, which is a 45° angle, would be approximately $(.707)(-32)(ft./sec^2)$. If we begin with the standard position equation, we can derive the constant of acceleration using the second derivative. We can also simulate a lower gravitational force using the same principle as Galileo did when he derived the acceleration constant in the first place, and that is by using a ramp.

The *position* equation for a falling object:

$$s(t) = -16t^2 + v_0 t + s_0$$

The *velocity* equation for a falling object

$$s'(t) = \frac{ds}{dt} = v(t) = -32t + v_0$$

Constant of *acceleration* for a free falling object

$$v'(t) = \frac{dv}{dt} = a = -32$$

Constant *acceleration* (angle θ) for a sliding object

$$a_{angle} = -32\sin\theta$$

If we now use the angle of the path between points (1,1) and (0,0) we can calculate the angle and the resulting sine value. By multiplying the approximate sine value by the acceleration constant, we can calculate the approximate diagonal acceleration of the particle along the path from (1,1) to (0,0)

Figure 3.1: Vertical Versus Diagonal Acceleration

$\theta = 45$; $\sin 45 \approx .707$
$a \approx (-32)(.707)$
≈ -22.624 ft./sec^2

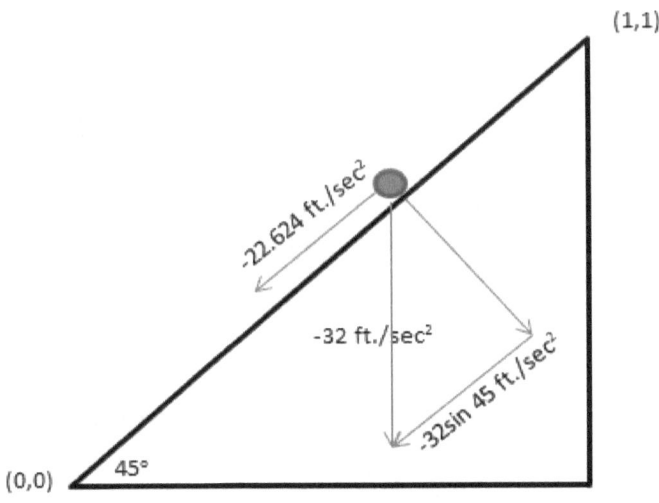

Because the angle of the path imposes a directing force of some magnitude that delimits gravitational force, the resulting acceleration for the particle following the 45 degree path is substantially lower. Let us now suppose we wanted to calculate the time it takes for the particle to free fall 1 foot compared to the time it takes to travel 1 foot along the diagonal path. Using the accelerations for each of the paths, we could calculate the time necessary for a particle to free fall 1 foot is .25 seconds while the particle traveling 1 foot along the diagonal path is approximately .297 seconds. This is no surprise since the acceleration being applied to the free falling particle is higher so we could expect the free falling particle to complete a 1 foot displacement faster. It is now simple to conclude that two particles traveling the same diagonal path would complete a given displacement in the same amount of time.

Now, let us examine a longer path; one connecting the same two points but broken into two contiguous segments that are angled on the circle. The vertex of the angle created between the two segments lies on the bisected arc of a circle passing through the two points. Figure 3.2 illustrates the paths that each of the particles would be following. Clearly, particle 2 has farther to travel and therefore should ostensibly take longer to complete the displacement. We will use this discrete example to test if a longer path can actually be completed in less time based on dynamic acceleration.

(Diagram can be found on the following page)

Figure 3.2: Paths of 2 Particles Completing the Same Total Displacement

Note: The path for Particle 1 is approximately 1.414 feet
       The path for Particle 2 is two segments of approximately .76531 feet or 1.53 feet

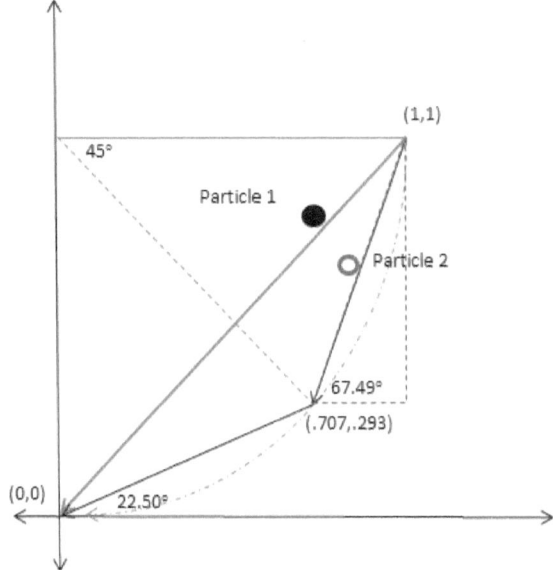

Particle 2 will travel along the 2-segments shown in Figure 3.2. The segments were selected based on chords of a unit circle that subtend 45° arcs, making the segments lengths approximately .76531 feet each. The segments intersect a circular path at the point (.707,.293). The angle for each segment (with respect to the positive x-axis) was then calculated using the arctangents of the coordinate ratios of y/x and x/y. The path originating at point (1,1) has an opposite side component of -.707 and an adjacent side component of -.293. Arctan(-.707/-.293) results in an angle of approximately

67.49°. Using the same process for the lower segment (opposite side of -.293 and adjacent side of -.707) results in an angle of 22.5°.

Now that the preliminary segment lengths and angle measures have been established, we will use the position functions for each path to determine the total time of displacement for each particle. Note that Particle 2 will already have accumulated substantial speed by the time it begins its path down the second segment. Normally, we would expect this particle to bounce, which would disrupt the time variable so we will assume for the sake of this investigation that the transfer will be fluid.

The time calculation for Particle 1 is a simple matter of deriving the position equation using the values in Figure 3.2. The time calculation for Particle 2 will involve two equations with the total time being the sum of the time on the two individual paths. Each calculation will use the total distance traveled by the particles as the initial position s_0.

Time Calculation for Particle 1:

Position equation for Particle 1 taking into account the angle of the path:

$$s(t) = -16(\sin \theta)t^2 + v_0 t + s_0$$

We now substitute the path angle to determine acceleration and also the initial position in terms of displacement:

$$s(t) = -16(\sin 45°)t^2 + 1.41$$

Final position equation based on a 45 degree path:

$$s(t) = -11.312t^2 + 1.41$$

Substituting 0 for the final position where the particle reaches its destination, we can factor the resulting expression and solve the quadratic equation for time:

$$0 = -11.312(t^2 - .12465)$$

Displacement time for particle 1:

$$t \approx .3531 \; seconds$$

Time Calculation for Particle 2 (Segment 1):

Position equation for the first segment of Particle 2:

$$s_1(t) = -16(sin\theta)t^2 + v_0 t + s_0$$

We now substitute the path angle of the upper segment and the initial starting position:

$$s_1(t) = -16(\sin 67.49°)t^2 + .76531$$

Final position equation of upper segment

$$s_1(t) = -14.781t^2 + .76531$$

Substituting 0 for the final position where the particle reaches its destination, we can factor the resulting expression and solve the quadratic equation for time

$$0 = -14.781(t^2 - .051776)$$

Displacement time for upper segment

$$t_1 \approx .22754 \; seconds$$

Time Calculation for Particle 2 (Segment 2):

We must calculate the velocity of the particle at the end of segment 1 in order to find v_0 in the equation for segment 2

$$s'_1(t) = \frac{ds_1}{dt} = v(t) = -29.56t$$

We substitute the time result from the end of segment 1 into the first derivative to determine the velocity at the end of segment 1. We will then use this value as v_0 for the next calculation:

$$v(t) = -29.56(.22754) ft/sec$$

Initial position equation for segment 2:

$$s_2(t) = -16(\sin 22.51°)t^2 - 6.7261t + .76531$$

Final position equation for segment 2:

$$s_2(t) = -6.1255t^2 - 6.7261t + .76531$$

We now use the quadratic formula to extract a usable root as a solution for time:

$$t = \frac{6.7261 \pm \sqrt{45.2404 + 21.3451}}{-12.251}$$

$$t = \frac{6.7261 \pm 8.15999}{-12.251}$$

We use the positive root for elapsed time, so 0.117 is the displacement time for the particle on segment 2:

$$t_2 = .117; \ -1.2151$$

$$t_1 + t_2 = .22754 \ seconds + .117 \ seconds$$

$$t(particle \ 1) = .3531 \ seconds$$
$$t(particle \ 2) = .34454 \ seconds$$

It is clear from the calculations that the path for particle 2, despite being a greater distance, is affected by gravitational acceleration in such a way as to complete the displacement in slightly less time. Archimedes began his investigation in a similar fashion. Based on this result, it would be logical to proceed using four even segments instead of two, again calculating the time for each segment and adding the results. By continuing in this fashion where additional segments are added each time, it is easy to see why Archimedes believed that the arc of a circle was the fastest path, but it was not until the calculus of variation was a usable tool that the true path for the shortest time was revealed. At the time, the problem was presented by Johann Bernoulli (who had already solved the problem). Only four other mathematicians of the time would solve it. They were Jacob Bernoulli (Johann's brother), Leibniz, L'Hopital, and Newton. According to Newton's biographer, Newton solved the problem in a single evening after returning home from the Royal Mint. This was no small feat since the time originally posed by Bernoulli for the completion of the problem was six months.

As correctly demonstrated by each of the mathematicians listed above, the brachistochrone, as it turns out, is an inverted *cycloid*. If a point on a circle is tracked as the circle is rolled along a straight line, the result is a cycloid. Figure 3.3 illustrates how the cycloid is generated. This path would then be flipped to create the brachistochrone as an inverted cycloid where an object like a ball could roll inside on the curved path.

Figure 3.3: Inverted Cycloid from a Rolling Circle

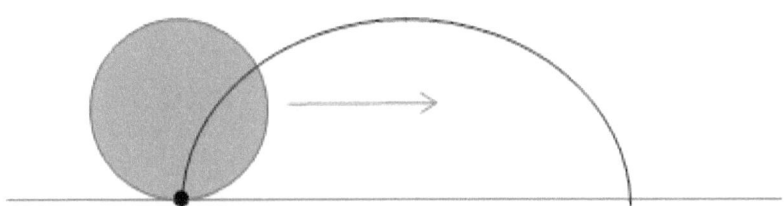

The derivation of the cycloid path relies on some ideas from applied physics, specifically those equating the quantities of gravitational potential energy and kinetic energy using the Law of Conservation of Energy.

Derivation of the Cycloid Path

Formulas equating kinetic and gravitational potential energy

$$\frac{1}{2}mv^2 = mgh$$

We solve for v in the equation and substitute y (the height of a function) in place of h

$$v = \sqrt{2gy}$$

The time needed to travel from point A to point B is given by the integral. The top represents the length of a curve and the bottom is the velocity. This is simply the rate, time, and distance equation.

$$t_{AB} = \int_A^B \frac{\sqrt{1+(y')^2}}{\sqrt{2gy}}$$

We now use the Beltrami identity where c is a constant. We then define the differential equation, substitute and simplify.

$$f - y'\frac{\partial f}{\partial y'} = c$$

Defining our partial differentials and simplifying gives us the following:

$$\frac{\partial f}{\partial y'} = \frac{y'\sqrt{1+(y')^2}}{\sqrt{2gy}}$$

Squaring both sides and simplifying allows us to define a new constant n^2 in terms of c

$$c = \frac{1}{\sqrt{2gy}\sqrt{1+(y')^2}}$$

This equation is now solved by the parametric equations

$$n^2 = [1 + (y')^2]y = \frac{1}{2gc^2}$$

Which produce the parametric equations of a cycloid

$$x = \frac{1}{2}n^2(\theta - \sin\theta)$$
$$y = \frac{1}{2}n^2(1 - \cos\theta)$$

The calculus involved in this derivation is fairly complex. It assumes a solid understanding of partial differential equations and also the assumptions involved in defining the initial integral. A number of additional steps would be necessary, starting with the introduction of Beltrami's identity, to make this derivation perfectly clear and so it is suggested that you do additional research if you wish to verify the problem on your own. There are a number of good resources online to be consulted for details.

It turns out that the inverted cycloid has another unique property when used as a track. Suppose that we place two particles in random locations on the inverted cycloid track. Some additional mathematics can verify that if the particles are released simultaneously, they will reach the vertical axis at the origin at the same time (see Figure 3.4). This is true no matter where the initial placements are located if we assume a frictionless environment.

Figure 3.4: Two Particles on an Inverted Cycloid Track

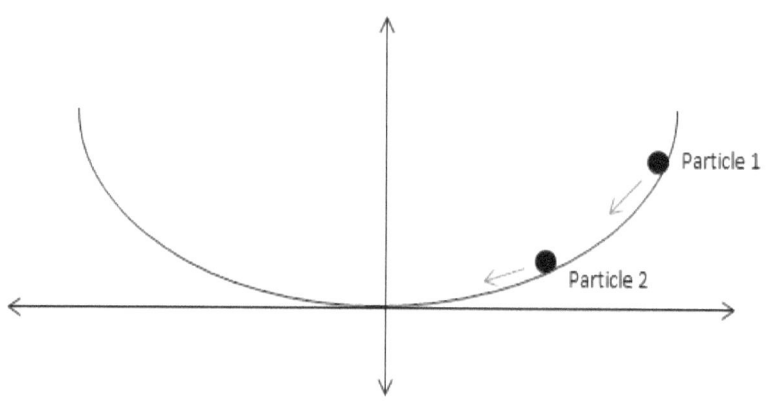

SUMMARY

It is not difficult to see that problems such as the brachistochrone problem can be very simple to represent but extremely difficult to solve. Complex problems in engineering and applied science almost all require the consideration of a number of dynamic variables, which is what makes them so difficult. More research into the brachistochrone problem will reveal additional proofs that incorporate practical variables such as surface friction and air resistance. We often find that more practical investigations such as those considering friction are needed, particularly in engineering where some variables may be very difficult to observe and yet important to consider.

ADDITIONAL READINGS

Ricky, V. F. (Reviewed Jan. 2013) History of the Brachistochrone. *Historical Notes for Calculus Teachers.* Retrieved 2013 from: http://www.Dean.usma.edu/departments/math/people/rickey/hm/CalcNotes/brachistochrone.pdf

Wesftall, R. S. (1980). *Never at Rest. A Biography of Isaac Newton.* Cambridge University Press. Cambridge, England.

ARTICLE 4: GUILLOCHE PATTERNS AND APPLIED PARAMETRIC EQUATIONS

ABSTRACT: *Guilloche patterns* are little known geometric graphs that have influenced cryptography, art, architecture, and other historically significant mathematical findings. These patterns are created from translated parametric equations that fall within a class of functions known as roulettes. The patterns can also be seen in planetary motion and mechanical engineering. They are investigated here as patterns within circles.

INTRODUCTION

The word Guilloche (pronounced Gill'-oh-shay, Gee'-o-shay, or even Ga-lowsh' depending on who you ask) is a French word for an intricately painted or carved ornament. The patterns typically consist of a series of overlapping or intertwining set of curves or circles. These patterns can be observed in Greek, Assyrian, Roman, French and English art and architecture. Because of their unique styling, Guilloche patterns have been recognized as a special artistic art form that began with techniques related to engine turning for detailed metal engravings.

Because of their prominence in the artistic world, it is unusual for people to immediately recognize how complex the mathematics involved in Guilloche patterns is. In fact, the graphs of the functions themselves is most often (but not uniquely) related to a larger family of functions called roulettes. Specifically, Guilloche patterns are illustrated as hypocycloid and epicycloid functions.

These roulettes, as functions including the hypocycloids and epicycloids, are also closely associated with a unique pattern design instrument known as *spirograph*. In fact, an interesting side note is that spirograph was one of the most popular toys in America in the mid-1960's.

As the story goes, in 1962, a mechanical engineer from England named Denys Fischer reportedly discovered the idea of spirograph by observing the unique and predictable overlapping curved patterns on an oscilloscope as part of his job in designing bomb detonators for NATO. With an acknowledgement that making the leap from bomb detonators to spirograph is significant, one should still recognize that the mathematics involved in the curving designs of spirograph is the manifestation of some very complex *parametric equation* graphing. But this roulette patterning is not unique to spirograph or even of an oscilloscope. It can also be seen on the paper currency of almost every modern country in the world.

According to the United States Bureau of Printing and Engraving, there was a time when anyone with $50,000 to spare could start a bank and issue their own bank notes. Of course, if the bank failed, the notes they issued would become worthless and so it became necessary for the banks to protect their notes against forgery. Guilloche patterns were used to do this because they were very difficult to reproduce. The wheel within a wheel function that is used for spirograph is the exact same process that is used to create the spider web patterns on paper money only more wheels are used. Today, the colored watermark and the ultraviolet and infrared printing techniques add another layer of security that makes unauthorized duplication of paper notes very difficult. These new anti-forgery techniques are, of course, necessary because the Guilloche patterns, no matter how complex, can be easily copied by today's basic color ink-jet printer technology. However, if you try to copy money on a networked printer, there are points within the Guilloche patterns that many modern printers recognize like a finger print, that will not only shut the printer down, but will also automatically send a message to the United States Secret Service, who are likely to visit you shortly thereafter.

One other place you can expect to see Guilloche patterns is on the famous eggs designed by Karl Faberge. In many eastern European cultures, eggs were decorated as a celebration of the onset of spring. This has influenced the cultural combination of the celebration of Easter as a religious holiday and iconic cultural celebrations related to the Easter bunny, which is a ritual celebration of spring that also involves eggs. Nevertheless, in Russia during the late 19th and early 20th centuries, Czar Alexander III and followed by Nicholas II, who continued the tradition, annually commissioned jeweled eggs to be fashioned by Karl Faberge for the czars. The decoration technique use by Faberge included Guilloche machining, which turned the egg on a lathe-type device in order to engrave the design on the metallic surface. The complexity of the pattern was determined by calibrating the size and rotational coefficients for the gears. Basically, calibrating the gear size on the lathe was analogous to changing the coefficients in a set of parametric equations. The difficulty in this process however, was that the etching pattern was on an ellipsoidal surface rather than a flat plane where we typically represent graphs. Still, the machines necessary for planar engraving of curved patterns create interesting engineering problems; moreover, they create a justification for parametric equations as a tool for science and engineering.

INVESTIGATION AND NOTES

To get a flavor of the graphs created by overlapping functions, let us begin by creating a simple curved pattern by using only straight lines. Linear equations do not really give us a lot of latitude in creating overlapping curves but they do illustrate how a series of tangents can be used to represent a curve in much the same way as was done in Article 2 - Figure 2.7, with the envelop method for constructing an ellipse. We will begin this process by manipulating the transformational coefficients of slope and y-axis intercepts for a series of six linear equations. Note how the slopes change predictably as do the y-axis intercepts for the equations (Figure 4.1).

Figure 4.1: Straight Line Curve

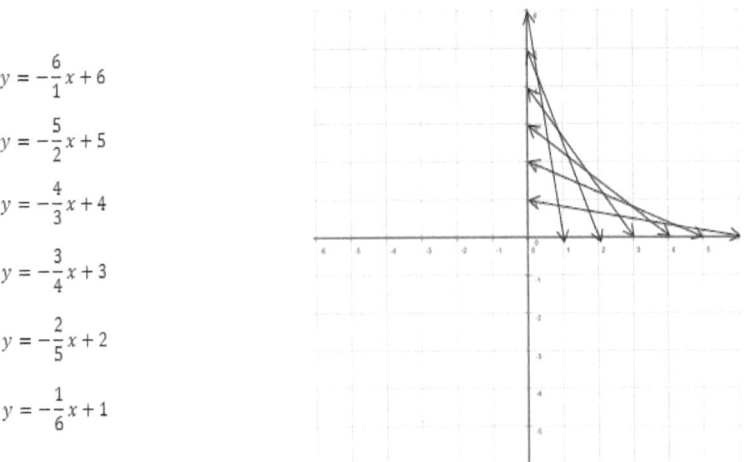

$y = -\frac{6}{1}x + 6$

$y = -\frac{5}{2}x + 5$

$y = -\frac{4}{3}x + 4$

$y = -\frac{3}{4}x + 3$

$y = -\frac{2}{5}x + 2$

$y = -\frac{1}{6}x + 1$

It is easy to see how a combination of straight lines creates what looks like a curve. This technique is used extensively in civil engineering with the construction of bridge supports that essentially look like curved support beams but are actually a series of straight line beams. Another exercise with parabolic graphs will continue in roughly the same fashion of manipulating the transformational coefficients of different curves. We will do this to illustrate how the process slowly evolves into the parametric equations that represent Guilloche patterns. In Figure 4.2, the same basic process is done, but because we are using parabolic functions, the overlap involves curves instead of straight lines, which makes the resulting pattern a little bit more difficult to see but also a bit more interesting.

Figure 4.2: Overlapping Pattern of Parabolic Graphs

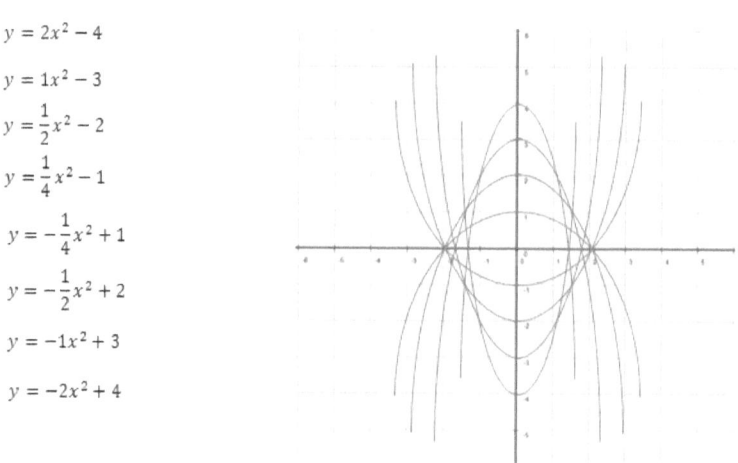

$y = 2x^2 - 4$

$y = 1x^2 - 3$

$y = \frac{1}{2}x^2 - 2$

$y = \frac{1}{4}x^2 - 1$

$y = -\frac{1}{4}x^2 + 1$

$y = -\frac{1}{2}x^2 + 2$

$y = -1x^2 + 3$

$y = -2x^2 + 4$

In this example using parabolic graphs, only two of the coefficients for a standard parabolic function were manipulated but there are certainly more that could have been changed (e.g. the vertex point). These would obviously add different flavors to the pattern depending on how they are adjusted. By adding a mesh overlay to the solid form in the center of the graph, we could even begin to create a three-dimensional model as well. Still, though, the curves do not look like those commonly seen in the hypocycloid functions of Guilloche patterns. To create those functions, we first need to experiment with trigonometric functions and then finally with a set of parametric equations.

In looking at basic trigonometric patterns, one of the most popular, but oversimplified, representations of a sine function is to roll a disk along a straight edge while mapping the curve that follows a fixed point somewhere between the center and the edge of the rolling disk. Though this is not actually a sine wave, it does illustrate the oscillation factor of some basic trigonometric functions. The curve described is a cycloid-type curve; the same type of cycloid curve in the Brachistochrone problem. More complex patterns can then be created by rolling the circle along a curve instead of a straight line. The most complex patterns are created by having several different disks of varying size and shape rolling along or inside of one another simultaneously. Very simple versions of this can be seen by using the spirograph disks drawn on paper, while the more complex forms were, at one time, constructed with very complicated machinery and produced things like the Faberge eggs.

As we continue to move toward using parametric equations as a way to approach Guilloche patterns, it is probably appropriate to discuss the idea of parametric equations and exactly what they imply. A parametric equation is simply a method of establishing a relationship between two or more variables using a common parameter. Many people confuse the idea of polar equations and parametric equations because standard functions are explicitly stated and do not need to be represented in terms of some other parameter. Polar equations are often represented in parametric form so the assumption is understandable, but the truth is that nearly any function can be represented in parametric form. For example, a simple parabola can be represented in a parametric form by relating the x and y coordinate values to a common parameter, say t, for instance. The value for t can then be manipulated within a certain domain and the outcomes of the function are determined with each t value. The same is true for graphs such as circles. The circle is a little more sophisticated parametric set because a circle is not a function, which is exactly why parametric forms are so useful. The following examples illustrate how a parabola and a circle can both be represented in parametric form:

Parabola:

$$y = x^2 \text{ so } x = t \text{ and } y = t^2$$

Circle:

$$x^2 + y^2 = 1 \text{ so } x = \cos t;\ y = \sin t$$
$$\therefore (\cos t, \sin t) \text{ for } 0 \leq t \leq 2\pi$$

In each of the examples shown above, we *parameterized* the equation using a floating value for t. The first example with the parabola is obvious because the equality is explicitly stated. The parameter t, for the circle relies on the trigonometric ratios of the Pythagorean Theorem, and for the most part, it is also fairly natural to associate the floating parameter with the rotations of polar constraints as is done in the circle example. So, if we now continue with an example of overlapping trigonometric graphs it becomes more evident of how the patterns are slowly evolving into Guilloche patterns even though this particular example is not in circular form. Figure 4.3 demonstrates how a sine function that is translated along the x-axis at $\pi/4$ increments creates the flowing patterns of cyclic curves.

Figure 4.3: Overlapping Sine Waves

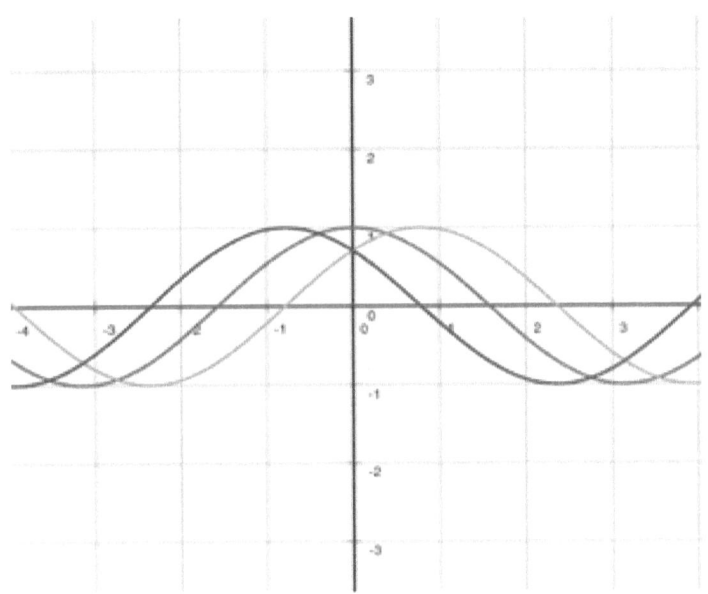

Although there is nothing tremendously exciting about unlabeled overlapping sine graphs, they do give us a better sense of how parameterized functions tend to look. Parameterizing functions will also allow us to define a complex overlapping set of curves as a single function rather than as a series of overlapping individual functions. The final steps in the evolution of graphical functions, then, is to transition from a series of overlapping functions as we did with the lines, parabolas, and sine waves, to a single parametric function based on a parameter t. To do this, we will derive a set of parametric equations for a single *roulette function* called a hypocycloid. This function will look very similar to the overlapping spirograph curves seen in Guilloche patterns.

A *hypocycloid* is a graph generated by following a fixed point P, anywhere inside or on the small circle, which rolls without sliding, inside a larger circle. Figure 4.4 shows part of a hypocycloid path defined by the small circle A, having radius r and point P at a distance of d. The small circle A rolls counterclockwise (but rotates clockwise) inside a larger circle B, having radius R.

(Diagram can be found on the following page)

Figure 4.4: Hypocycloid Curve

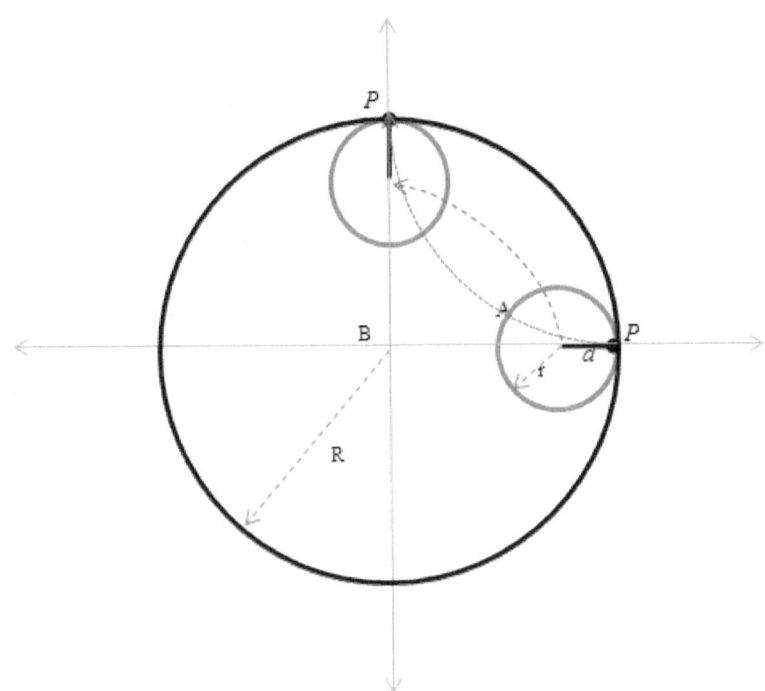

In this case, d = r in the small circle, but the point P could be anywhere on or inside the small circle A. The curve produced by the fixed point P on the smaller circle would continue in the same fashion through each quadrant as the small circle rolled inside the larger one. The curve for this kind of hypocycloid (where $r = d$) would eventually close as long as R/r is a rational number. Further, if R/r simplifies to a whole number, you could expect to see R/r cusps in the resulting graph. For example, the radius of the large circle in Figure 4.4 is four times that of the smaller circle, so the resulting graph would have four cusps.

Now that we have a sense of how the curve could look if we continued to roll the small circle inside the large one, we can begin to define the position of a given point P through a set of parametric equations. In order to do this, we need to define our parameter *t* in terms of angles θ and α. We can do this intuitively by calculating the distance in the x direction from the center of the large circle to the center of the smaller circle. We then add or subtract another x quantity based on the reference angle between the center of the smaller circle and the point P on the edge of the smaller circle. Let us suppose that the reference angle between the center of the large circle and the center of the small circle is represented by θ. The reference angle between the center of the small circle and the point P is α. Figure 4.5 illustrates how the x and y coordinate locations are derived intuitively.

(Diagram can be found on the following page)

Figure 4.5: Defining the x and y Coordinate Positions

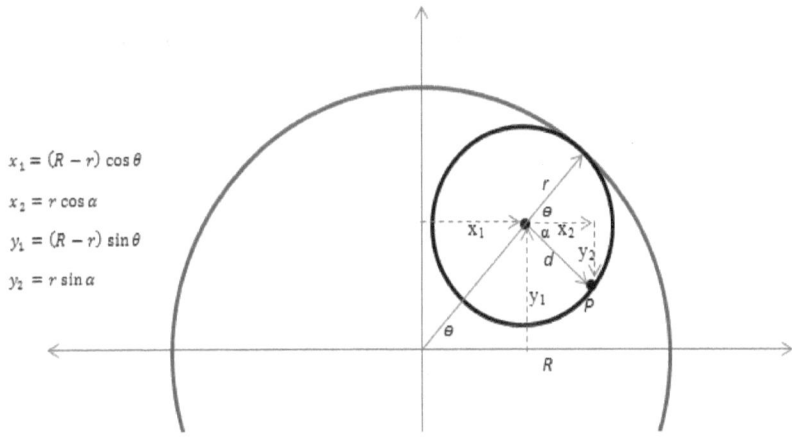

$x_1 = (R - r) \cos \theta$
$x_2 = r \cos \alpha$
$y_1 = (R - r) \sin \theta$
$y_2 = r \sin \alpha$

    The x-coordinate of the point P can be found by adding the cosine components of the two circles. The y-coordinate of the point can be found by adding the sine components. The difficulty then becomes how to identify the individual components in each of the x and y directions. Locating the center of the small circle with respect to the center of the large circle is fairly simple. Let us assume that the center of the large circle is at the origin. The polar form of a point is then easily represented as the magnitude of the radius (the hypotenuse of the right triangle defined by the point) multiplied by the horizontal and vertical ratios of cosine and sine. Because the point P is defined by d at a length of $(R - r)$, the radius of the large circle minus the radius of the small circle for all $R - r > 0$, and a reference angle of θ, x_1 and y_1 are thusly defined in Figure 4.5. Components x_2 and y_2 are also simple with respect to the angle α, but angle α put in terms of angle θ is a bit more difficult to define.

To do this we must recognize that any arc of the large circle must have arc length of $R\theta$. Similarly, the small circle rolling inside the large circle over the same arc must have arc length $r(\theta+\alpha)$. We can then equate these two arc representations: $R\theta = r(\theta + \alpha)$ and solve for α, which gives us $\alpha = [(R - r)/r]\theta$. Our final parametric set becomes:

$$x(\theta) = (R - r)\cos\theta + r\cos\left[\frac{R - r}{r}\right]\theta$$

$$y(\theta) = (R - r)\sin\theta - r\sin\left[\frac{R - r}{r}\right]\theta$$

These are the parametric equations of the hypocycloid with the angle θ being our parameter (assuming that the small circle rotates with a constant angular velocity, which would essentially make θ analogous to an incremental time parameter t). Note also that the y coordinate defined by the small circle must be subtracted from the center point coordinate because as the small circle rolls, α is measured clockwise while θ of the large circle is measured counterclockwise. With these equations we are now ready to create Guilloche patterns. Remember that if the ratio of R/r is a rational number, the pattern eventually closes, so Figure 4.6 illustrates two closed curves that are roughly Guilloche patterns.

Figure 4.6: Hypocycloids where R/r = 3.6 and 7.2

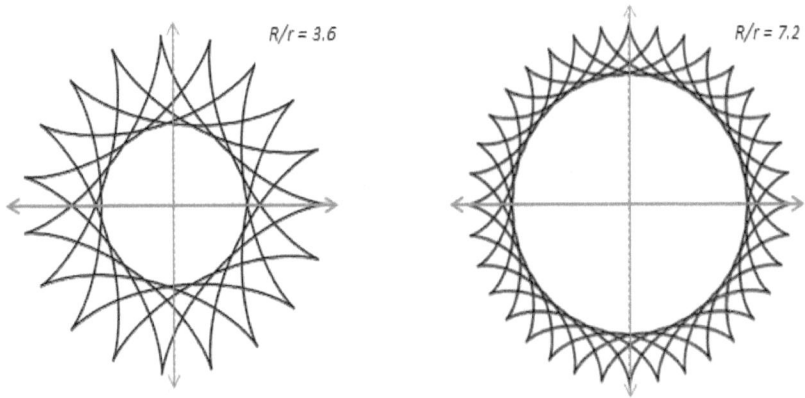

The hypocycloid patterns that are created in Figure 4.6 are beginning to look like Guilloche graphs that you might find on a certificate or on paper money but they are limited because they must fit inside a circle so they are much more like spirograph. Extending on the idea of the hypocycloid, we can also look at *epicycloids*. The *epicycloid* graphs are very similar in form to the hypocycloid but they are drawn from a small circle rolling along the outside of a larger circle rather than inside. The derivation of the parametric formulas for epicycloids is very similar to that of hypocycloids but the radii are added instead of subtracted. Also, the small circle rolling outside of the larger circle both rotates and revolves counter clockwise. Because the derivation of epicycloids is so similar to the hypocycloid, the derivation will not be provided here; however, the parametric equations are provided and Figure 4.7 is shown to illustrate how the patterns of epicycloids are different than hypocycloids.

Figure 4.7: Epicycloid Equations and Patterns R/r = 5.5 and 3.8

$$x(\theta) = (R + r)\cos\theta - r\cos\left[\frac{R+r}{r}\right]\theta$$

$$y(\theta) = (R + r)\sin\theta - r\sin\left[\frac{R+r}{r}\right]\theta$$

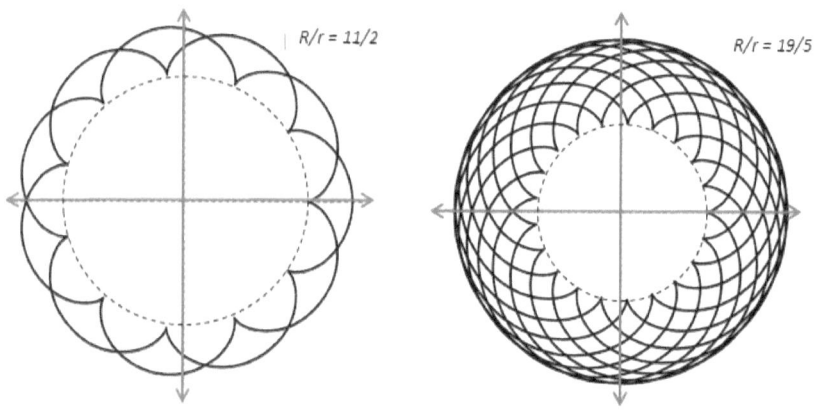

SUMMARY

Combining the graphs of linear equations, quadratic equations, trigonometric equations and finally the parametric equations for hypocycloids and epicycloids, we can see the evolution of curves that develop slowly into a complex pattern that looks somewhat like what you might see on paper currency. For another great look at applied Guilloche patterns, check out an episode of the television series NUM3RS titled *Counterfeit Reality*.

Most importantly, there are a number of mechanical and computer engineering applications associated with Guilloche patterns. Specifically, engine turning, and of course the computer software needed to guide the machinery, is often used for metal engraving. Although the technology has advanced significantly, geometric lathes are still used for making metal ornamental and security patterns. The U.S. Bureau of Printing and Engraving still uses the same basic geometric engraving techniques for the paper currency printed in the United States although again, the technology has advanced beyond engine turning. Yet, in the future mechanical interactions that rely on circular motion will remain prominent.

ADDITIONAL READINGS

Fenn, Amor (2010). *Abstract Design and How to Create it*. Dover Publications. ISBN – 9780486276731

Pfeffer, S. (1998). Faberge Eggs. Universe Publications. ISBN - 97808836309

ARTICLE 5: PI

ABSTRACT: The application of Pi to science, engineering and technology may not be immediately obvious because Pi has generally been associated with analytic geometry. Pi, however, has a rich history and many applications in science, engineering, technology, statistics, and even provides historical clues in the early development of mathematics.

INTRODUCTION

The Greek letter Pi, as we now use it in the geometry of a circle, has only been popular for about three hundred years. There is some evidence that the ancient Greek mathematicians knew about the value 22/7. It was not until Leonard Euler, a Swiss mathematician, used the Greek symbol Pi to represent a constant value meaning half the circumference of a circle of radius equaling 1 unit that the symbol Pi became popular. Euler's regular communication of mathematical proofs to the learned community of mathematicians in Europe created a need for the symbol and Pi, which has been used regularly to represent the ratio of the circumference of a circle to its diameter ever since about 1748.

Pi has a rich history and has been interesting in that at one point, the relentless pursuit of more undiscovered digits of Pi represented an intellectual "race" (in some sense not too different from the USA vs. USSR space race of the 1960's). The search for algorithms that would extend the digits of Pi out as far as possible was seen as a worthy academic goal. As of late 2011, Pi has been calculated out to a little over 10 trillion digits so the computation of

Pi's digits is still seen as a worthwhile mathematical pursuit. It is interesting to note that the search for the digits of Pi continues even though most applications of computational mathematics require fewer than fifty digits. In fact, physicists suggest that approximately 40 digits of Pi are adequate to calculate the circumference of the visible universe with a margin of error that is approximately the width of a proton. Even the anomalous magnetic dipole movement of the electron would require only about 15 decimal places to verify the theoretical prediction used in the study of particle physics.

In most mechanical design settings, five places of Pi would be overkill. Nevertheless, Pi is tremendously useful in mechanical calculations because circular motion and circular structures are both very common in machine technology environments.

INVESTIGATION AND NOTES

Pi is a non-terminating, non-repeating decimal that represents the ratio of the circumference of a circle to its diameter. It is easily the most familiar irrational number in mathematics and has an approximate applied value of 3.1415926536. Pi is a *transcendental number* which is a number that is not the root of any non-zero polynomial having rational coefficients. Mathematicians such as Archimedes explored geometric approaches to finding values of Pi by squeezing circles between inscribed and circumscribed polygons. Later on (approximately 15th century), algorithms based on infinite series improved the mechanism for searching for the digits of Pi. Like all irrational numbers, Pi cannot be accurately represented as a simple fraction (i.e. 22/7 or 355/115 which were two of the earliest estimates of Pi), but it can be relatively accurately represented by an infinite series of nested fractions known as *continued fractions*.

There are a number of series-based representations of Pi such as the Gregory-Leibniz series and the Nilakantha series. Both of these series are fairly simple to comprehend and converge to Pi after a number of iterations. Of course, the most profound breakthroughs in finding the digits of Pi did not occur until the mid-20th century when computers revolutionized the search techniques. A team of mathematicians led by George Reitwiesner and John von Neumann calculated Pi accurately to over 2000 places using an arctangent infinite series calculation that took 70 hours of computer time on the ENIAC computer (Arndt & Haenel, 2006). Two infinite series methods are presented below.

Examples Converging Infinite Series for Pi:

Gregory-Leibniz series: $\pi = \frac{4}{1} - \frac{4}{3} + \frac{4}{5} - \frac{4}{7} + \frac{4}{9} - \frac{4}{11} + \cdots$

Nilakantha Series: $\pi = 3 + \frac{4}{2\times3\times4} - \frac{4}{4\times5\times6} + \frac{4}{6\times7\times8} - \frac{4}{8\times9\times10} + \cdots$

In searching for the proofs related to the irrationality and transcendence of Pi, Leonard Euler solved a related problem (though he may not have known it was related at the time) known as the *Basel* problem in 1735, although the outcome was in question until 1741 when he produced a rigorous proof of the solution. The Basel problem did not address the transcendence of Pi specifically, but rather used Pi in the solution. The Basel problem is simply stated as the precise summation of the reciprocals of the squares of the natural numbers (i.e. the sum of $1/1^2 + 1/2^2 + 1/3^2 + ...$). Euler's solution created the foundation for one of the most famous problems in mathematics, the Riemann Zeta Function.

Euler's Solution of the Basel Problem: $\dfrac{\pi^2}{6} = \sum_{n=1}^{\infty} \dfrac{1}{n^2}$

The *Monte Carlo methods*, which are designed to evaluate the results of multiple random trials of an experiment, can also be used to create approximations of Pi. One of the simplest of the Monte Carlo methods is very simple to understand and makes perfect sense from an experimental point of view. Figure 5.1 illustrates how this method works. Assume that we have inscribed a circle in a large square having sides of length $2r$, where r is also the radius of the circle. For our experimental purposes, we will also define a value for the radius, $r = 6$ (within this environment, we can expect "border disputes" so we must also define how we count points). The area of the large square is $4r^2$, and is illustrated by breaking the large square into four smaller squares (defined by quadrants) each having sides of length r and areas of r^2. Knowing that the area of the inscribe circle is πr^2 allows us to verify the value of Pi by setting up a proportion related to a simple random event. Let us suppose that we use the squares and circle as a landing platform for a random set of coordinates that are finite and countable (perhaps little dots generated in a random matrix within the square). If we count how many of the total dots fall within the circle we should be able to approximate Pi based on the ratio we would expect, pi/4 ≈ .7854.

Figure 5.1: Estimation of Pi based on the Ratio of Circle/Square Area

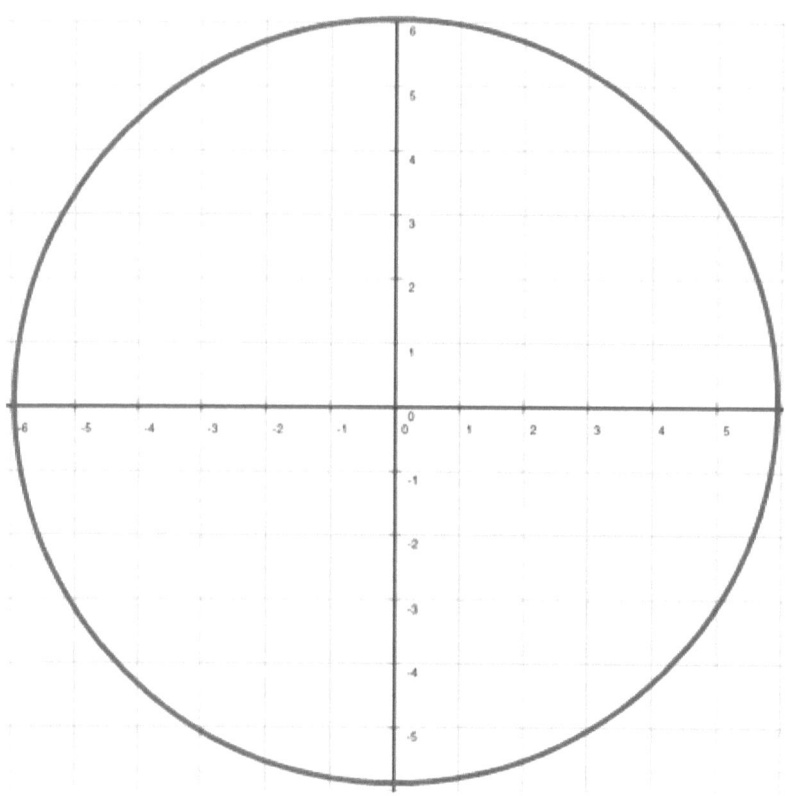

Notice if we count the ordered pairs within the circle and divide by the total number of ordered pairs falling within the square, we can calculate a constant value as a ratio. In order to avoid the issue of how to count the ordered pairs falling on the border of each shape, we will simply count half of the border points for each shape.

Using this method, the number of ordered pairs enclosed within the circle shown in Figure 5.1 is 111. The number of ordered pairs falling within the large square is 144. Assuming that, until we make the calculation, Pi is a variable we can solve as follows:

Area of the square: $\qquad A_s = 4r^2$

Area of the circle: $\qquad A_c = \pi r^2$

Proportion of circle to square: $\qquad \dfrac{A_c}{A_s} = \dfrac{\pi r^2}{4r^2}$

Canceling the r^2 factors: $\qquad \dfrac{A_c}{A_s} = \dfrac{\pi}{4}$

Substituting constants: $\qquad \dfrac{111}{144} \approx \dfrac{\pi}{4}$

Solving for pi: $\qquad \pi \approx 3.0833$

Our estimate of Pi is less than .06 from the actual value. Had we counted the border points on the top and bottom of the circle, our estimate would have been approximately 3.1388. Better estimates could of course be achieved from more accurate graphs using hundreds of thousands of points rather than just hundreds. The probability calculation that relates to this method assumes that in time, an infinite number of random points would fall with an even distribution analogous to how we counted the ordered pairs from the graph above, ultimately resulting in Pi. There are other Monte Carlo methods that yield very close approximations as well. Some are fun probability experiments to try. One such example is *Buffon's needle problem* (in the classroom, use toothpicks). Buffon's problem asks to find the probability that a needle of length L will land on a line, given a floor with evenly spaced parallel lines that are D units apart. See Figure 5.2.

Figure 5.2: Buffon's Needle Problem

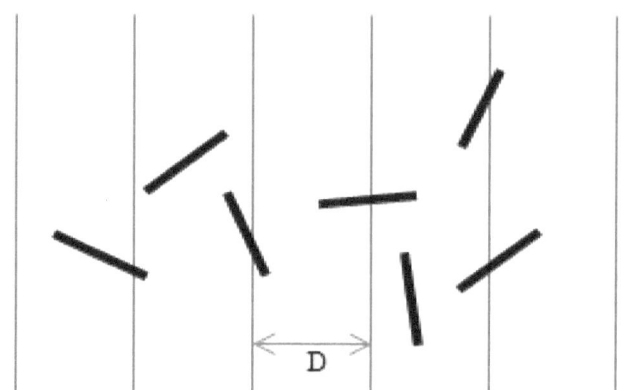

The probability, of course, depends on ratio defined by the length of the needles and the distance between the lines. Note that when we define the integral, the parameters of Pi and the trigonometric function cosine are used because each needle represents a possible diameter of a circle and can fall in any position representing the rotation of a diameter within a circle. We present the solution as follows for a ratio where the length of the needle is less than the distance between the lines:

Defining a ratio parameter x:

$$x = \frac{L}{D}$$

Define the probability with the integral:

$$P(x) = \int_0^{2\pi} \frac{L|\cos\theta|d\theta}{D2\pi}$$

Simplifying the integral (quadrant 1):

$$P(x) = \frac{2L}{\pi D} \int_0^{\pi/2} \cos\theta \, d\theta$$

Evaluating the integral:

$$P(x) = \frac{2L}{\pi D} [\sin\theta]_0^{\pi/2} = \frac{2}{\pi} \cdot \frac{L}{D}$$

Substituting our ratio parameter x:
(solving as x approaches 1)

$$P(x = 1) = \frac{2}{\pi} \approx 0.63662$$

    Among all of the unique methods for calculating the digits of Pi, there are also a number of historical examples of how Pi might have been used in engineering and science. These examples are certainly worth exploring, but I would offer one note of caution to anyone wanting to find Pi in strange places. A good scientist, mathematical or otherwise, cannot assume the existence of Pi (or anything else for that matter) in a given situation and then go about looking for it. Pi must emerge unsolicited from a pattern or computation to truly be considered a mathematical or scientific *discovery*. For that reason, I consider some of the following examples to be a bit *suspicious*. Nevertheless, anything that makes us think mathematically is worth exploring in my view.

If we go way back in history, we find that the Great Pyramid at Giza is uniquely connected to Pi. This is a bit counterintuitive at first considering that the surfaces are all triangular and have square bases, but Egyptologists suggest that the values appearing in the ratios of the pyramid are so close to those approximating Pi that it is difficult to deny the connection. In the pyramid at Giza, the ratio of the length of the one side to the height is approximately $\pi/2$. This is particularly interesting since the value of this ratio is represented much more accurately in the pyramid than the Egyptians of the time were supposed to have had known about the value of Pi. The writings of Herodotis, a fifth century BC Greek historian, suggest that the pyramid was built such that the area of each of the lateral triangular sides was equivalent to a square that had each side equal to the height of the pyramid. They claim that ultimately Pi can be distilled from this relationship, but that it takes some imagination to see how Egyptologists came to their result. It turns out that Herodotus was either misquoted or not very well versed in geometry.

To verify this finding, we would first need to better understand the relationship as stated by Herodotus. If the square of the height of the pyramid is equal to that of any of the triangular surfaces as stated, then the area of half of the square of the height would have to be equal to half the lateral surface. Triangle ABC as shown in Figure 5.3 (half of the area of a square of the height of the pyramid) would suggest that the triangle on the interior must be equivalent to the triangle ABD which represents half of the lateral surface of one side. This equivalence comes from the stated equivalence of a square having sides the height of the pyramid being equal to the lateral sides. If we cut each of our figures in half, we get triangles ABC and ABD. Let us now assume that segment AC, the height of the pyramid, has a value of *h*, and segment CB from the center of the pyramid to the middle of a side is half the length of the side *S*. Based on this information, we can quickly see a contradiction developing. In order for this relationship to be accurate as stated, the slant height of the pyramid would have to be equivalent to the altitude of the pyramid. Thus the derivation of Pi using this method must be false. See Figure 5.3.

Figure 5.3: Pyramid with Interior Triangle ABC Equal to Surface Triangle ABD

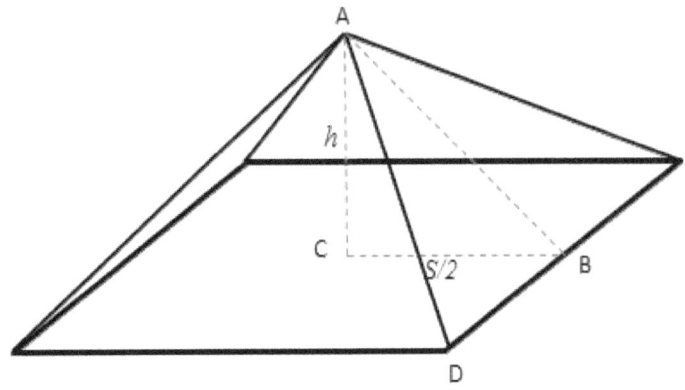

A second derivation of Pi based on actual measurements taken from the pyramid suggests that the ratio between the perimeter of the pyramid and its height is approximately 2π. This is much more plausible. Let us suppose that the pyramid shown in Figure 5.3, has a height of 1 non-standard unit. Based on the measurements given, the apothem of the square base S/2 would have a value of S/2 = π/4. Using these values, it would be fairly simple to verify the lateral slant of the pyramid, even using a picture.

Lateral slant angle of the great pyramid at Giza:

$$\arctan\left(\frac{h}{S/2}\right) = \arctan\left(\frac{1}{\pi/4}\right) \approx 51.85°$$

Starting with a known slant angle for the lateral triangular surfaces, we could derive Pi. It is interesting in some sense to think about this problem as one we know is geometrically impossible using a straight edge and compass… squaring the circle. If the stated relationship indicates that the ratio of the perimeter of the pyramid to its height is 2π, then what if a circle was drawn from the center of the base of the pyramid with a radius of h? The circumference of that circle would have to be 2πh. In essence, if the ratio of the perimeter of the pyramid to the height is 2π, then a circle using h as the radius of the circle would also have a perimeter of 2πh, and thus, the circle has been squared!

In truth, this example is somewhat of an anomaly because the pyramids we admire as engineering marvels from ancient civilizations do not all have the same slant height and therefore do not all have the same ratio of perimeter to height. But engineering in general is where we can expect to find Pi applied over and over. Many of the mechanical machines we use apply Pi because of their tendency toward converting circular motion into other types of motion. Further, the very space around each of us must be viewed in a fashion consistent with circles and spheres. Our existence on a spherical planet demands we know and use Pi.

SUMMARY

There is probably as much mysticism and misinformation surrounding Pi as there is hard evidence of how it is appropriately used in science and engineering. There are also some great stories surrounding Pi, but again, it is worth extensively researching the things we read in order to verify their authenticity. One such story has many different versions, but based on several cross referenced sources there are probably at least kernels of truth in the version presented here. The story tells as follows. In the 1890's in Indiana, a legislative bill (Bill #264) attempted to legally define the value of Pi, incorrectly I might add. Allegedly, a physician and self-proclaimed mathematician Edwin J. Goodwin believed that he had discovered a way to solve the "squaring a circle" problem with only a compass and straight edge (this problem had already been proved impossible). He also believed that he had successfully solved several other impossible problems, but those were not presented in the bill other than as passing notions intended to establish his credibility. The bill mentions several different values for Pi, all different and all proven by Goodwin's methods. Among these values were $\pi = 4$ and $\pi = 3.2$. The most troubling part of this story, however, is not that one person could produce such enormously convoluted and clearly incorrect solutions, but rather that the bill came very close to passing.

When the bill was introduced to the Indiana House of Representatives it was examined and passed through various committees, which for the most part, reported favorably on the proposal. Ultimately it passed without a single dissenting vote. When the bill reached the Indiana Senate, it went through similar committee reviews, some of which reported favorably and others unfavorably, but it was finally sentenced to a slow death based on doubt and confusion about the goal of the bill. At one point, it was reported that the bill nearly passed but one senator observed that the General Assembly lacked the power to define mathematical truth.

There are also some interesting excerpts from the O.J. Simpson trial in which the defense attorney attempts to discredit one of the detectives by pointing out that his calculations were incorrect. The attorney asked the detective for the value of Pi. The detective was unable to answer correctly, and even the sitting judge misquoted the value. What these examples tell us is not that the value of Pi is misunderstood or forgotten, but that understanding how mathematical situations are defined and verified should be much more a part of our mathematical education than simply knowing values. Had Dr. Goodwin had a better sense of the responsibilities involved in mathematical proofs, the Pi Bill never would have happened. Pi and other popular mathematical constants are certainly simple to memorize to a few decimal places, but our search for Pi using mathematically appropriate methodologies is the only approach that will allow us to understand what it means and build new knowledge based on authentic prior knowledge and sound reasoning.

ADDITIONAL READINGS

Arndt, J, & Haenel, C. (2006). Pi Unleashed. Springer-Verlag. ISBN 978-3-540-66572-4

Beckman, P. (1989). History of Pi. St Martin's Press. ISBN 978-0-88029-418-8

Blatner, D. (1997). The Joy of Pi. ISBN 978-0-0827-7562-7

Hallerberg, A.E. (1977). Indiana's squared circle. *Mathematics Magazine*, Vol. 50, 136-140.

ARTICLE 6: THE PYTHAGOREAN THEOREM

ABSTRACT: Named after the Greek mathematician Pythagoras, the *Pythagorean Theorem* is one of the most perennial concepts taught in intermediate and secondary school geometry. The theorem is reported to be one of the most proved theorems in mathematics. The following manuscript illustrates a number of geometric and algebraic proofs and extends the mathematical relationships of the theorem to trigonometry, integral calculus and several other science and engineering topics.

INTRODUCTION

The Pythagorean Theorem is unique in the study and communication of mathematics in that it represents both a formula and a series of proofs. This can be somewhat confusing to amateur mathematicians because on one hand, it is simply a statement of equality, while the other meaning has its foundations in demonstrating how the equality is derived and how we verify it. The word theorem, in fact, comes from the Greek word meaning to *observe* or to *contemplate*, and is not so different from the derivative of the word *theater*.

The theorem itself is typically credited to Pythagoras (circa 570-490 BC) although there are a number of ancient sources that suggest that the discovery of the relationship predates Pythagoras. There is significant evidence that the Babylonians understood the relationship that the formula represents, but there is apparently little surviving evidence that they used it as a formal mathematical framework. Instead, it was written as a fact set forth in a table used for architecture and perhaps for educational/cultural reasons as well. A Babylonian cuneiform tablet from approximately 1800 BC, known as Plimpton 322 (represented by the collection in which it resides at Columbia University) is basically a trigonometric table that lists a series of trigonometric ratios as a rule for calculating the hypotenuse of a right triangle. Included on the tablet are a number of Pythagorean triples, about 15 rows, but the entire list uses constants and so no algebraic representation, as we currently know the theorem, is present. Euclid, too, demonstrated the relationship in *The Elements* (circa 300 BC) and stated the relationship formally as the square described upon the hypotenuse of a right angled triangle is equal to the sum of the squares described on the other two sides.

The simplicity of the Pythagorean Theorem encourages exploration, and even many of the algebraic and geometric proofs can be done and easily understood in a very short time. But there are a number of extended applications and proofs that are indeed very complex. The fascination with the theorem is also fairly obvious considering how critically it connects to the sciences and engineering.

INVESTIGATION AND NOTES

According to some sources, there are nearly 400 unique proofs of the Pythagorean Theorem. Of course, not all of them relate to the standard coordinate geometry we see in secondary schools. Other applications and proofs can be found in vector relations, polar geometry, hyperbolic geometry, and even in the geometry of solids. Common adaptations and formulaic uses include the distance formula in algebra, Pythagorean trigonometric identities and derivations, and arc length calculations in integral calculus. Because of our familiarity with the basic premises of the Pythagorean Theorem, many learned mathematicians assume there is little more to know, but nothing could be further from the truth. Figure 6.1 illustrates one of the most basic, and earliest, proofs of the theorem using proportions of similar triangles. Though the proof shown in Figure 6.1 is simple and illustrates the continuity between geometric and algebraic methods, it is also the subject of speculation and debate among many mathematics historians. In fact, Euclid used a different proof that relied less on the idea of proportions, perhaps because proportions were not explored until later sections of the book, *Euclid's Elements*. Note also that no geometric squares are represented in this proof.

Figure 6.1: Proof of the Pythagorean Theorem Using Triangle Proportions

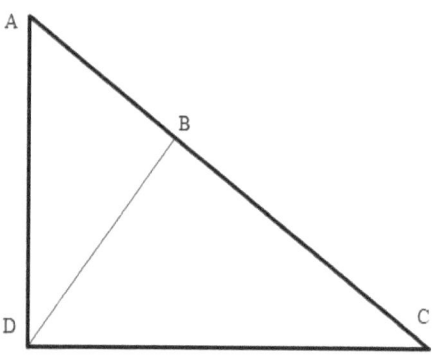

Assume triangle ADC is a right triangle
Triangles ADC, DBC, and ABD are similar

Therefore equating cosines give us:
$$\frac{DC}{AC} = \frac{BC}{DC} \text{ and } \frac{AD}{AC} = \frac{AB}{AD}$$

Rewriting the proportions and summing:
$DC^2 = AC \cdot BC$ and $AD^2 = AC \cdot AB$
$DC^2 + AD^2 = AC \cdot BC + AC \cdot AB$
$DC^2 + AD^2 = AC(BC + AB)$
$DC^2 + AD^2 = AC^2$

A different, and algebraically based, proof that involves squares is a nice exercise in introductory algebra. It illustrates the Pythagorean notation through polynomial multiplication and uses the squares we are so accustomed to seeing. This proof is particularly descriptive on a Cartesian coordinate graph and can even be used to prove the distance formula in algebra courses. Assume the large square has sides that are the sums of segments of length A and segments of length B. The square inscribe at an angle has sides of length C. Figure 6.2 illustrates this simple proof.

Figure 6.2: Algebraic/Geometric Proof using Polynomials

Area of the large square: $A = (a + b)(a + b) = a^2 + 2ab + b^2$

Area of the center square: $A = c^2 + 4\left(\frac{1}{2}ab\right) = c^2 + 2ab$
from the sum of the parts
where each triangle's area is $ab/2$

Equating the area forms: $a^2 + 2ab + b^2 = c^2 + 2ab$

Subtracting $2ab$ from: $a^2 + b^2 = c^2$
each side give us the
Pythagorean Theorem

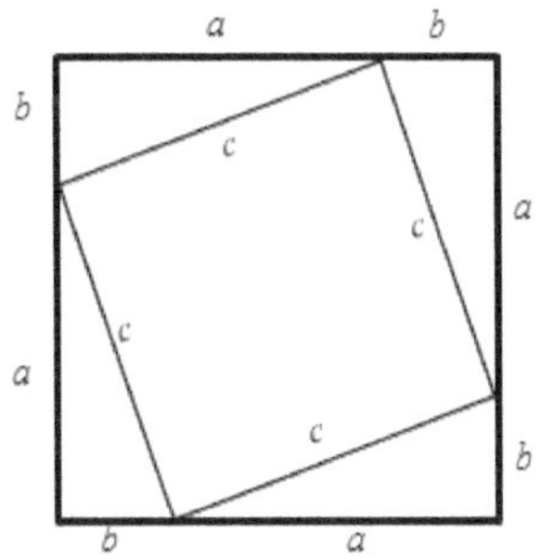

The proofs tend to continue on in this fashion, most relying on a combination of geometry and algebra to complete the task so we will now move on to application of the theorem within other mathematical structures. We can apply what we know about the general form of the Pythagorean Theorem to derive a general form of a distance formula on a coordinate system using the differences of the horizontal and vertical components of the points as the legs of a right triangle. Figure 6.3 illustrates an intuitive derivation of the distance formula.

Figure 6.3: General Cartesian Distance Formula

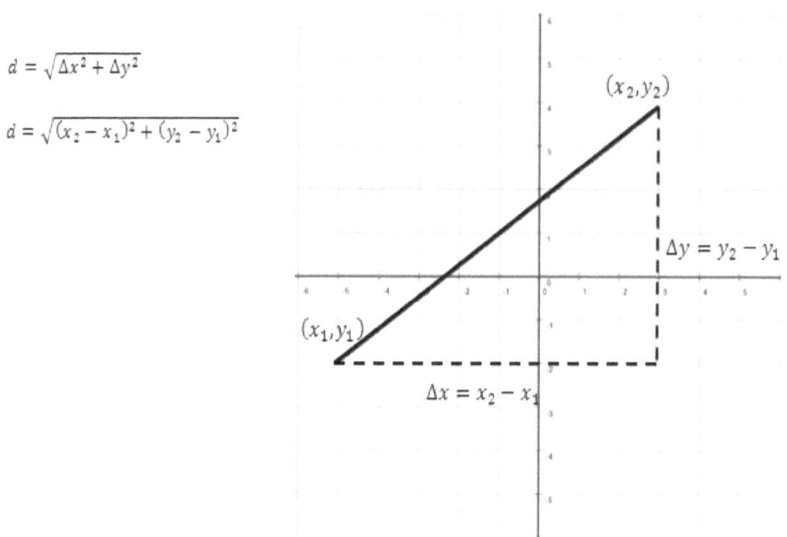

This distance formula derivation is going to be helpful even though it is fairly familiar and simple to understand. In fact, it will be used several more times to help generate additional formulas and theorems but there are a few other relationships we need to establish before we move on. In particular, we want continue with some special visual applications of the Pythagorean Theorem, and those for the purpose of identifying some other critical relationships within the unit circle. We will do this prior to deriving any more formulas because we need to set the stage for some trigonometric identities and relationships.

First, we will apply the theorem to some of the circle segments we explored in Article 1 so we can create a visual representation of the trigonometric identities. If we revisit the circle diagram (Article 1, Figure 1.10, page 29) with the various trigonometric segments given, we can easily see how the Pythagorean identities emerge from the triangles. Let us assume that we are using a circle having a radius of 1 unit in length. We can derive the following Pythagorean identities from the circle segments in Figure 6.3 simply by finding right triangles. Look for triangles made by sets of trigonometric segments.

Figure 6.3: Key Pythagorean Identities

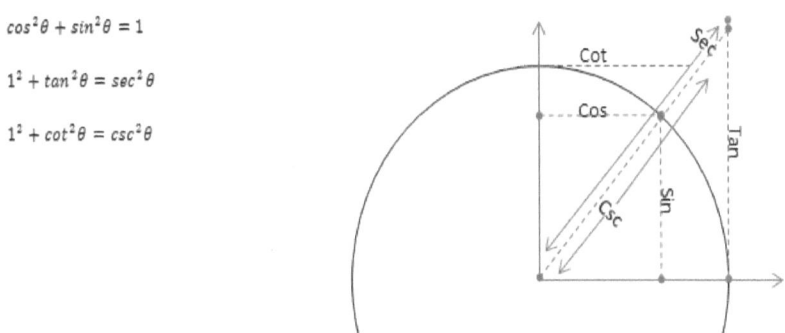

Though there is no formal proof of the identities listed with this diagram, we can be fairly confident in claiming them to be true. By inspection we can see that it is appropriate to apply the Pythagorean Theorem because it involves segments intersecting at right angles on the rectangular coordinate system to which they are applied. As a result, any triangle partially represented with the horizontal and vertical components of a rectangular coordinate system is automatically connected to Pythagorean solutions.

As we continue our exploration of the Pythagorean Theorem, you will find that the more advanced formula and identity derivations appear to be exclusively mathematical in their profile. It is important to keep in mind that the theorem itself has a number of useful applications to other STEM disciplines, and not just in subjects like physics where triangle rules are often used for processes such as vector and matrix calculations. For example, carpenters often use the Pythagorean triple 3-4-5 to *create* right triangles. This is an excellent mathematical strategy simply because the theorem has reflexive properties between algebra and geometry. If a 3-4-5 Pythagorean triple can be derived from a right triangle, then we also can define measurements of 3, 4, and 5 arranged in a triangle to establish a right angle.

    Our next strategy will be to complete a more advanced proof of the Pythagorean Theorem using a combination of the trigonometric identities from Figure 6.3 and the distance formula shown in Figure 6.2. We will begin this process by defining three points and deriving a way to calculate length using the Law of Cosines. The *Law of Cosines* relates the lengths of the side of a plane triangle and is a generalized form of the Pythagorean Theorem. It is an extremely simple derivation if we plot the points that define the triangle on a coordinate system and then use the distance formula. Figure 6.4 shows three points, the first at (0,0), the second on the *x*-axis at a distance of b from the origin (b,0), and the third at a distance of a from the origin (a·cos θ, a·sin θ). The sides of the triangle are then defined as a, b, and c where c is an unknown.

Figure 6.4: Derivation of the Law of Cosines using the Distance Formula

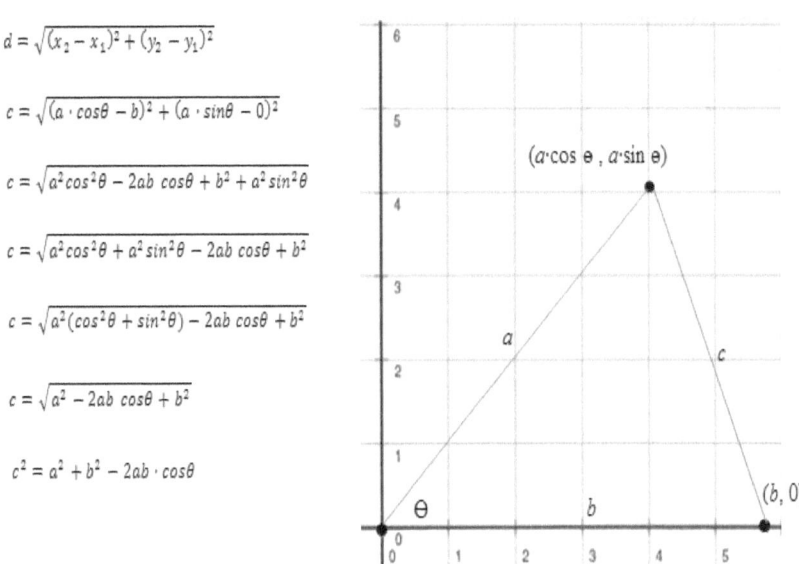

Now that we have developed several formulas and relationships using the Pythagorean Theorem, we can explore some practical extensions. It is important to understand that many mathematical situations equating areas can be represented by the Pythagorean Theorem. For example the geometric representation of the Pythagorean Theorem shows an arrangement of three squares where the sides of the squares represent the sides of a right triangle. The squares can also be multiplied by a scalar constant across the equation and still maintain the equality. Having the ability to multiply constants through the equation justifies us in suggesting that there are an infinite number of Pythagorean triples. For example, the 3, 4, 5 triangle dimensions can be doubled to produce a

6, 8, 10 triangle or tripled to produce a 9, 12, 15 triangle. Scalar multiplication also allows us to manipulate other equations that are quadratic. For example, the kinetic energy equation can be used within the Pythagorean equation to estimate or predict stopping distances for cars. Figure 6.5 illustrates how the differences in energy for cars travelling at different speeds can be calculated using the Pythagorean Theorem.

Figure 6.5: Energy Calculations for a System of Motion

$K.E. = \frac{1}{2}mv^2$ is the kinetic energy equation.

If we assume that half of the mass of the car is a constant, then we can equate three velocities (v_1, v_2, and v_3) using the Pythagorean Theorem. Sample velocities of 30mph, 40 mph, and 50mph are illustrated here.

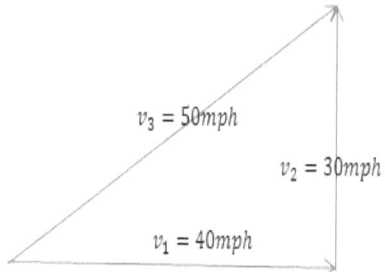

Using $\frac{1}{2}m$ as a constant, we can represent the system of kinetic energy using the Pythagorean Theorem

$$\frac{1}{2}mv_1^2 + \frac{1}{2}mv_2^2 = \frac{1}{2}mv_3^2$$

Factoring out the mass constant allows us to equate the velocities.

$$\frac{1}{2}m(v_1^2 + v_2^2) = \frac{1}{2}mv_3^2$$

What this roughly suggests is that a single car of a constant mass contains the same amount of kinetic energy as two other cars of the same mass given that their velocities satisfy the Pythagorean Theorem. Put in practical terms, a car traveling 50 mph has the same amount of kinetic energy as two other cars combined where one is going 30 mph and the other going 40 mph. This lesson becomes especially powerful when it is translated to stopping distances. Suppose we manipulate the Pythagorean Theorem to represent the differences in velocities.

Assuming that the kinetic energy in the system can be represented using the Pythagorean Theorem:

$$\frac{1}{2}mv_1^2 + \frac{1}{2}mv_2^2 = \frac{1}{2}mv_3^2$$

We can represent the slowing of a car by simply subtracting the velocities:

$$\frac{1}{2}mv_1^2 = \frac{1}{2}m(v_3^2 - v_2^2)$$

Again, using our sample velocities of 30 mph, 40 mph, and 50 mph, we can make substitutions to calculate the amount of energy necessary to slow a car to a given speed. For example, in order slow our car from 50 mph to 40 mph it takes as much energy as slowing our car from 30 mph to 0 mph. This can be illustrated by the change in velocity from v_3 to v_2 in the equation. That change in velocity represents the same amount of energy as v_1. Also, slowing our car from 50 mph to 30 mph takes as much energy as slowing from 40 mph to 0 mph. If we translate this energy into a Pythagorean diagram, we could easily translate the energy into sliding distances on a slippery surface such as an icy road. What this would mean is that if you slammed on the brakes upon seeing an object in the road while going 40 mph and you were able to stop inches before hitting the object, the result would be much different at a higher speed. Consider the same scenario going 50 mph. If we stopped inches short of the object at 40 mph, an original velocity of 50 mph for the same conditions would mean that we would hit the object with a force equivalent to 30 mph because the additional kinetic energy must satisfy the Pythagorean equation. The Pythagorean Theorem, then, gives us a nice tool for describing the energy left in a system when slowing from one speed to another. For example, a popular interstate highway speed is 75mph. If we want to know the amount of energy (in terms of speed) that it would take to slow our car to, say, 55mph, we could simply calculate the square root of the difference of the squares of each of our speeds:

$$75^2 - 55^2 = v^2 \approx 51 mph$$

Let us suppose that two drivers slam on the brakes at the same point in the road, in order to avoid an object in the road; one is traveling 75mph and the other at 55mph. If the 55mph driver is able to avoid the object by mere inches, the 75mph driver will still be traveling nearly 51mph when he hits the object. The triangular model using the Pythagorean Theorem is illustrated in Figure 6.6.

Figure 6.6: Stopping Distance Model using the Pythagorean Theorem:

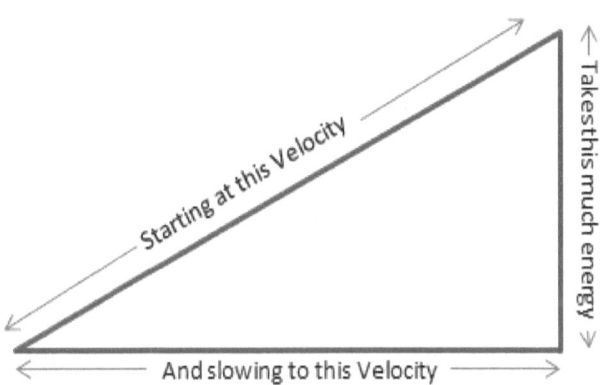

Of course this model does not represent exact stopping distances because there are so many other factors that need to be considered in such a calculation, such as the road conditions, the quality and technology related to the car's brake system, the driver's skill and reaction time, et cetera. However, what this also tells us is that the recommended following distance of 2 seconds behind the car in front of us becomes less and less safe as the speed of the traffic increases. This is because velocity, which is calculated as distance over time, is a linear measurement. Kinetic energy from increased speeds, however, is a quadratic measurement since the energy increases as the square of the velocity. Essentially cars following at a distance of two seconds at 60 mph, for instance, have a much more reliable safety buffer than cars following at a distance of two seconds at 75 mph.

Our final look at an application of the Pythagorean Theorem will be to examine how it helps us establish accurate measurements along a curve. In general, linear distances are fairly simple to calculate while distances defining curved paths are a bit more difficult. If we do not mind a "method of exhaustion" such as that employed by Archimedes in the calculation of Pi, we could trace our curve with a series of straight line estimates. If you recall, we started to do this in the Brachistochrone problem (Article 3, figure 3.2, page 55). In this scenario, we would add the values of each tiny line segment along the curve and use the total as an estimated length of the curve. The more tiny line segments there are, the better the estimate of the length of the curve. Figure 6.7 illustrates a discrete version of this method for a random curve through multiple iterations. Again, suppose we are attempting to calculate the length of a curve on a graph from the point A to a point B.

(Diagram can be found on the following page)

Figure 6.7: Curved Path Defined by Segments

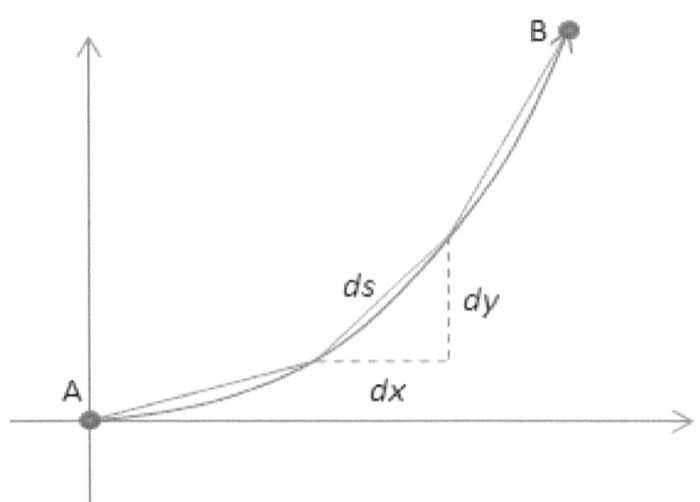

Note that the displacement (length) of a given segment *ds* can be defined by the Pythagorean Theorem (distance formula) in terms of the slope of the line where we use the displacement or change in *x* and *y* as *dx* and *dy*:

$$ds = \sqrt{dx^2 + dy^2}$$

Adding all such segments would give an estimate of the length of the curve. Better estimates could be obtained by using smaller and smaller segments

Putting our function in terms of the Pythagorean Theorem under the radical will now provide us with a function we can integrate. We do this by factoring dx^2 from each term under the radical:

$$ds = \sqrt{\left(\frac{dx^2}{dx^2} + \frac{dy^2}{dx^2}\right)dx^2}$$

Integrating with respect to x will essentially add all of the tiny segments together giving us the length of the curve:

$$s = \int_a^b \sqrt{1 + \left(\frac{dy}{dx}\right)^2}\, dx$$

This can also be written in a more familiar form as:

$$s = \int_a^b \sqrt{1 + (f'(x))^2}\, dx$$

Given our new formula, let us now look at an example. Suppose we want to find the length of the curve $f(x) = x^{3/2}$ from (0,0) to (4,8). The curve is, of course, only a gentle curve so the measurement should not be much longer than a straight segment connecting the points. The distance of an actual straight segment would be $4\sqrt{5} \approx 8.944$. The length of the curve should be just slightly longer and would be found by using our arc length formula as follows:

We would first find the derivative of our curve:

$$f(x) = x^{3/2}; \quad f'(x) = \frac{3\sqrt{x}}{2} = \frac{3}{2}x^{1/2}$$

We now substitute our derivative into our formula:

$$s = \int_0^4 \sqrt{1 + \left(\frac{3x^{1/2}}{2}\right)^2}\, dx$$

Simplifying the integral gives us the following:

$$s = \int_0^4 \sqrt{1 + \frac{9x}{4}}\, dx$$

We use u-substitution to rename the integrand:

$$u = 1 + \frac{9x}{4}, \quad du = \frac{9dx}{4}, \quad dx = \frac{4du}{9}$$

Remember that in doing this we also need to rename our limits of integration in terms of u. Further, we will write the integrand in exponential form:

$$s = \int_1^{10} u^{1/2} \frac{4du}{9}$$

Substituting the *du* form of *dx* and pulling the constant out gives us a function we can integrate.

$$s = \frac{4}{9} \int_1^{10} u^{1/2} \, du$$

Integrating and substituting our upper and lower limits gives us the approximate length of the curve:

$$\frac{4}{9} \left[\frac{2u^{3/2}}{3} \right]_1^{10} = \frac{8}{27} \left[(10)^{3/2} - (1)^{3/2} \right] \approx 9.07$$

SUMMARY

There are of course many, many more proofs and applications of the theorem, but the main purpose of this chapter was to demonstrate just a few brief examples of how it is applied within many different disciplines including algebra, geometry, trigonometry, physics, and calculus. It should also be noted that the arc length example using the function $f(x) = x^{3/2}$ is a very common example shown in calculus books. The presentation given for arc length was more an effort to illustrate how the simplicity of the Pythagorean Theorem has evolved into newer forms of mathematics so as to be useful in entirely new ways and at increasing levels of complexity. This is the case with many of the mathematical topics we routinely think of as *only* algebra, or *only* geometry. As you progress through the remainder of this book, expect to see the Pythagorean Theorem appear several more times. It really does epitomize the power, flexibility, utility, and complexity of mathematics throughout the realms of numbers, algebra, and geometry.

ADDITIONAL READINGS

Bernhoic, E. (2011). The Pythagorean Theorem: The Way of Truth. Ancient History Encyclopedia. Retrieved at

Davenport, C., & Woolner, K. (1999). Revisiting the Pythagorean Theorem: Putting Bill James' Pythagorean Theorem to the Test. Baseball Prospectus. Retrieved from www.baseballprospectus.com/article.php/articleid=342

Kaplan, R., & Kaplan E. (2012). Hidden Harmonies: The Lives and Times of the Pythagorean Theorem. Bloomsbury Press. ISBN: 978-1608193985

Maor, Eli. (2010). The Pythagorean Theorem: A 4000-Year History. Princeton Science Library. ISBN: 978-0691148236

SECTION 2: MATHEMATICAL "DEVICES"

The term *engineering* is typically one that conjures visions of people engaged in a process of creating tangible devices, from the very large to the very small. Just about everything we use in the modern world, from bridges and airplanes to calculators and doorknobs, are all the products of some form of engineering or design efforts. Engineering in all of its forms is really about innovation and design cycles but the products that result from engineering often begin as nothing more than mathematical symbols and models on a page. These mathematical models can themselves be devices and so the term *mathematical engineering* can aptly describe the efforts that produce mathematical products. Mathematical engineering is the result of the engineering process being applied to the synthesis of mathematical ideas in a way that something useful emerges. In some cases, this may be as simple as the production of a special formula. In other cases, it may result in a complex diagram that allows us to make useful decisions about how to measure or calculate with numbers. *Section 2: Mathematical Devices* provides an overview of how the tangible products of mathematics emerge from engineering design heuristics. The mathematical concepts presented in Section 2 are as follows:

    Article 7: Nomographs: An Introduction to Mathematical Engineering
    Article 8: The Solution Shark: A New Ruler Technology
    Article 9: Napier's Bones and Lattice Computation
    Article 10: Consul the Educated Monkey and Number Pyramids
    Article 11: Basic Sundials and the Measurement of Time

ARTICLE 7: NOMOGRAPHS: AN INTRODUCTION TO MATHEMATICAL ENGINEERING

ABSTRACT: Nomographs are mathematical tools that have their function in the interplay of mathematical relationships. The narrative presented herein illustrates how mathematics defines the utility of engineering based tools and coins the term *mathematical engineering*. Familiar concepts related to geometry are leveraged to create interactive mathematical relationships including several unique ways to use number lines and quadratic graphs to do calculations that involve multiplication, root extraction, and even identifying rational exponents.

INTRODUCTION

Nomographs are *simple* mathematical tools based primarily on the use of number lines. *Simple*, however, does not necessarily mean popular or even familiar in today's world; although, there was a time when nomographs were very popular. For the most part, number lines are now thought of as early mathematical learning devices and are not typically explored much past the elementary grades. Nomographs, however, probably should be explored in much greater depth in schools because of the way they can connect topics from simple mathematics to topics in more complex forms mathematics. For example, a nomograph can, through a series of interconnected developmental explorations, describe how addition evolves into multiplication, then to exponential and logarithmic notation. Additionally, the concepts associated with nomographs are what make certain kinds of charts and matrices work. In fact, they are most often associated with numeric tables, graphs, and charts. An example might be a graphical matrix that helps us to determine values for variables such as wind-chill index. This use of mathematical relationships to create informational tables, graphs, and charts can, to a large degree, be thought of as the process of *Mathematical Engineering*.

The word *nomograph* is formally defined as a diagram representing the relations between three or more variable quantities by means of a number of related scales. This kind of nomograph-based product is, in essence, the outcome of engineering heuristics applied to numeric, algebraic, and geometric ideas in much the same ways that new kinds of gears or bridge supports are the outcome of innovations in mechanical and civil engineering. Nomographs are usable mathematical products that come from innovative ways of looking at numeric and spatial relationships.

There are of course, many kinds of nomographs. Some involve the use of straight lines, while others combine straight lines and curves. To a small degree, the overlapping vesica piscis from Article 1, which illustrated segments lengths of incremental roots, was a kind of nomograph using the spatial relationships of intersecting circular regions to establish segment lengths. Most nomographs, however, allow us to have a bit more control over how we select and compare the data points because they allow us to choose the values to be compared. In fact, most nomographs are thought of as calculators, and were initially used largely in engineering. They were first brought into use in the late 1800's by a French engineer named Philbert Maurice d'Ocagne and were used extensively in the engineering field to provide engineers with graphical calculations of complex formulas. Most nomographs use a parallel coordinate system rather than a Cartesian coordinate system, but there are exceptions. Nomographs were also especially popular through the first part of the 20th century among people who did not own sliderules and were not well versed in simplifying mathematical expressions where values were substituted into algebraic formulas.

INVESTIGATION AND NOTES

The nomographs illustrated herein will start with a simple process of addition and slowly evolve into a non-sliding sliderule. Other nomograph models will be explored as well, such as parabolic nomographs, which can also be used to multiply and extract roots. The linear nomograph used for simple addition is constructed by establishing three evenly spaced lines and then creating evenly spaced increments on the lines. Figure 7.1 illustrates a basic addition nomograph using positive integers. To use the nomograph, a transversal (sometimes called an *isopleth*) is extended across all three lines. The outside number lines contain the addends of the problem. The solution can be found where the isopleth crosses the center line. Figure 7.1 illustrates the expression $3 + 5 = 8$.

(Diagram can be found on the following page)

Figure 7.1: Addition Nomograph Illustrating 3 + 5 = 8

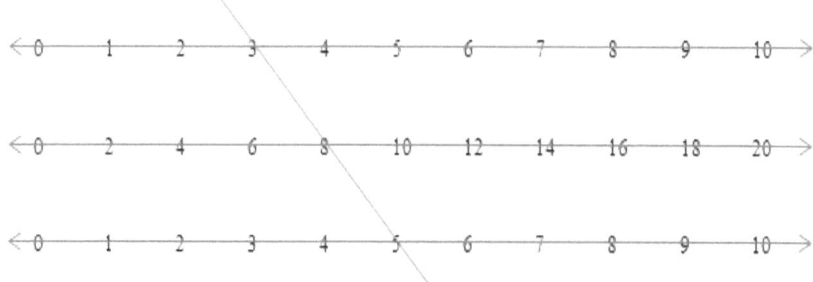

Note how the number line in the center is incremented with values that are double the value of their counterparts from the outside number lines. Geometrically, the point on the center line is essentially an average of the outside distances. By doubling the values, we create a sum. The reason this works is based on a very familiar geometric idea associated with triangles. Assume that we are looking at a right triangle. If we bisect the vertical segment of the right triangle and extend a segment parallel to the base until it intersects the hypotenuse, the intersection point of the hypotenuse not only bisects the hypotenuse, the intersection point is directly above the midpoint of the base. The 1 to 2 ratios are maintained. Generating a nomograph is essentially a process of creating a series of similar triangles. This idea will be explored in depth in Article 9 in a section that illustrates the process of multi-secting line segments. Ultimately, the relationships within similar triangles and circles are responsible for many of the mathematical tools that are used in various charts and tables.

Now, to create a nomograph that is more accurate, we would simply provide evenly spaced increments between the numeric values on the center line. The increments really only provide points of reference for us. We could add numbers defined by any random point on the outside lines (even if they were not labeled) and expect the sum (also not necessarily labeled) to be accurately represented as an intersecting point on the center line. Additionally, we could label the increments on the three lines to represent any fraction or decimal we desired. Figure 7.2 illustrates the addition of fractional values. Note that the nomograph in Figure 7.2 includes the additional increments on the center line.

Figure 7.2: Fraction Nomograph illustrating ½ + 1¼ = 1¾

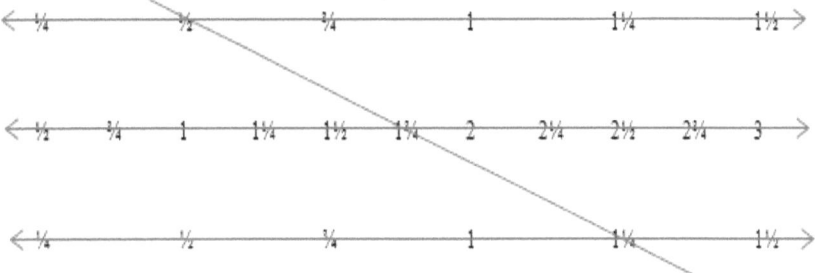

The nomograph concept can be adapted to include the addition of negative numbers by extending the three number lines in the negative direction. So, we can see with the various modifications of the number lines, the nomograph has slowly evolved from whole number addition to the addition of fractions and finally, negative values. This evolution suggests that the concept could possibly be adapted further to a model that works for multiplication. All that would need to be done is for the multiplication process to be represented as addition. This should not be too difficult of a task given that multiplication is often represented as repeated addition. Labeling the increments on the number line, however, is not quite as intuitive as it might first appear. In order for us to represent multiplication as a process of addition, we need to recall an algebraic rule for multiplying polynomials with identical bases, but different exponents. Recall that $x^n \cdot x^k = x^{n+k}$ for all real numbers n and k. This algebraic property provides a way for us to multiply polynomials using a process of addition, so we should be able to adapt the process to our nomograph. Figure 7.3 illustrates this process for the multiplication problem $x^2 \cdot x^4 = x^6$. Note that the distances along the number line are now represented as exponents, so our scale is no longer linear in the strictest sense.

Figure 7.3: Polynomial Nomograph Illustrating $x^2 \cdot x^4 = x^6$

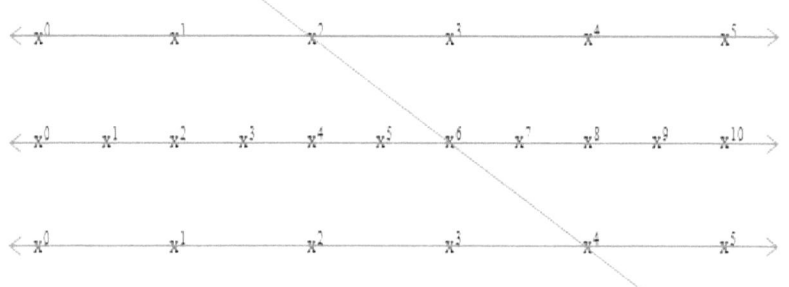

We can now adapt our polynomial model to create a multiplication nomograph by substituting any value greater than one in for x. Values less than one will work, but represent multiplication of small decimal numbers, and we are not quite to the point where we want to do that. Additionally, other non-integer rational values will make the increments difficult to label, so for now, we are going to substitute a small value for x such that our increments are integers. We will start our substitutions with $x = 2$. Figure 7.4 illustrates a multiplication nomograph using 2 as a base. Using the same transversal (isopleth) we can see that $x^2 \cdot x^4 = x^6$ (i.e. 4 x 16 = 64 where $x = 2$). Of course the same procedure could be used regardless of the value of x.

Figure 7.4: Multiplication Nomograph for Increasing Powers of 2

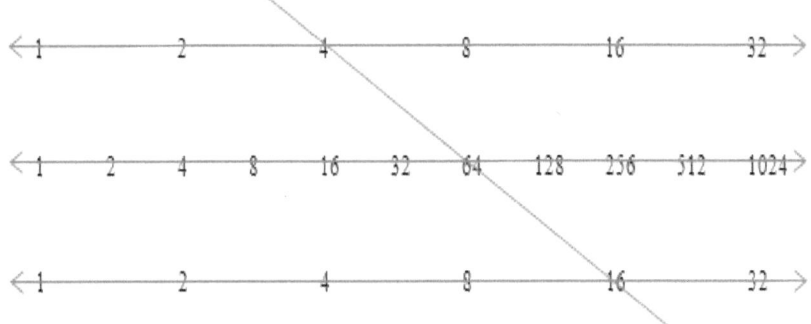

The nomograph shown in Figure 7.4 certainly represents a tool that can be used for multiplication, but our need to multiply numbers that are not multiples of two make this particular model impractical from an applied standpoint. For instance, if we wanted to multiply 5 by 11, we would end up doing a lot of guessing and interpreting. The question then becomes, how do we create a multiplication nomograph that can multiply any pair of numbers? The answer lies in the fact that we know the current nomograph only really works on an addition principle, so we need to explore a more efficient way of representing sums as products. We can do this by taking a step back and looking at our polynomial nomograph. In Figure 7.3, the distances of the increments on the nomograph were represented by the exponents. Given that we know this model works (we just demonstrated it in Figures 7.3 and 7.4), we should also be able to represent the distances as *logarithms*.

Suppose we have an exponent that is represented by a distance N on the top number line. Also, let us assume that this distance N corresponds to x^3. This is a measured distance or increment from a starting point of zero. We will do the same thing on the bottom number line with a distance K, which we will assume represents a value of x^4. If $N = x^3$ and $K = x^4$, then $3 = log_x N$ and $4 = log_x K$. The sum, represented on the middle number line would then be the sum of the logs. By revisiting the rules of logarithms, we recall that $log_x N + log_x K = log_x (NK)$. Note that the values of N and K have essentially been multiplied in this process. This model is represented in Figure 7.5.

Figure 7.5: Nomograph Representing Multiplication Using Logarithms

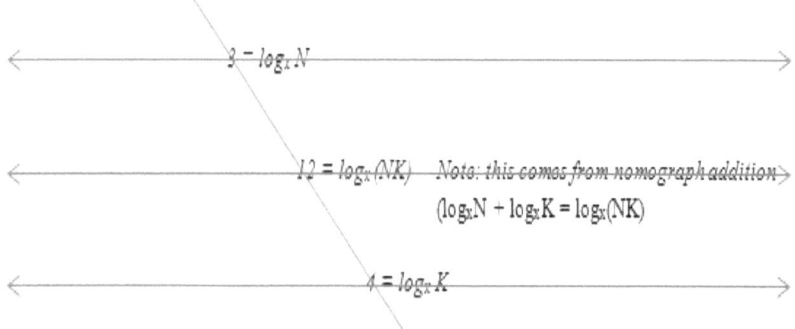

The process of using logarithms can now be generalized where we would use the logs of the numbers we want to multiply, namely, 1-10. And because these log values represent measurements, we could easily use a standard ruler to build the physical model of the multiplication nomograph. All we need is a fairly accurate log table and a ruler to create the increment on the number line (Figure 7.6).

Figure 7.6: Table of Logarithms for Incrementing the Exterior Lines

log 1 = 0   This increment would be at the left end of the exterior number lines
log 2 = .3010   The number 2 would be .3010 of the way down the exterior number lines
log 3 = .4771   The number 3 would be .4771 of the way down the exterior number lines
log 4 = .6021   The number 4 would be .6021 of the way down the exterior number lines
log 5 = .6990   The number 5 would be .6990 of the way down the exterior number lines
log 6 = .7782   The number 6 would be .7782 of the way down the exterior number lines
log 7 = .8451   The number 7 would be .8451 of the way down the exterior number lines
log 8 = .9031   The number 8 would be .9031 of the way down the exterior number lines
log 9 = .9542   The number 9 would be .9542 of the way down the exterior number lines
log 10 = 1.00   The number 10 would be on the right end of the exterior number lines

Our nomograph can now be created using the measurements listed in Figure 7.6. The product line (center) of the nomograph can be incremented by using the rules of logarithms as well. Let us suppose that we are extending a vertical isopleth through the nomograph at some distance A. We know that by summing the logs we would calculate *log A + log A = log (A·A)*. This can, of course, be written as *log A²*, and by extension, *2log A*. What this means is that we can use the same increments and simply square the center line numbers, or create new measurements that double our original log measurements (i.e. log 2 = .3010, so 2 log 2 = 2(.3010) = .602 = log 4). What we have created is a non-sliding *sliderule*. Figure 7.7 illustrates a completed multiplication nomograph with two multiplication expressions.

Figure 7.7: Multiplication Nomograph Illustrating 3 x 5 = 15 and 2 x 8 = 16

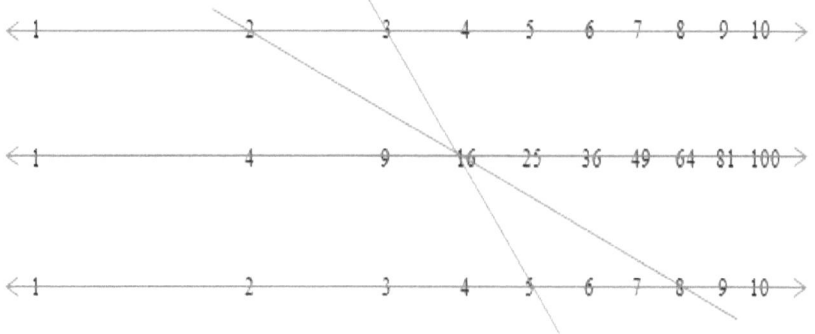

The multiplication nomograph in Figure 7.7 obviously still requires that we interpret our results because not all answers are represented on the number line in the center. Note specifically how the isopleth passes through the center line at a point just shy of 16 when multiplying 3 and 5, as opposed to the point of intersection of the product of 2 and 8. Using additional log calculations to create more increments on the number lines would, of course, result in more precise multiplication calculations.

Another advantage to the log nomograph in Figure 7.7 is that numbers of any size can be multiplied simply by moving the decimal in the factors we want to multiply. For example, if we wanted to multiply 18 x 34, we would need the graphical positions on the number lines of log 1.8 and log 3.4. These distances would be read as two digit factors. The center line where the product would be located would also need to be labeled with appropriately precise increments.

The next step of our nomograph investigation will extend our multiplication process into a way to calculate rational exponents. We have already explored how logarithms can be used to represent whole number exponents, so if we continue to exploit the power of the log calculations, we can create a new nomograph that is capable of calculating fractional exponents by modifying our nomograph model such that a logarithmic scale is set next to a linear scale and two isopleths are used. Consider the exponential expression $2^3 = 8$. We can represent this exponential expression as a log expression $log_2 8 = 3$ and apply the same principles as we did when multiplying. Using a change of base formula, we can verify the log/exponential relationship *log 8/log 2 = .903/.301 = 3*. This is a powerful relationship because it allows us to calculate the value of rational roots. Let us try a more difficult problem and represent it on a log/linear nomograph. Figure 7.8 illustrates $5^x = 8$.

(Diagram can be found on the following page)

Figure 7.8: Calculation of a Rational Exponent $5^x = 8$

Suppose: $5^x = 8$
Log form: $\log_5 8 = x$
Change of Base: $\log 8 / \log 5 = x$

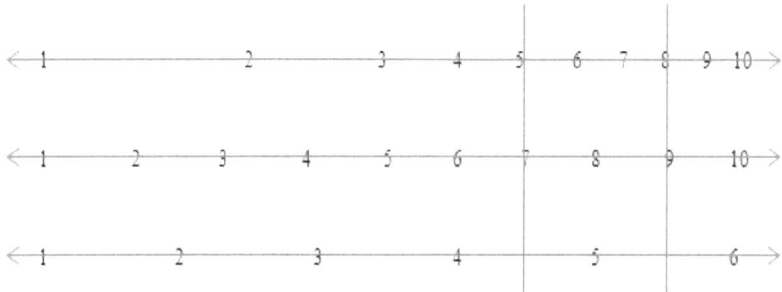

By using two vertical isopleths, we can determine the ratio of *log 8/log 5* as a rational equivalent. Note that in this example, the isopleth passing through *log 8* corresponds to a linear measurement (on the middle line) of approximately 9 while *log 5* corresponds to approximately 7 on the same scale. Using the linear ratio of 9/7, we can calculate the resulting exponent as approximately 1.2857. The actual exponent value is approximately 1.292. Our approximation using the linear scale is very close to the actual exponent. The estimate would be closer the more accurate we are with our linear measurement. With a little more exploration, we discover that the unit length of the linear scale is actually irrelevant because the ratio of distances of log 8 to log 5 is the same regardless of the linear scale being used. Notice that the scale on the third line in Figure 7.8 is different than that of the second line, but the ratio of the isopleth values on the third line of 5.5/4.4 = 1.25 still gives us a very close approximation of the actual exponent in $5^x = 8$.

Another lesson we learn from the nomograph model used in Figure 7.8 is that a nomograph does not necessarily have to be a comparison of two linear scales. In some instances, it is just as effective to compare a linear scale with a log scale or exponential scale. In fact the first two lines of the nomograph model shown in Figure 7.8 are simply a comparison of y-values of the function $f(x) = 10 \log x$. If we extend the idea of comparing linear scales to non-linear scales, we can derive other geometric models of nomographs that are non-linear. For example, if we look back at the process of multiplication, we can use a parabolic model. Figure 7.9 illustrates how the function $f(x) = x^2$ can be used with a linear isopleth to determine products from y-axis intersections.

(Diagram can be found on the following page)

Figure 7.9: Parabolic Nomograph Illustrating 1 x 2 = 2 and 2 x 1.5 = 3

Initial Function: $f(x) = x^2$
Isopleth Function: $g(x) = x+2$
Resulting Function: $h(x) = x^2 - x - 2$

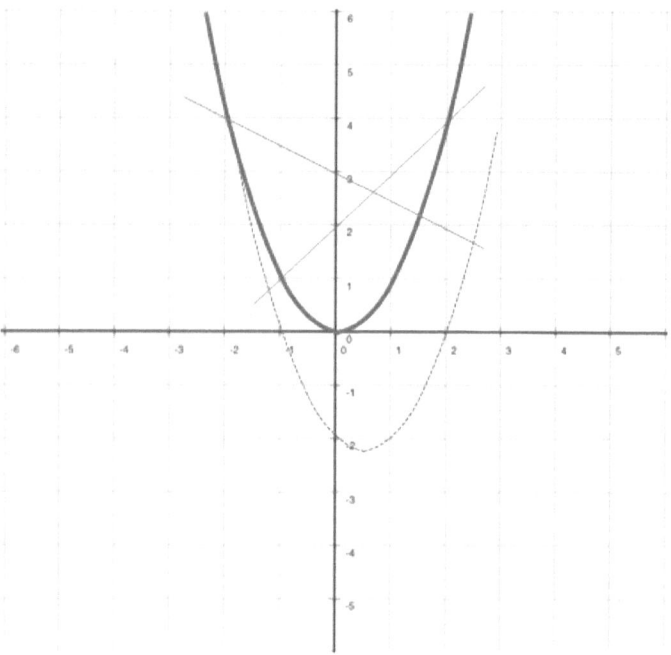

The examples illustrated in Figure 7.9 represent expressions where the factors of any given multiplication expression can be read from the intersections between the function and the isopleth. In the expression (1 x 2 = 2), note that the isopleth intersects the function at 1 on the left side of the y-axis (but it is read as positive 1 rather than negative 1) and intersects at 2 on the right side of the y-axis. The y-axis intercept provides the product. This process works as a combination of functions. Let us suppose that $f(x) = x^2$ (the function) and $g(x) = x + 2$ (the linear equation of the isopleth). At the intersections of the function and the isopleth $f(x) = g(x)$. If we translate this pair of functions to $f(x) - g(x) = 0$, we can see that it results in a parabola $x^2 - x - 2 = 0$, which has solutions at -1 and 2 (our factors), and if we graph the parabola, a y-axis intercept at -2 (the product of the intercepts). You will find the same holds true for a parabolic function representing the intersections of 1.5 and 2.

SUMMARY

The exploration and discovery of geometric relationships that are presented in the creation of tools such as nomographs can be thought of as including the same kind of design heuristics as those used in more formally recognized engineering processes. For this reason, *mathematical engineering* becomes a very real discipline. This kind of mathematical heuristic is not necessarily done in pursuit of new mathematics, but rather in the development of task-specific tools within the realm of existing, computational mathematics. What distinguishes the mathematical engineering aspects of the tools that are created is that the tools themselves have no moving parts. The functionality of the mathematical tools is primarily dependent on the spatial relationships established within the positioning of static physical structures such as lines, angles, and curves. Prior to the digital age, the development of mathematical tools that relied on the interplay of spatial relationships set the stage for the more advanced technologies we enjoy today. Devices such as sliderule calculators and sundials made humankind consider a larger sphere of possibilities in the physical universe.

ADDITIONAL READINGS

Almack, J.C., & Carr, W.G. (1926). The principle of the nomograph in education. The Journal of Educational Research. Vol. 14(5). 340-355.

Douglass, R. D. (1947). Elements of Nomography. McGraw-Hill Book Co; 1st Ed. ASIN: B0007DR6C0.

Evesham, H.A. (2010). The History and Development of Nomography. *CreateSpace Independent Publishing Platform.* ISBN-13: 978-1456479626

Levens, A. (1959). Nomography. *John Wiley & Sons; 2nd Ed.* ASIN: B0000CKG42.

Ostler, E. (2013). Exploring Logarithms with a ruler. The Mathematics Teacher. Vol. 106(9). 669-673.

ARTICLE 8: THE SOLUTION SHARK: A NEW RULER TECHNOLOGY

ABSTRACT: The Solution Shark is an educational ruler set that represents a multi-faceted analog mathematics technology. The concepts represent an extension of the ideas related to *mathematical engineering* as presented in Article 7. The Solution Shark combines a number of capabilities within a single mathematical tool that allow a user to measure, calculate, graph, and reference using a series of uniquely arranged geometric and spatial representations.

INTRODUCTION

The *Solution Shark* is included in this section on mathematical devices because it is a defining example of how mathematical functions can be leveraged into a practical tool that uses a number of different relationships within a single device. You might call it the Swiss Army Knife of ruler technology. The design process associated with the development of this ruler set is also a good example of mathematical engineering. The device itself has no moving parts, although the ruler set periodically relies on special positioning of one ruler with respect to the other for completing a number of the calculation and measurement functions. The ruler set was originally conceived to demonstrate the interplay between mathematical ideas involving algebra and geometry, and to help middle school and high school level mathematics students generate an understanding of how numbers, geometry, and algebra are related and interdependent.

The Solution Shark has seven primary functions, but can actually do much more. In fact, one of the main design distinctions of the ruler set is that it illustrates the articulation of simple mathematical ideas and strategies to more complex concepts by relating the majority of key concepts of secondary level mathematics to *measurement*. Nearly all of the functionality of the ruler set falls within some aspect of *measurement* including simple calculations involving whole numbers, decimals and fractions; conversions between different measurement systems; developing trigonometric ratios and relationships; doing slope calculations for lines; carrying out geometric constructions; and even in the generation of 3-8 sided regular polygons. The rulers can also function as a protractor, compass, or reference tool.

INVESTIGATION AND NOTES

The primary applications of the Solution Shark ruler set are focused on computational forms of geometry. Computational Geometry, as defined for secondary school applications, focuses on the empirical measurement elements of the physical world and verifying those relationships through algebraic and numeric patterns. The tool is not intended to aid in the understanding or development of geometric proofs or axiomatic systems. That is to say, numeric and algebraically represented relationships and concepts are the intended targets of learning to use the rulers instead of the formal reasoning associated with proof. The narrative hereafter is focused on the design parameters of the ruler set.

The Solution Shark ruler set consists of a pair of double sided rulers that can operate independently or interact in several unique ways to produce the following functions: English/Metric ruler, compass, protractor, calculator, numeric/geometric reference, bar graph constructor, and polygon constructor. The rulers are each 9 inches long and 1.5 inches wide to accommodate some operations that will be presented later on. Figures 8.1a and 8.1b show both the obverse and reverse diagrams of each ruler.

(Diagram can be found on the following page)

Figure 8.1a: Solution Shark Obverse

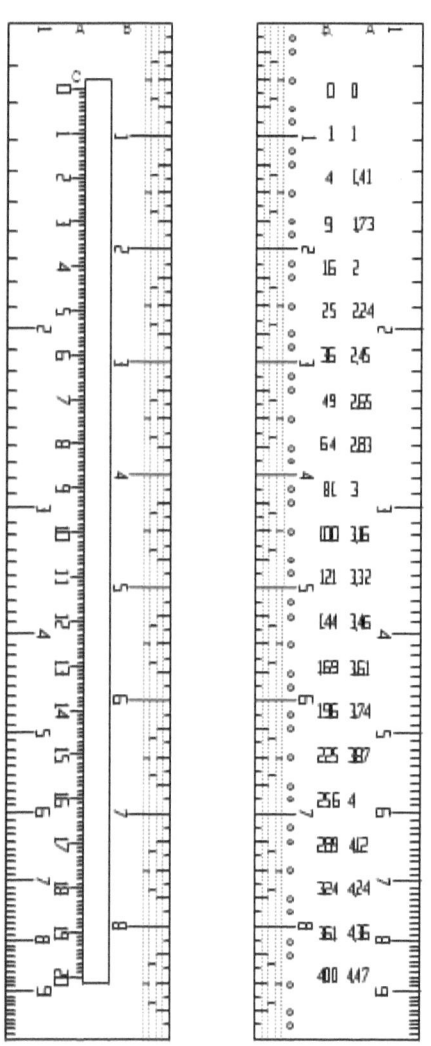

Figure 8.1b: Solution Shark Reverse

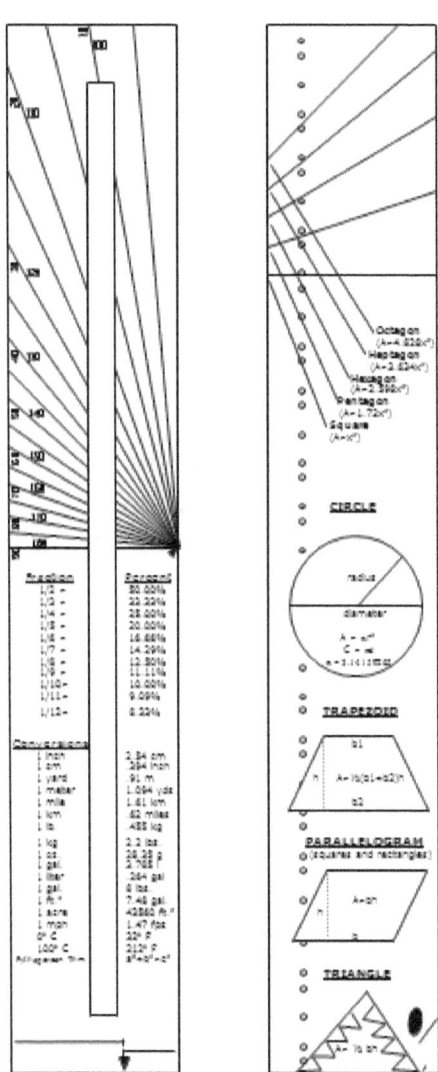

Function 1 – Linear Measurement: Notice in Figure 8.1a that there are three ruler systems represented on the ruler set. Both rulers have a standard English ruler except that the fractional increments are represented in a brick pattern and include eighths, fourths, thirds, and halves. The brick pattern increments allow for more direct comparison of fractional sizes, particularly with the thirds increment, which is rarely seen on rulers even though it is one of the most common fractions we encounter in computation. Additionally, the inch scales (B-scales) of each ruler can be positioned to illustrate the addition and subtraction process of whole numbers and fractions as represented by a kind of sliderule calculation.

The middle scale (C-scale) on the slotted ruler contains a metric ruler in centimeters and millimeters. This scale also acts as a guide in some of the calculation functionality related to roots and exponents. There is one other simple measurement instrument and that is on the reverse side of the slotted ruler. At the bottom of the reverse side of the slotted ruler (left ruler at the bottom of Figure 8.1b), there is a partition with an arrow that breaks the ruler into an inch segment and a half inch segment. This partition is available for one of the ruler functions related to measuring the slope of a line.

Function 2 – Computation: The Solution Shark is not intended to replace traditional methods or technologies in the process of calculation, but rather to illustrate what is happening when calculations are done. For example, when constant numbers (i.e. 1½ + 2¾) are added, repetition and practice overshadow the idea of what is happening. Each of the addends listed above are quantities. Those quantities could be distances, masses, volumes, etc. The sliderule function allows us to stack the distances of 1½ and 2¾. By placing the two rulers together as illustrated in Figure 8.2, we can see the addition process illustrated by the specific positioning of the rulers. If the two rulers are aligned so the ruler scales are together, sliding the top ruler to the right so that the left end of the top ruler is aligned with 1½ creates the first addend. We define this value as a measurement of 1½ inches on the bottom ruler. If we now look back at the top ruler at 2 ¾ (the other addend), we can see the sum of the two values on the slotted ruler, directly below our second addend.

Figure 8.2: Addition of 1½ + 2¾ Using a Sliderule Function

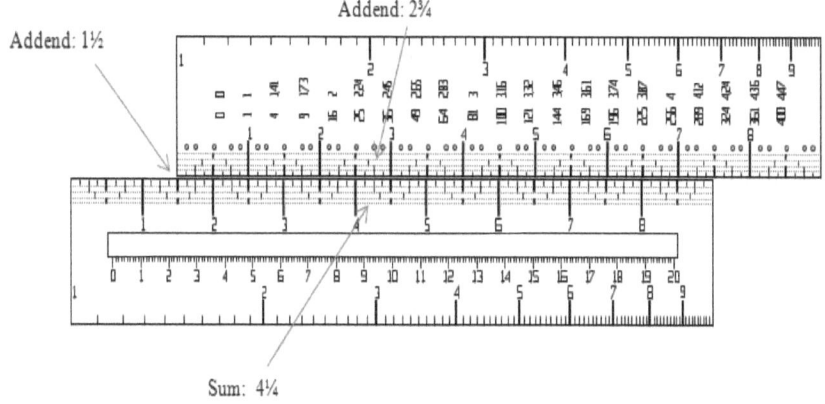

Subtraction would be done in a similar manner where we would align the minuend and subtrahend and then read the difference at the end of the top ruler. We can even arrange the rulers such that you read positive answers on the top ruler and negative answers on the bottom ruler.

The computation process continues into multiplication/division process by aligning the logarithmic scales on the opposite sides of each ruler. You may notice that the log scales read slightly differently, with the end of the ruler representing a value of 1 rather than 0. Also, the log scale collapses onto itself over and over as higher place values are represented. For example, the first nine numbers are simply located at each labeled increment on the scale. But the number 12, for example, would be represented by the increment shown 2 marks after the 1. Similarly, we could represent the number 27 by looking at the mark that is 7 units after the 2. Larger numbers, then, can only be estimated because they are only able to use the first two digits of a number. For instance, the number 345 would be located approximately half way between the 4th and 5th marks after the three. Reusing the scale in this way makes the multiplication and division processes a bit more complex too. If we want to multiply 8 x 7, we need to read from the right end of the ruler rather than from the left end as was done when we were adding. The reason is that if we slide the top ruler all the way over to the 8 increment on the bottom ruler, nothing would be below the 7 on the top ruler. We would simply run out of real estate on our bottom ruler. Instead, we would slide the top ruler in the opposite direction until we positioned the right end of the top ruler above the 8.

Figure 8.3 illustrates the multiplication process using factors of 7 and 8. Note specifically that we have repositioned the rulers so that the right end of the top ruler is aligned with 7 on the bottom ruler. The 7 on bottom ruler represents the first factor. If we now look to the top ruler to find 8, you can see that the product is represented immediately below the 8. Note that the 8 on the top ruler is lined up with the 6th mark after the 5 on the bottom ruler, which is of course, our product of 56.

Figure 8.3: Multiplication of 8 x 7 Using a Sliderule Function

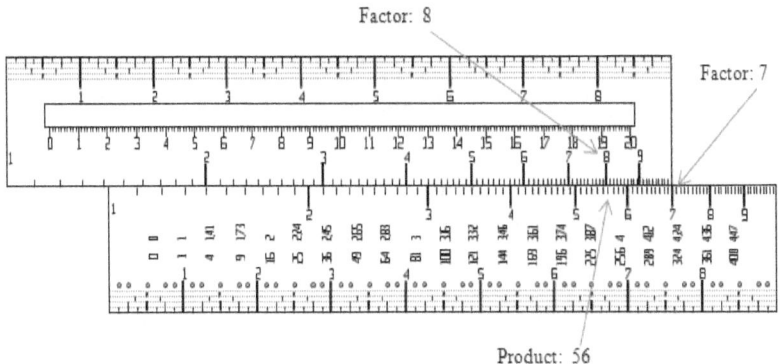

Division works in a similar fashion. We find our dividend on one of the rulers and align the divisor with it. This will produce the quotient at the end of the ruler. In the case of our multiplication problem, if we align 56 and 8 on the top and bottom rulers as our dividend and divisor, the quotient of 7 can be seen above the right end of the top ruler. As you might have surmised, computation of very large and very small numbers (in the form of decimals) is largely guesswork because we can only position the rulers to be accurate to two or three place value positions.

The next example of a calculation function of the ruler set also uses both rulers but in a different sort of way and involves the computation of squares and square roots. The computation itself is done by reading a table. That is to say that the calculation is not traditional in that the rulers do not need to be moved to different positions to do different calculations. Instead, we will reposition the rulers so that they arranged vertically with the slotted ruler literally resting on top of the solid ruler. The rulers should be positioned so that either of the two center columns of numbers on the solid ruler can be read through slot of the slotted ruler. Also, the slotted ruler should be positioned such that the metric ruler reads from small numbers to large numbers as you go from the top to bottom.

Figure 8.4 illustrates the arrangement of the rulers. Note that the slotted ruler would be placed on top of the solid ruler so the numbers from the solid ruler could be read through the slot; however, the diagram in Figure 8.4 shows how the alignment of the rulers allows numeric square and square root calculations to be done. To find the numeric square or square root of a number from 1-20, find the number on the centimeter scale from the slotted ruler and read the square (left column) or square root (right column through the slot on the solid ruler.

(Diagram can be found on the following page)

Figure 8.4: Using the Slot to Calculate Squares and Square Root

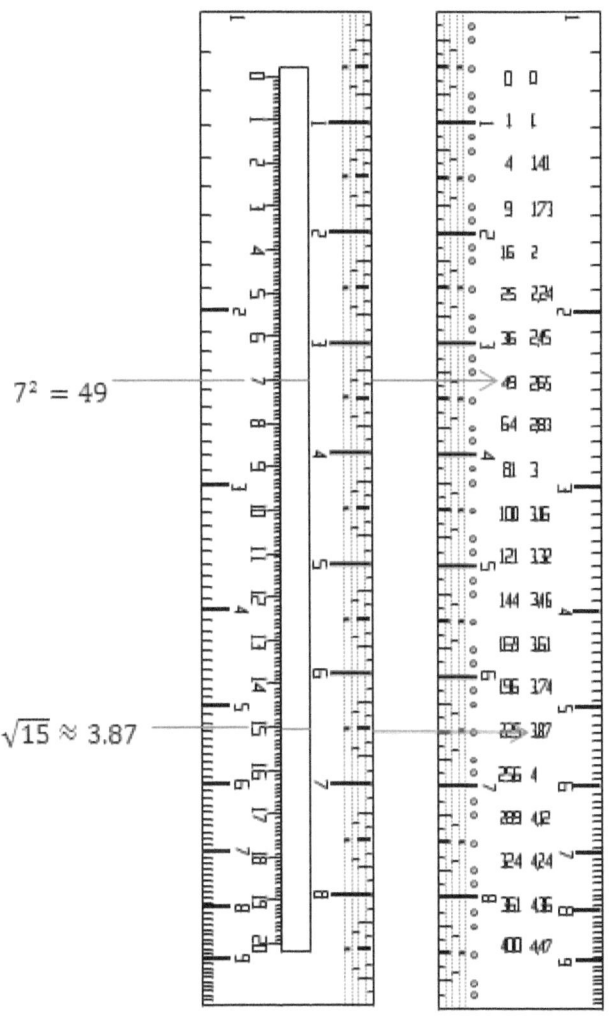

The limit of this functionality is that the ruler only represents the numbers from 1-20. For numbers higher than 20, the log scales can be used with a little additional effort. There are some other computational geometry based methods for calculating the roots using exponential rules that are interesting as well. For the most part, the alternative root extraction methods involve writing roots as products where one of the factors is the largest perfect square that can be extracted, which leaves the other factor as a smaller number.

Function 3 – Angular Measurement: On the reverse side of the slotted ruler there is a non-conventional protractor inlaid with two sets of numbers, one upright and the other sideways. The numbers are arranged in such a way that only the *upright* numbers are read during a measurement. One scale is for acute angles and the other is for obtuse angles. Also, in order to measure both acute and obtuse angles, both rulers are needed, but only the protractor ruler is necessary for determining the measurements. The second ruler acts only as a guide. Figures 8.5a and 8.5b illustrate the measurements of acute and obtuse angles.

(Diagrams can be found on the following page)

Figure 8.5a: Measurement of an acute angle

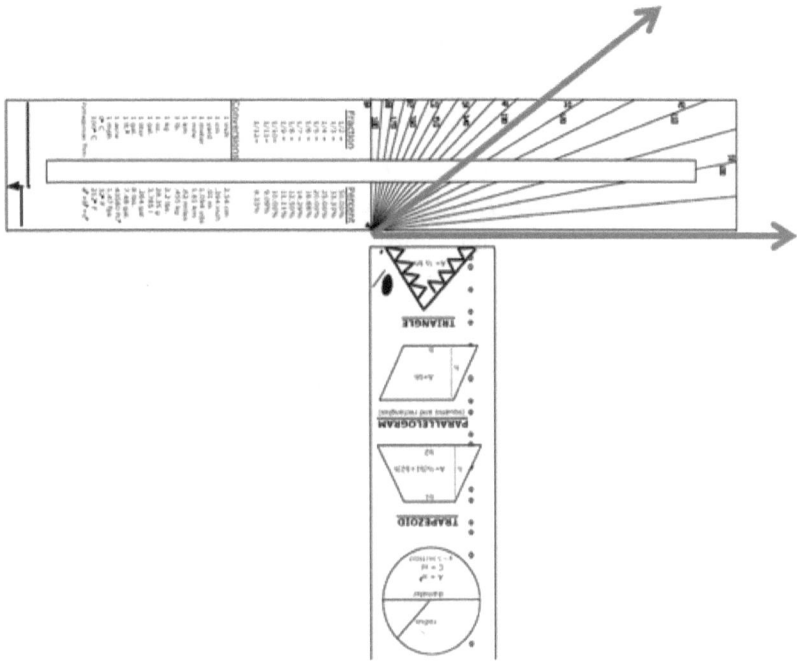

To use the protractor, we first position the "shark face" on the reverse of the solid ruler such that the *nose* of the shark is next to the vertex and the flat end of the ruler (the mouth of the shark) is aligned with the initial side of the angle. Next, the slotted ruler is positioned so that the tiny arrow in the middle of the ruler is also pointing at the vertex of the angle and the base of the ruler follows the initial side of the angle. Basically, the horizontal ruler in Figure 8.5a can simply be set flat against the shark face to create a working protractor. The angle is then read where the terminal side of the angle meets the opposite side of the ruler. Note that the measurement scale has a set of *upright* or readable numbers and a set of numbers that is readable when the ruler is positioned vertically. To measure an angle, only the upright scale is used. Finally, Figure 8.5a shows a slight gap between the rulers so that the angle is clear, but when measuring an actual angle, the rulers would be pushed flush against one another.

To measure an obtuse angle, we simply rotate the slotted ruler in Figure 8.5a so that it is positioned vertically. Notice that the tiny arrow on the slotted ruler is still pointing at the vertex and that the shark face is still aligned with the initial side of the ruler. The slotted ruler is then rotated 90 degrees counterclockwise from the image shown in Figure 8.5a. After this rotation, the scale used to measure obtuse angles shows the upright numbers and crosses the terminal side of the angle. Figure 8.5b illustrates the measurement of an obtuse angle.

(Diagram can be found on the following page)

Figure 8.5b: Measurement of an obtuse angle

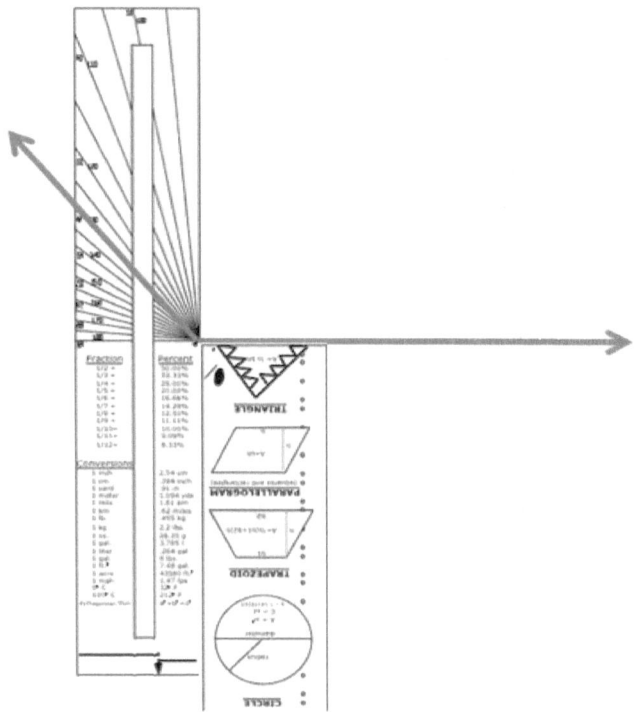

The method may appear to be a bit cumbersome but the upside is that the user must pay close attention to the parts of the angle, which may reduce the number of positioning errors and scale errors that occur with a standard protractor. This is primarily because of the rectangular shape, which is fairly unusual in a protractor but has some benefits. In fact, the rectangular shape provides several other advantages including the power to act as a tool for estimating simple trigonometric ratios. What makes this possible is the fact that the measurement gradations for the protractor intersect the top edge of a ruler along a straight line. This means the point at which they intersect the top line can be measured from the center of the ruler to the point of intersection.

Given that width of the rulers are a standard 1.5 inches, the basic sine, cosine, and tangent ratios can be derived by measuring the distance from the center of the slotted ruler to the intersection of any given angle along the top of the ruler and then using that measurement in a proportion with the 1.5 inch measurement of the width of the ruler. The same technique could be used by measuring the actual angle line from the vertex to the intersection at the top of the ruler. Figure 8.6 illustrates this process using an angle of approximately 30°.

Figure 8.6: Trigonometric Derivation of Sine, Cosine, and Tangent Ratios

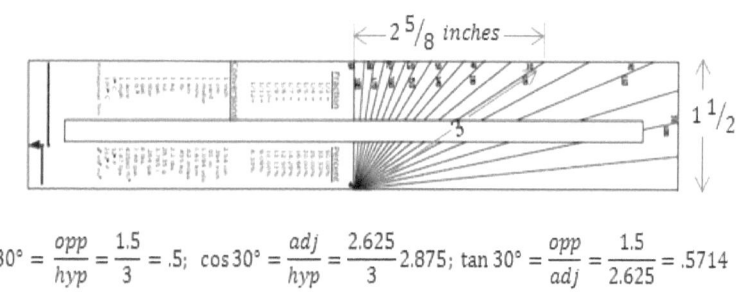

$$\sin 30° = \frac{opp}{hyp} = \frac{1.5}{3} = .5; \quad \cos 30° = \frac{adj}{hyp} = \frac{2.625}{3} = 2.875; \quad \tan 30° = \frac{opp}{adj} = \frac{1.5}{2.625} = .5714$$

As you can see, the calculations are not perfect, but they do create accurate enough ratios to provide decent estimates needed for various applied settings. The distances used for each angle can literally be measured using the other ruler, so the measurement aspect of these ratios can be easily reinforced. The only exceptions for the ratios are for the 5, 10, and 15 degree angles, which do not intersect the top side of the ruler. For those particular angles, the 1.5 inch height measurement cannot be used. They would each need to be measured individually for determining the value to be used for the *opposite* side of the triangle.

The final measurement based calculation that has been designed into the ruler specs is the arrow on the bottom of the slotted ruler. The arrow and the accompanying offset marks on either side of the arrow allow the user to make rough one-inch or half-inch measurements. This design aspect is primarily used for measuring the slope of a line on a graph. Suppose that a line is graphed on an unmarked coordinate system. Normally the slope would be difficult to obtain in terms of a rational number if the gradations are not available. The rulers, however, can be arranged so that the slope can still be determined.

Figure 8.7 illustrates how the rulers can be arranged to measure the slope of a random line. Note that both rulers are needed, but there are several ways they can be arranged to measure the slope with satisfactory accuracy. First, the reverse side of the slotted ruler must be positioned so that the arrow is pointing down and the tip of the arrow must be pointing at (touching) the graph of the line. The left side of the slotted ruler must simultaneously run along the y-axis. The solid ruler is then used to measure the distance from the base of the slotted ruler to the y-axis intercept of the line. This positioning of the rulers essentially creates a right triangle having a base measuring 1 inch. Given that slope is calculated as the change in y-values divided by the change in the x-values, any rational number created by using the ruler measurements would have an x-value change of 1, thus making the slope the measured y-value. This would happen because the slope represented by this system would automatically be Δy/1. See Figure 8.7.

Figure 8.7: Measuring Slope of a Random Line on an Unmarked Coordinate System

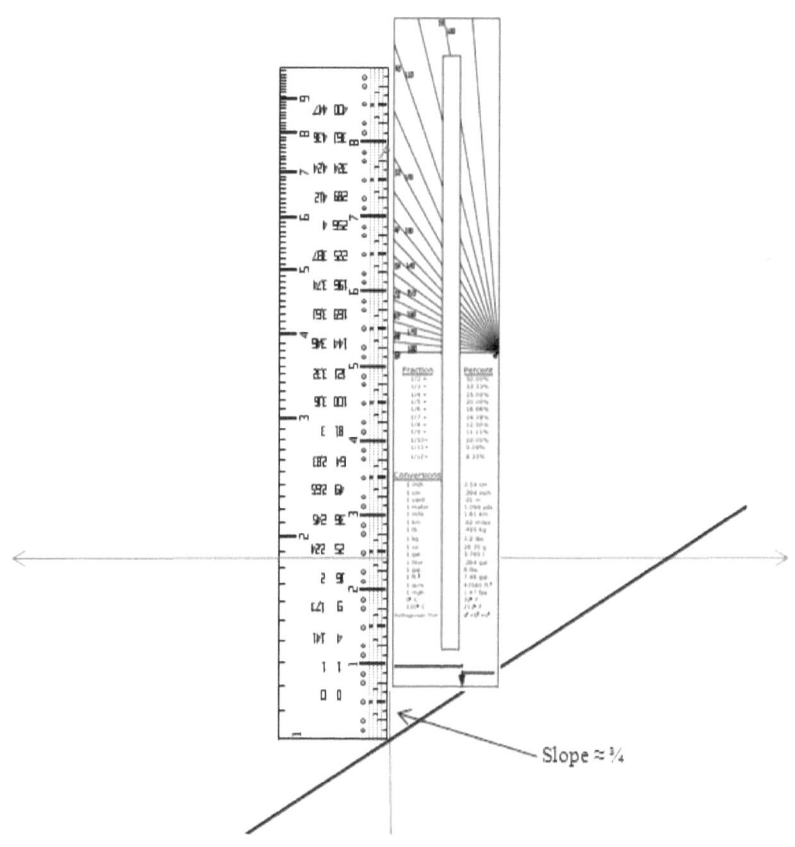

Note that a small triangle is created between the line and the rulers. The inch scale on the solid ruler (which is also aligned with the y-axis) is used to measure the distance along the y-axis from the y-axis intercept of the line to the point at the corner of the slotted ruler. Because the slotted ruler measures one inch from the edge to the tip of the arrow, the x-component of the slope (which is also the denominator of the slope ratio) will always be 1, and thus, the measurement of the numerator will automatically be the slope based on the identity for multiplication and division. In Figure 8.7, the measurement along the solid ruler is approximately 3/4, which represents the slope of the line for this particular example.

Function 4 – Compass: The solid ruler is offset with a series of holes, which are aligned with the ruler in ¼ and ½ inch increments. The holes are specifically designed for creating arcs and circles. This functionality allows the user to create circles within ¼ inch radius measurements. Two pencils or pens are needed to construct a circle or arc. One pencil or pen should be placed at the point where the center of the circle is to be located. The other is placed at the desired distance and rotated as far as needed to complete a given arc or circle. Figure 8.8 illustrates the initial position needed for the arc/circle function. Note that the pencils do not have to be placed at the end of the ruler and then at the given distance; but rather, only separated by a distance that represents the desired radius.

(Diagram can be found on the following page)

Figure 8.8: The Arc/Circle Function with a 3 Inch Radius

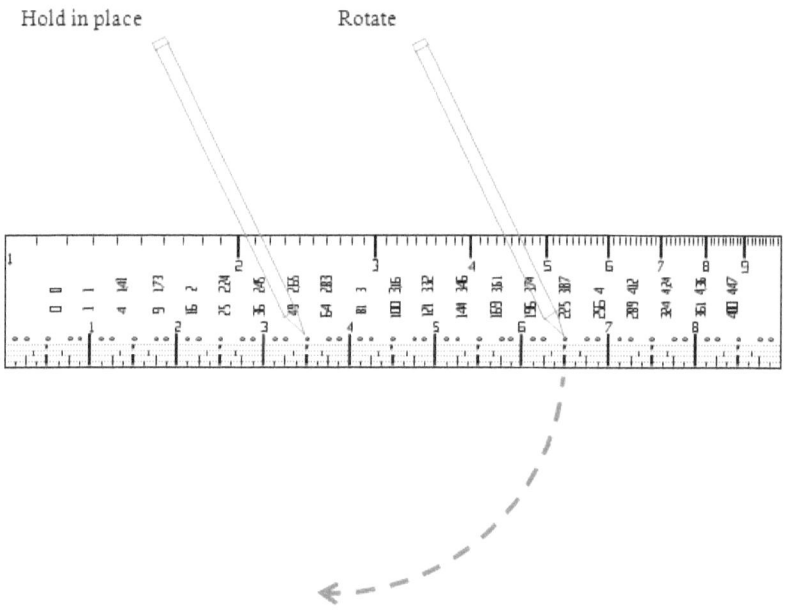

Function 5 – Polygon Construction: On the reverse side of the solid ruler is a series of lines that cross the ruler at a diagonal. These lines are positioned to create angles that allow for the construction of regular polygons including squares, pentagons, hexagons, heptagons, and octagons. The hexagon line can also be used to create an equilateral triangle if the direction of the construction is reversed from what is shown in Figure 8.9. Each *polygon line* is also accompanied with a formula that allows for the calculation of the area of the respective polygon based on the side length. The construction of the polygons requires a series of steps, and it is possible to create polygons with sides of any length, but again, it requires additional steps. Figures 8.9a-8.9d illustrates the rotations and ruler placements needed to construct a pentagon.

Figures 8.9a-8.9d: Positions and Rotations Needed to Construct a Pentagon

Figure 8.9a – Locate the Pentagon Line and mark points P1 and P2 on each side of the line.

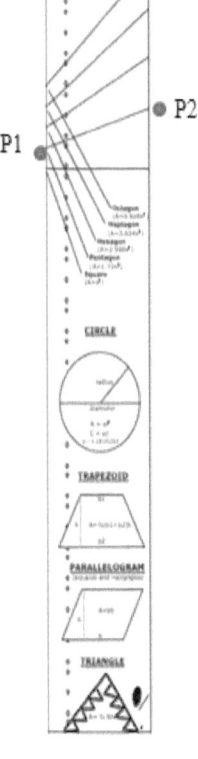

Figure 8.9b – Using the original two points, rotate the ruler clockwise until the dots are aligned with the top side Making sure P2 is at the end of the pentagon line, draw in P3 at the other end of the pentagon line.

Figure 8.9c – Rotating clockwise again so that the edge of the ruler is aligned with P2 and P3, draw P4 on the opposite end of the pentagon line.

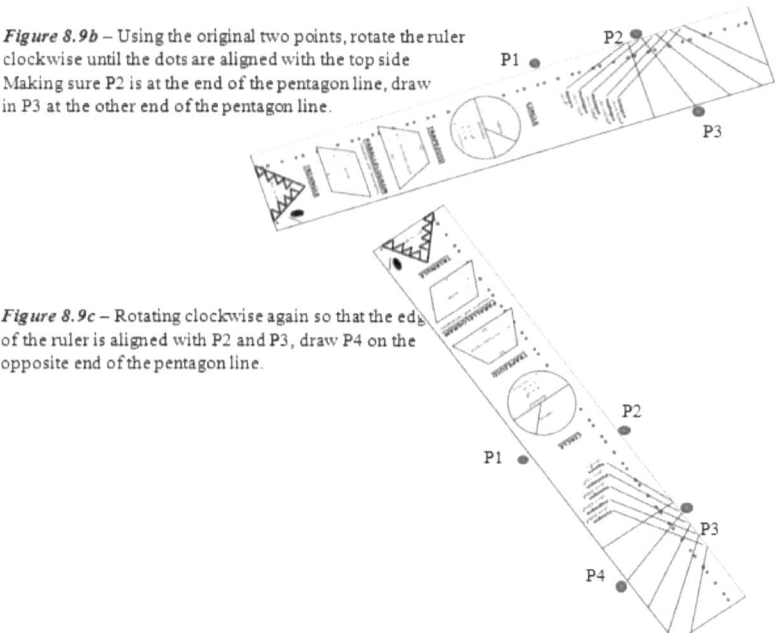

Figure 8.9d – Rotate the ruler clockwise one last time such that P3 and P4 are aligned with the edge of the ruler and mark the final vertex, P5

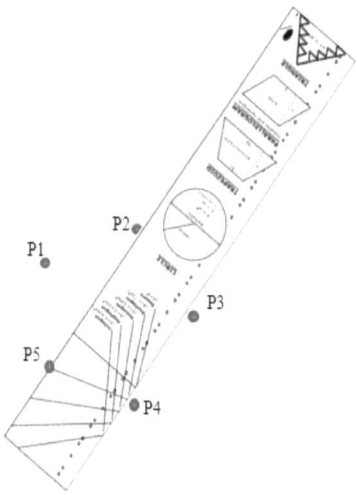

The five points we marked during this process are the vertices of the pentagon. Using the straight edge of the ruler, we can sketch the sides of the pentagon between the vertices that we have marked. The same process is used for creating a square, hexagon, heptagon, or octagon. Polygons with sides of a given length can be created using the same technique but an extra step is required for each vertex. For instance, suppose we wanted to make a pentagon with sides of length 3 inches. Rather than marking a vertex on both sides of the pentagon line, we would make a very light mark where P2 would have been, and then align the edge of the ruler with P1 and the temporary mark to define the edge of the pentagon. We would then measure 3 inches from P1 to P2 along the edge of the ruler. We would then reposition the ruler as we did in Figure 8.9b to define the next vertex P3, and so on.

Function 6 – Bar Graph Construction: One of the most basic functions of the ruler set is that the slotted ruler is designed to be used with a standard chisel tip marker to make bar graphs. Starting with a pair of axes, the slotted ruler can be aligned with the side along the y-axis, and with the bottom of the slot in the ruler aligned with the x-axis. The marker is then placed in the slot and filled down. This can be done for as many bars as needed for the graph. The height of each bar corresponds to the units in the centimeter scale.

Function 7 – Rational Exponent Calculator: Both rulers (that is to say, either ruler) can be used to calculate rational exponents using the technique illustrated in Article 7, Figure 7.8 on page 80. The reason is that both rulers have a log scale on one edge and a linear scale on the other. A simple change of base formula for logarithms is used to convert a logarithmic ratio into a linear ratio. Suppose we want to calculate the exponent in the equation, $3^x = 5$. To make this process work, we would first need to convert the equation to log form and then use the change of base formula to rewrite the ratio. We can then use the ruler to measure a linear distance for each log and simply divide to calculate the exponent. The process for the equation $3^x = 5$ is illustrated in Figure 8.10.

Figure 8.10: Calculating a Rational Exponent

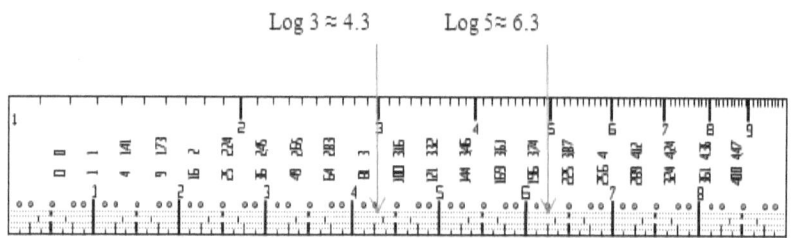

Starting with the equation $3^x = 5$, we convert to log form $log_3 5 = x$ and then rewrite using the change of base formula:

$$\frac{\log 5}{\log 3} = x$$

Recall that both logs can be written as measurements on a linear scale. To do this we will locate the linear equivalents of each log on one of the rulers. Dividing the linear equivalents 6.3/4.3 gives us an exponent of approximately 1.465

SUMMARY

The tool shown in this article is a patented device used in many computational geometry settings at the middle and secondary school levels. The device illustrates how geometric relationships can be leveraged into some very powerful computing, measurement, and construction capabilities through a process of *mathematical engineering*.

Many of the engineering tools we use today have gone through several iterations of improvement, and each time this is done, mathematical modeling is used to describe the functionality. By paying close attention to the interplay between numbers, algebra, geometry, we can generate powerful models that emulate the engineering process without actually building a physical device. This alone justifies engineering-based modeling as a way to learn applied mathematical investigations.

ADDITIONAL READINGS

Ostler, E. (2013). Exploring Logarithms with a ruler. The Mathematics Teacher. Vol. 106(9). 669-673.

ARTICLE 9: NAPIER'S BONES AND LATTICE COMPUTATION

ABSTRACT: Napier's Bones, or Napier's Rods as they are sometimes called, are mathematical tools that rely on special positioning in order to function. For the most part they are designed for multiplication and use the concepts of lattice structures to align the numbers in a matrix. The narrative that follows illustrates the basic processes involved in lattice multiplication and division and extends these procedures to show how Napier's Rods can be used to do numeric and algebraic computation.

INTRODUCTION

The mathematical work of 16th century Scottish mathematician John Napier is most commonly associated with the development of logarithms. Though the need for logarithms is now somewhat different than in Napier's time, they revolutionized the process of engineering and scientific calculations by representing difficult multiplication problems as table-based addition problems. Within the past decade or so, the log tables have all but disappeared from advanced algebra, trigonometry, and calculus books (mostly because of advanced calculator technology), but there was a time when they were frequently used.

The common logarithm tables essentially represented the exponents required to raise a base number 10 to a given value. *Napier's Rods*, however, though not based on logarithms, are excellent examples of *mathematical engineering* because they can be used to multiply, divide, represent exponents, and even extract square roots. They function based on the special alignment of numeric lattices. This lattice based process is sometimes referred to as *gelosia multiplication* or sieve multiplication. Occasionally you will even hear them called *Venetian Squares*. The process is algorithmically similar to the standard multiplication processes that are taught in schools, but it is broken into a series of smaller steps where the multiplication and addition aspects of the solution are not mixed. That is to say, all factors are multiplied first and then the remaining products are added for the final result. You might say, given that they were invented about 400 years ago, that they represent one of the first digit-based calculators. Of course there are much older computing devices such as the abacus, which some scholars suggest dates as far back as 2700 BCE, but the abacus predates the popular use of numeric symbols for computation. Because Napier's Rods use a unique arrangement of numeric symbols, they can be thought of as an algorithmic calculator rather than as a systematic way to accumulate groups of markers, as the abacus does. This kind of numeric-geometric interplay creates an interesting and inventive look at the multiplication and division of numbers and variables.

INVESTIGATION AND NOTES

For this investigation, it is appropriate to begin by describing the process of lattice multiplication and division for both numbers and symbols. The earliest lattice process can be thought of as a calculation using a matrix of intersecting lines (or oblong markers such as a popsicle stick) where each line has a value. Given that each marker has a value, the intersections of the markers can represent a product of any two markers. Let us suppose for example that we want to multiply the numbers 3 and 4. If each marker has a value of 1, 3 sticks could be arranged horizontally and 4 would be arranged vertically. In this example, we would simply count the intersections. Now suppose we want to multiply larger numbers such as 12 and 23. It would be cumbersome to line up 12 markers in one direction and another 23 in another direction and then count the intersections. However, if we can find a way to limit the number of markers, the process could still be very practical. Figure 9.1 illustrates the problem 12 x 23. In this problem, a dark marker represents a value of 10 and a white marker represents a value of 1. This being the case, a dark marker intersecting another dark marker would represent a 10 x 10 intersection and would have a partial product value of 100. A dark marker intersecting a white marker would represent a 10 x 1 intersection and would have a partial product value of 10. Finally a white/white intersection would have a value of 1. To find the product of our two factors, we would simply add the intersection values.

(Diagram can be found on the following page)

Figure 9.1: Matrix Multiplication of 12 x 23

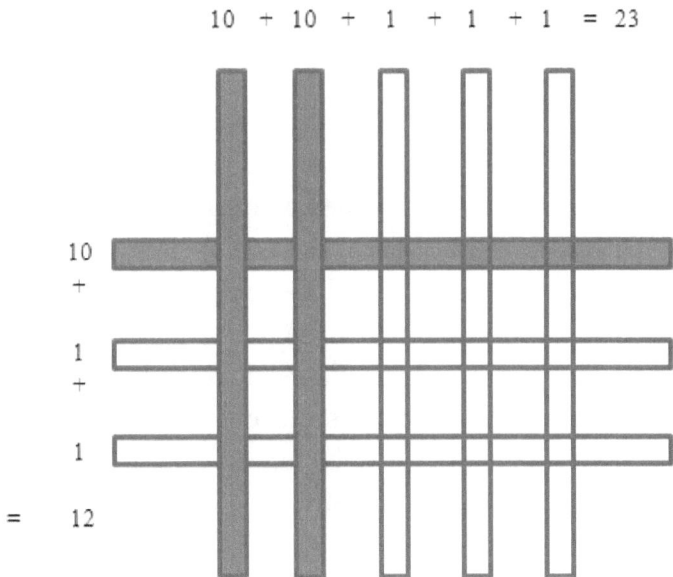

Aligning the markers such that each marker represents a place value unit, we can simply count the number of intersections of each value and total them to determine the product. In the problem illustrated above, the number 23 is represented by two markers having a value of 10 and 3 markers having a value of 1, all arranged vertically. Likewise, the number 12 is represented by one marker of value 10 and two additional markers of value 1. Counting the intersections, we can see two dark/dark intersections (value 10 x 10 = 100) totaling 200, seven dark/white (value 10 x 1 = 10) totaling 70, and six white/white (value 1 x 1 = 1) totaling 6. Adding the partial products give us the final product of 276. By adding different colors to the markers, we can multiply numbers of virtually any size.

A similar process is done with lattice multiplication, but the lattice process uses the numeric symbols instead of using markers. Suppose that we want to multiply the numbers 53 and 37. Again, we arrange the numbers both vertically and horizontally, but the intersections are now somewhat *virtual*, and require us to enter the partial products in a lattice. Figures 9.2a-9.2c illustrate a process where a lattice is drawn in so that the partial products can be recorded. Note that the individual products are entered into the lattice with a square where the tens place of an individual product is entered above the diagonal line and the ones place is entered below the diagonal line. After the partial products are recorded, they are added along the diagonals. Each diagonal path represents a specific place value starting with the ones place in the lower right hand corner and proceeding to the tens, hundreds, thousands, etc. as more diagonals are added from right to left.

(Diagram can be found on the following page)

Figure 9.2a-9.2c: Lattice Product of 53 x 37

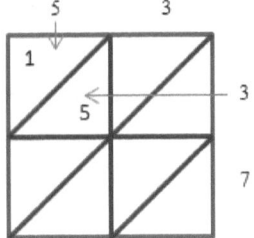
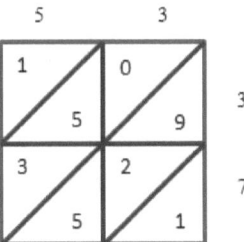

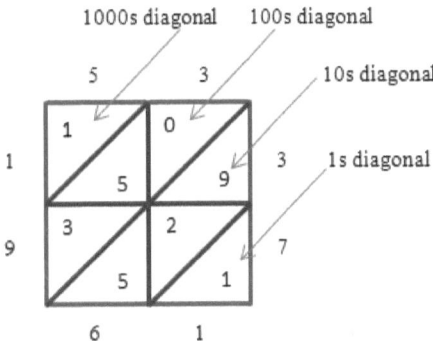

The partial products are placed into the boxes where the vertical and horizontal numbers meet. For example, the 5 digit from the 53 and the 3 digit from the 37 cross in the box in the upper left hand corner. The product of 15 is entered so that the tens place is above the diagonal line and the ones place is below the diagonal line for that particular box. Each successive partial product is completed and entered in the same way. The partial products are then added on the diagonals. Note how each diagonal represents the place value of the products they represent. For example, the 5 digit from the 53 and the 7 digit from the 37 have a product of 35 that is entered into the lattice; however, because the product is 50 x 7, the location of the diagonals of the box represent the 3 in the 100s diagonal, the 5 in the 10s diagonal, giving this part of the lattice a total value of 350 in the context of the larger problem.

The methods shown in Figures 9.1 and 9.2 can also be used in various forms to multiply algebraic polynomials. If we consider the form of a typical two digit number, say 47, we can write it in expanded form as 40 + 7 in much the same way that a binomial is written, for instance *4x + 7*. Multiplying a pair of two-digit numbers that are in expanded notation is really analogous to *FOILing* an algebraic binomial, which by no coincidence is the algorithm used with standard multiplication. Consider the problem posed in Figure 9.1, 12 x 23. If you recall, the number 23 was represented by two dark markers and three white markers and the number 12 was represented with one dark marker and two white markers. Suppose as an alternative, the numbers were not 23 and 12, but rather *2x + 3* and *x + 2*. The problem could be represented in the exact same way as it was in Figure 9.1, but instead of a dark marker representing a set of 10, it would represent a set of *x*. A dark/dark intersection would then represent x^2, while a dark/white intersection would represent *x*. The result of counting the intersections would give us $2x^2 + 7x + 6$. The example is illustrated in Figure 9.3.

(Diagram can be found on the following page)

Figure 9.3: Matrix Product of (2x + 3)(x + 2)

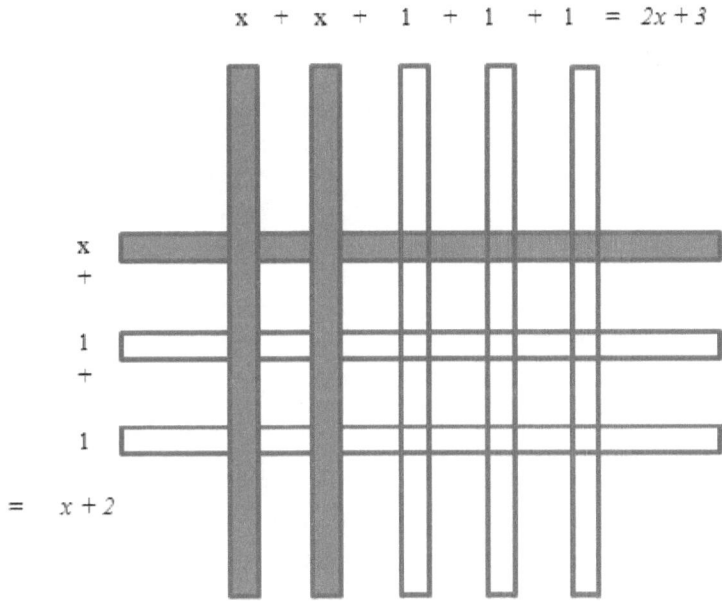

The lattice process used for multiplying polynomials is similar, with the exception that the diagonal lines in each box that represent place values are unnecessary since place values cannot be determined when multiplying variables. Instead, we rely on exponents to help us determine the appropriate place values for a polynomial. This is why they are also written in descending exponential order of some variable. Higher exponents represent higher place values. Figure 9.4 illustrates polynomial multiplication. Note that diagonal addition still has to take place for the linear terms.

Figure 9.4: Polynomial Multiplication using a Lattice

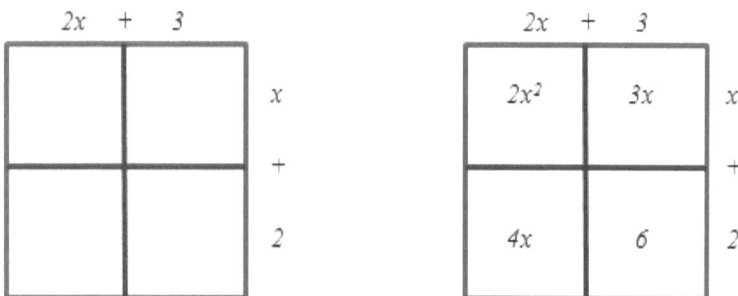

The lattice multiplication method is the principle on which the functionality of Napier's Rods rests. Imagine an oblong lattice that represents the integer multiples of a given number. If this was done for each of the digits from 0 through 9, the result would be a large square matrix of Napier's Rods. Figure 9.5 shows the matrix of individual lattices that are used to make up Napier's Rods. Notice that the matrix includes a column of zeros on the left side. This is necessary as a place holder when the rods are used to multiply larger numbers that have a zero element.

(Diagram can be found on the following page)

Figure 9.5: Napier's Rods Lattice

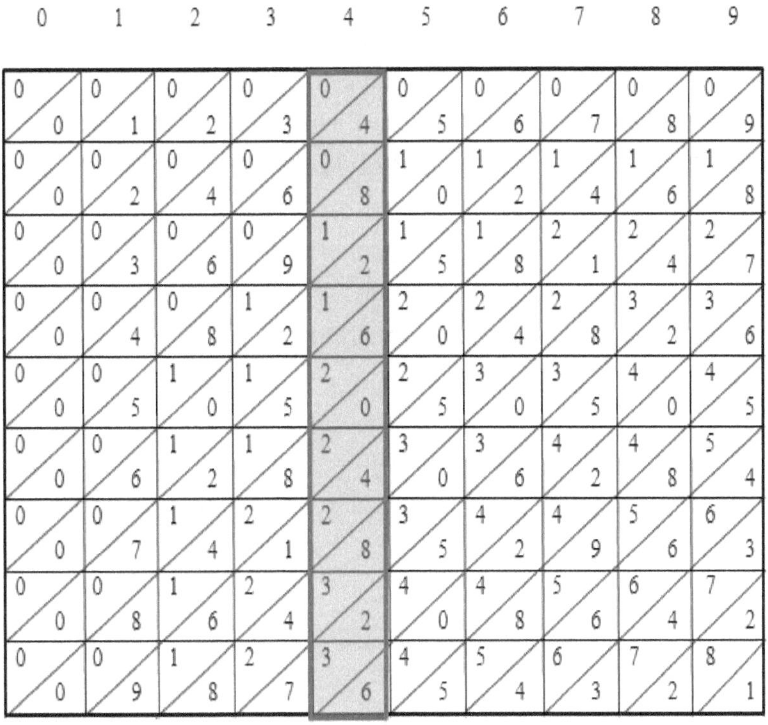

	0	1	2	3	4	5	6	7	8	9
	0/0	0/1	0/2	0/3	0/4	0/5	0/6	0/7	0/8	0/9
	0/0	0/2	0/4	0/6	0/8	1/0	1/2	1/4	1/6	1/8
	0/0	0/3	0/6	0/9	1/2	1/5	1/8	2/1	2/4	2/7
	0/0	0/4	0/8	1/2	1/6	2/0	2/4	2/8	3/2	3/6
	0/0	0/5	1/0	1/5	2/0	2/5	3/0	3/5	4/0	4/5
	0/0	0/6	1/2	1/8	2/4	3/0	3/6	4/2	4/8	5/4
	0/0	0/7	1/4	2/1	2/8	3/5	4/2	4/9	5/6	6/3
	0/0	0/8	1/6	2/4	3/2	4/0	4/8	5/6	6/4	7/2
	0/0	0/9	1/8	2/7	3/6	4/5	5/4	6/3	7/2	8/1

When the Napier's Rods are constructed together as a large matrix of numbers it can sometimes be difficult to see how the patterns might be used to multiply individual numbers. However, if you look at the individual columns below the top row of numbers, you can see that each vertical rod is actually an extended lattice containing the multiples of the first number. For example, in Figure 9.5, if you look below the number 4 from the top row, you can see that the highlighted vertical column of numbers contains the multiples of four in each box. The tens place of each multiple is located above the diagonal line while the ones place is written below it. The advantage to this layout is that the individual rods can be separated to show the multiples of a single number (through 9) or the rods can be combined and arranged to show the multiples of larger numbers. Suppose, for instance, that we want to multiply 47 x 6. We would combine the 4 rod with the 7 rod to create the number 47. We would then count down to the sixth block and add along the diagonals (only in the 6th row) just as we did when we added in the lattice multiplication process. Figure 9.6 illustrates the multiplication of 47 and 6. Larger sets of numbers can be multiplied as well using the same approach illustrated in Figure 9.6.

(Diagram can be found on the following page)

Figure 9.6: Multiplication of 47 x 6 using Napier's Rods

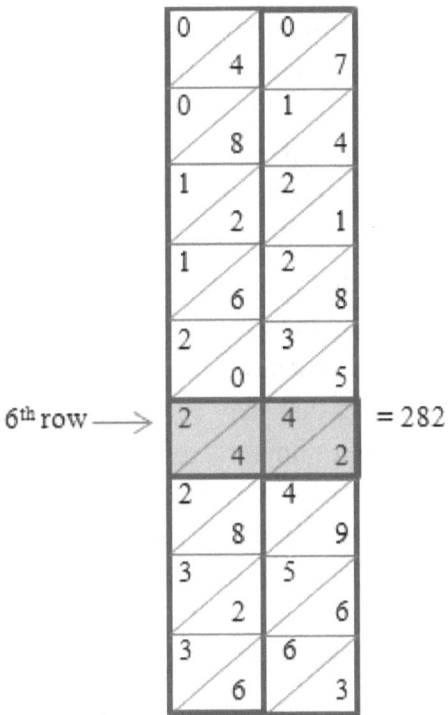

Notice how the two rods working together represent multiples of the number 47. This is true for every number that can be assembled using different combinations of the rods, including those that use zero as a digit. Also, because multiplication and division are inverse operations of one another, division can be done in a similar fashion, but in reverse order. The process of division is a bit more complex, however, because the divisor must be assembled from the lattice numbers in the matrix. For example if we wanted to divide the number 282 by 6, we would have to find the appropriate numbers to manufacture the number 282 in a 3-digit lattice at the 6th row. And because we may not initially know if the number we are attempting to divide is evenly divisible by a chosen row (divisor) we may not be able to find an exact integer quotient. Instead, we would have to represent partial quotients as remainders. This can be a worthwhile educational investigation but it is not particularly worthwhile as an applied technique.

So far, the examples that have been illustrated for multiplication have only been in the form of single digit multiples such as 7 x 4, but it is possible to multiply 2-digit by 2-digit numbers and beyond. To do this, we must again arrange the rods to represent one of the factors, and then locate each individual row that represents the digits of the other factor. The trick in this technique is to add the diagonals of rows that may be separated. Because we are multiplying a pair of 2-digit numbers, the order in which we add them can be important. One of the factors is going to represent the tens place of the second factor and so the diagonal addition of that number is going to have to be moved one position so that the appropriate place values are represented. The best way to do this is to reconstruct each row of the Napier's Rods into a lattice with the tens position on top. With some practice, it is possible to become proficient at adding the rows without reconstructing a new lattice, but for illustration purposes, we will reconstruct a lattice using the appropriate numbers. Figure 9.7 illustrates the multiplication of 47 x 38.

Figure 9.7: Multiplication of 2-digit by 2-digit Numbers (47 x 38)

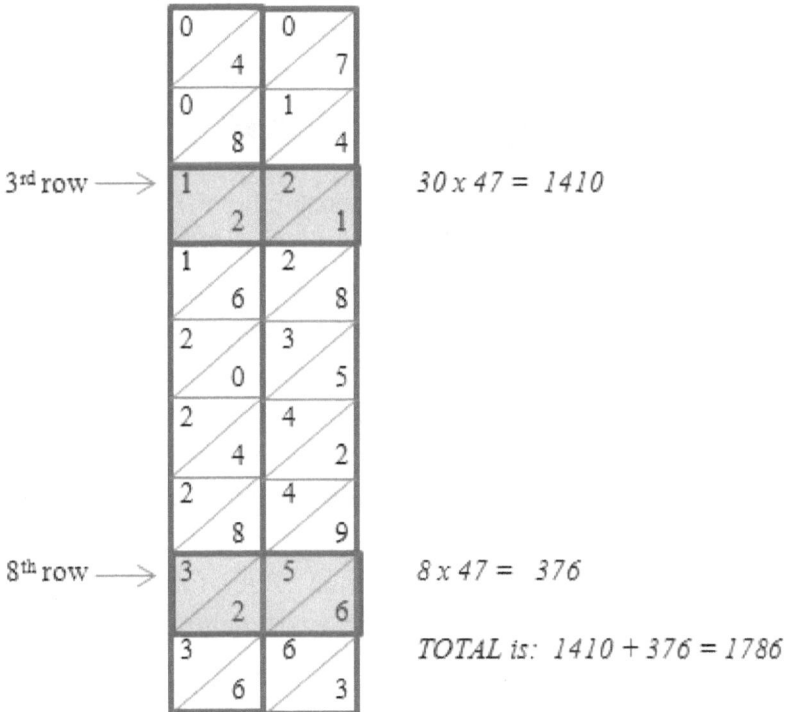

Note that the lattice in the third row represents 30 x 47 rather than 3 x 47 because we are multiplying a 2-digit number. The final addition process will need to include this extra place value position to derive the correct answer of 1786. If the two shaded rows from Figure 9.7 are placed together, the result is a lattice similar to the form illustrated in Figure 9.2. This technique works for numbers of any size but clearly will become more difficult to do mentally as the numbers get larger. One other important thing to remember is that the order of addition and place values change based on the form of the numbers we are multiplying. For example, the number 38 that we used as a factor had the number 3 in the tens position and the 8 in the ones position. We added the zero place-holder to the 3 in this example. However, had we multiplied by 83, we would have added the zero to the bottom number when we added. Again, this seems obvious until you try to add the lattice values mentally with large numbers.

Finally, perhaps one of the most unique functionalities of Napier's Rods is that they can be used to extract square roots. The matrix used for this process looks a bit different than the one used for simple multiplication because there is an additional rod with 3 columns on it. The extra rod will be placed on the right side of the original matrix, but some forms of the matrix include it at the bottom. The entire Napier's Rods matrix is shown in Figure 9.8 with the additional square root lattice highlighted on the right hand side of this example. The first column of the extra rod lists the numeric squares of each row number in lattice form. The second and third columns simply contain the even multiples of each row and the row numbers respectively.

Let us suppose, for example, that we want to calculate the square root of the number 2,387. We begin on the right hand side of the number and group the number in sets of two digits. In this example, the number would be written: 23 87. If we had an odd number such as 73,284, we would use the same technique, starting on the right side of the number and group the digits in sets of two until we run out of numbers (i.e. 7 32 84). At this point, the technique becomes a bit complex, so for our purposes, we are simply going to estimate the first two digits of our square root. The process demonstrated here will not use the 2nd or 3rd columns.

Figure 9.8: Using Napier's Rods to Extract the Estimated Square Root of 2,387

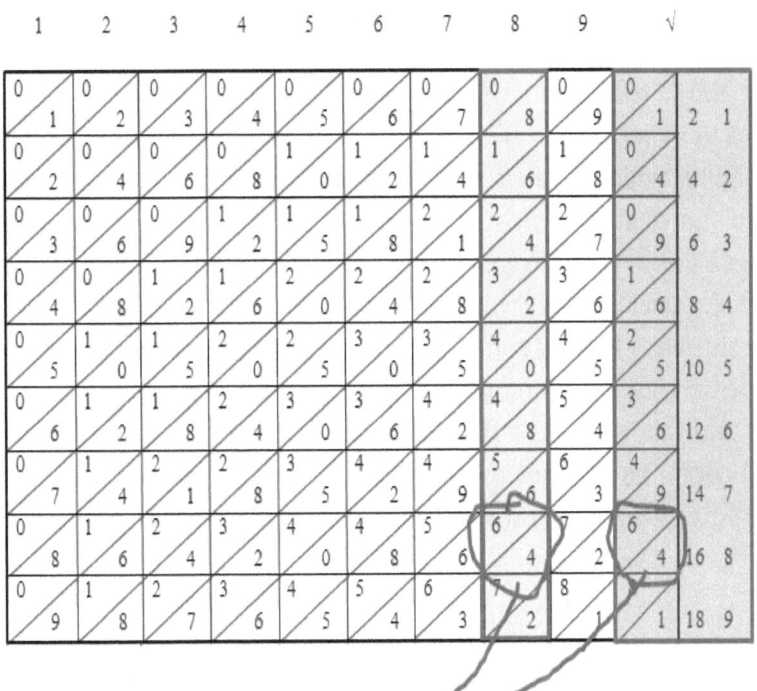

Add these lattices to get 704. This is in the 8th row so we use 8 as the second digit of our square root.

Our first step is to start with the leftmost group of two numbers; in this case 23. We will pick the largest square root row from the square root rod that is less than 23, which is the 4th rod down (because 16 is the largest square less than 23). This tells us that the first digit of our solution is 4. And because we started with a 4 digit number, the root is 40. We now create a new number by subtracting the square from the 4th row (16) from the first 2-digit pair of our original number but we fill in the second grouping of digits for the square with zeros before we subtract. This gives us the difference 2387 − 1600. The result is 787. Now, the middle column of the square root rod for the 4th row reads 8. This number tells us which rod or set of rods we need to use to get the next digit of our square root. We are going to use the highlighted 8 rod and add the lattice with the square root rod to get as close to 787 as we can get. Using the 8 rod and the square root rod we could add the 8th row lattices 6/4 and 6/4 which would give us 704 (adding along the diagonals), which is close to 787. You will have to search the lattice for the sum that is as close to the target number as possible. Because we used the 8th row to get as close to our target number of 787 as possible, our next digit would be 8. We are now at 48 for our square root estimate. If we subtract again, 787 − 704, we get 83. We are now down to a 2 digit number, we simply take the square root of our result and this gives us a final estimate that will be fairly close to the actual root. The square root of 83 is just over 9, so we use 9 as our next digit. Our final estimate is approximately 48.9 for our square root. If we check this value by squaring it, we find the result to be 2391.21, which is very close to the original number of 2387. Of course, this process only provides a rough estimate, but there are other similar methods that will provide exact results. Ultimately the methods used here are impractical other than to use as numeric investigations, so it is unlikely that they would be needed in an applied setting; however, it is worth knowing they exist.

SUMMARY

Despite the fact that Napier's Rods are not particularly practical for high power computation, they do illustrate how numeric and geometric factors can come together to create a *mathematical engineering* environment. The fact that the lattice method used for Napier's Rods can also be used to multiply algebraic polynomials rounds out the numeric/algebraic/geometric connections that make this kind of investigation so mathematically powerful from an instructional standpoint. Napier's Rods in general are great for pattern searches and can provide a rich environment for problem solving in algebra.

ADDITIONAL READINGS

Bently, P. (2008). The Book of Numbers: The Secret of Numbers and How they Changed the World. Firefly Books. ISBN: 978-1554073610

Haven, K. (1998). Marvels of Math: Fascinating Reads and Awesome Activities. Libraries Unlimited. ISBN: 978-1563085857

Murphy, D. (2011). Napier's Bones. ChiZine Publications. ISBN: 978-1926851099

Pappas, T. (1989). The Joy of Mathematics. QED Publications. ISBN: 978-0946544325

ARTICLE 10: CONSUL THE EDUCATED MONKEY AND NUMBER PYRAMIDS

ABSTRACT: Consul the Educated Monkey was a mathematical toy from the early 1900s that used a combination of mechanical operations and a unique arrangement of numbers in a pyramid form that functioned somewhat like a mechanical computer. The narrative that follows gives a brief history of the toy and illustrates how the mathematical arrangement of numbers in a pyramid can be used to do simple operations such as addition and multiplication with numbers and algebraic polynomials.

INTRODUCTION

In 1916 the *Educational Novelty Comp*any of Dayton, Ohio invented a toy known as *Consul the Educated Monkey*. The toy was a simple mechanical device made of tin that could be used to teach mathematical operations such as addition and multiplication. Consul (the real monkey) was a famous performing monkey who was trained to do things like ride a bike and use common utensils, such as silverware and a drinking glass, at the dinner table for eating. A few years before our monkey inspired the toy, however, (1909) Consul was featured in a movie *Consul Crosses the Atlantic*, which was allegedly the monkey's first trip to the United States. It is rumored that during this time his popularity inspired the educational toy, which represented an early mechanical computer. It is also rumored that during the 1950's a large version of Consul was re-created by a group of mechanical engineers from the University of Mississippi as a state fair exhibit. The exhibit was said to have evoked fear among the more superstitious of the fair goers, who thought it must be the work of the devil. What they witnessed was nothing more than a clever arrangement of gears coupled with a clever arrangement of numbers.

The number pyramids illustrated in this article are similar to what was used to make the toy work, but the actual caricature monkey with his little red vest is not needed to demonstrate how this particular mechanical computer worked. The device is shown in this section of the book because it represents a mathematical device that is a hybrid variety of computing machine. It relies on both mechanical interplay and the geometric positioning of sets of numbers. Using the toy meant that Consul's feet could be maneuvered to point at a pair of numbers in a row at the bottom of the device. The hands would move correspondingly to display the result of an addition or multiplication problem. It is easy to see why some people would have been intimidated by something that appeared to be so magical.

INVESTIGATION AND NOTES

For the most part, the devices so far have been focused on computation. Such is the case with this device, but it is done in a different way. The Consul toy makes use of a triangle to define the patterns for addition and multiplication. There are also some powerful pedagogical representations that can be helpful when using the device to teach computation. With the physical toy, the monkey was used as a mechanical overlay. Parts of the monkey could be manipulated to make other parts move through a simple gear arrangement. However, that in and of itself was not enough to make the toy function. A numeric template of specially arranged numbers was also necessary. For our example, in place of Consul, we will use a triangle as the overlay to demonstrate how the device generally worked. Figure 10.1 shows a basic number pyramid that when used with the triangle overlay will give the solution to an addition problem. There are a number of patterns that can be seen almost instantly in the pyramid, but the addition function of the device is not immediately obvious to most people. Basically, the triangular overlay can be moved over any part of the pyramid to highlight the two desired addends and the sum. The device works by arranging the overlay so that any two addends (numbers below the line at the bottom) fall adjacent to the sides of the triangle overlay. The sum can then be determined as the number to which the top of the triangle points.

(Diagram can be found on the following page)

Figure 10.1: Addition Pyramid Illustrating 2 + 7 = 9 and 4 + 8 = 12

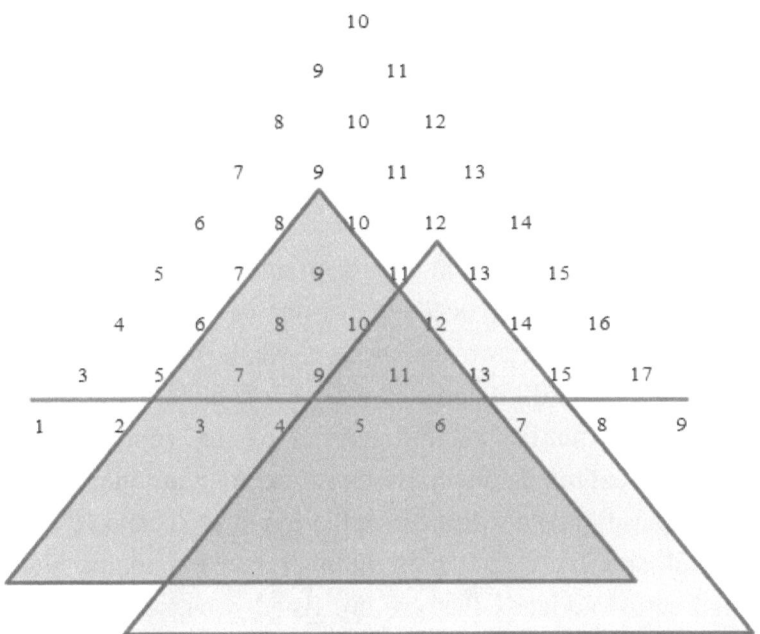

The triangle overlays used in this example are transparent so that the patterns within the pyramid can be examined closely, but for the addition problems here, you can see how the numbers at the edge of the darker triangle (2 and 7) are the addends that create a sum of 9, which is shown immediately above the top of the triangle. If the overlay is then moved, we can represent a different sum of 4 + 8 = 12. This process will work as long as the triangle overlay is the same shape as the number triangle.

One of the most interesting aspects of the device is that it holds of number of patterns and presents some interesting combinatorial problems as well. Notice that the rows and columns create patterns in almost every direction. For example the row numbers are either all odd or all even and increase by twos as we count from left to right. Vertical columns are all the same number. The sums of the numbers in the rows increase by 10 as we go from the top to the bottom. The sum of the top row is 10, the second row down is 20, the third row down is 30, and so on. Further, the outside numbers of each row have an average of 10. Additionally, if we start counting anywhere in the number pyramid going up and to the right, and then turn on a given number to start counting down and to the right, the numbers increment in order by one unit no matter where we start. Finally, because the number pyramid represents every possible sum of two addends, if we wanted to count how many positive single digit sums of 9 there are, all we would have to do is count the number of appearances of the number 9 in the pyramid. For example, we know there are four unique sums of 9 possible because there are four 9s in the pyramid, (1 and 8, 2 and 7, 3 and 6, 4 and 5). The even number sums actually have an additional set of addends that are not listed because of the double (i.e. $4 + 4 = 8$).

  The mechanical part of the Consul toy was really just designed to keep the overlay intact as a triangle so that the sums or products of the number pyramid beneath it showed up in the right spots. As Consul's feet were moved to represent various addends or factors, the position of his hands would change so that the three parts of the fact family would remain in a triangular form. The addition pyramid can also be changed slightly to represent the addition of fractions as well. Dividing each of the numbers in the pyramid by any denominator value would still maintain the integrity of the addition. Each rational value could be simplified to represent fractions of different denominators within the same pyramid. Of course, the pyramid works just as well for multiplication but the patterns look a bit different. Figure 10.2 shows a multiplication pyramid illustrating the product of 3 and 9 as 27.

Figure 10.2: Multiplication Pyramid Illustrating 3 x 9 = 27

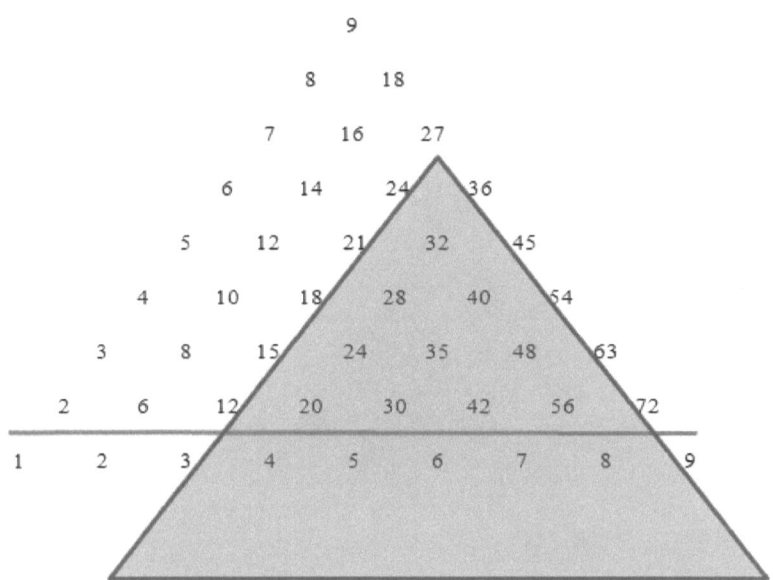

Because we now know that the number pyramid can be used for either addition or multiplication, we can transition the pyramid into a new algebraic tool that allow us to do both processes simultaneously. We know from Article 7 on nomographs that the multiplication of algebraic polynomials can be represented by the addition of exponents for a given base. What this tells us is that we may be able to create a multiplication pyramid that is represented by logarithms just as we did when we were exploring exponential number line values. Figure 10.3 shows a modified addition pyramid that simply uses the numeric values as exponents for a base of x. The pyramid itself functions in exactly the same way but we can actually substitute numbers for the x variable and use it to multiply different sets of numbers.

Figure 10.3: *Polynomial Multiplication Pyramid Illustrating* $x^3(x^8) = x^{11}$

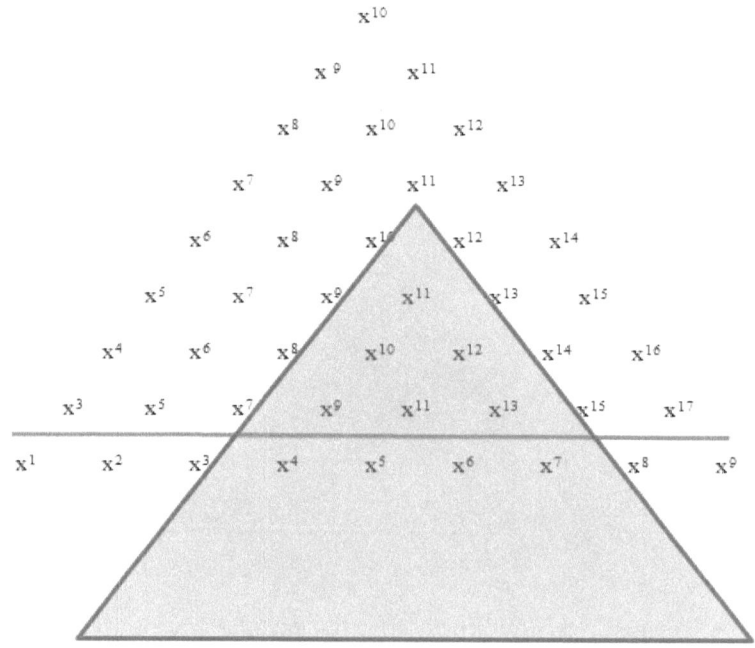

At this point, the multiplication process using the pyramid should be fairly intuitive. If a base number is now substituted for the x-variable, we have a new multiplication pyramid that can multiply much larger numbers than our first multiplication pyramid, which only used single digits. However, because we will only have multiples of that single chosen base, our pyramid is pretty limited in its practical applications. Again, if we wanted to get more advanced in the mathematics we are exploring, we could certainly represent the exponents in the pyramid as logarithms, but that exercise will be left to the reader.

SUMMARY

The fact that a simple repositioning of a series of numbers can be turned into a mathematical device is a great way to justify a connection between engineering and mathematics. Also, the Consul the Educated Monkey toy is worth showing to interested people because it represents a nice transition from purely mathematical interplay to a hybrid type of mathematical engineering device that may spur other ideas how different matrices of numbers may be repurposed as mathematical tools. The toy is shown here (Figure 10.4). It is still for sale by novelty shops on the internet and collectors may even have success finding original versions of it on popular auction sites.

(Diagram can be found on the following page)

Figure 10.4: Consul the Educated Monkey Toy

ADDITIONAL READINGS
Kolpas, S.J., & Massion, G.R. (2000). Consul, the educated monkey. Mathematics Teacher, Vol. 93. No. 4, 276-279.

ARTICLE 11: BASIC SUNDIALS AND THE MEASUREMENT OF TIME

ABSTRACT: Sundials are very familiar devices. We see them in gardens and museums but most people are not familiar with the mathematics that makes them work, nor are they aware of the number of different types of sundials there are. The narrative that follows describes some of the general mathematical principals needed for sundials to work and provides a brief history of the theory and development of various types of sundials.

INTRODUCTION

Humans have always been obsessed with measuring time. We have atomic clocks that can subdivide increments of time into billionths of a second. In fact, our most sophisticated clock is also one of the tiniest objects in the universe; to be more precise, the cesium atom. It may sound unusual that a simple atom could be so important in time keeping, but when the cesium atom is bombarded with energy it generates pulses of electromagnetic radiation 9,192,631,770 times per second. The National Institute of Standards and Technology in Colorado, who is the official time keeper for the United States, uses the predictable resonance frequency of the cesium atom to set the official time. The accuracy of this time piece is quite staggering when you consider that it means the cesium clock is accurate to within plus or minus 1 second in approximately 100 million years. Of course for most of us, the keeping of such accurate time is unnecessary, but how did the technology that keeps our time evolve?

It has been suggested by the academic community of physicists that the very first clock was the earth and that the divisions of time were simply the separations of day and night. Essentially this meant that the first clock only "ticked" once per day. But the transition to more accurate ways of telling time is a mathematical history in and of itself. The *sundial*, which has a history that dates back thousands of years, is still popular today. Sure, it only works during daylight hours, and that of course is also dependent on strong shadows from the available sunlight; but a well-constructed and well-designed sundial can keep extremely accurate time without any moving parts. This is because the earth rotates so predictably on its axis and revolves so predictably around the sun. The sundial is perhaps one of the best examples of mathematical engineering in the history of humankind because it involves somewhat complex mathematics, it has been continually improved over its two-thousand year history using various mathematical representations, and it serves a useful purpose in society. There are even various biblical and literary references indicating an ongoing interest in them. What is somewhat ironic, too, is that as the pendulum technology used to keep more accurate time was developed, it was checked and reset with a sundial!

INVESTIGATION AND NOTES

There are many different kinds of sundials and the complexity of the design of each varies, as does the mathematics that governs each one's functionality, so we will begin with the simplest version. A basic horizontal sundial has three parts, a dial plate where hour lines are laid out and the time can be seen, a gnomon (Latin for "one who knows") which is object that rests on the dial plate to cast a shadow, and the style, which is the sharp edge or point of the gnomon that casts the shadow. The gnomon and style can be as simple as a nail sticking out of a board. In fact, the simplest sundial design is a roughly horizontal (but not technically) board with a nail in the middle. For this design, the gnomon (nail) needs to point directly at the sun during *local apparent noon* (LAN). Local apparent noon is a term we use to define when the sun is directly overhead for a given location on the earth. The sun's rays must also be perpendicular to our board, which acts as the dial plate for our clock. Figure 11.1 illustrates the operation of our basic sundial. It should be noted that this particular sundial is very limited in its function, so you will not typically see it placed in a garden or museum. Still, it is a good way to show how a sundial operates.

Figure 11.1: Basic Sundial

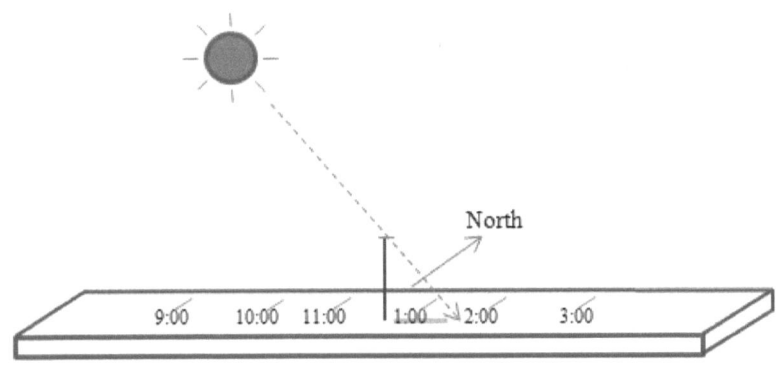

In this sundial model, the gnomon must protrude from the dial plate at a 90 degree angle and the dial plate must face the sun rather than resting horizontally on the surface of the earth where the sun's rays would otherwise strike the dial plate from an odd direction. The hour lines are marked on the dial plate perpendicular to the direction of the apparent east to west movement of the sun. Note, in Figure 11.1, how the hour lines also get farther apart as the time gets farther away from local apparent noon. This is based on trigonometric ratios related to circular versus linear motion.

Our next task is to derive some basic equations related to triangle proportions for the sundial in Figure 11.1. Because we know that the earth rotates $360°$ in 24 hours, we can assume an apparent movement of the sun over the surface of the earth at a rate of $15°$ per hour from the east to the west. Using this circular rate and knowing the height of the gnomon allows us to calculate the length of a shadow cast on the dial plate at any time during the day. The sundial can then be marked in hour increments based on our calculations. The formula for this is based on basic right triangle trigonometry. If a ray of light from the sun strikes the top of the nail, which casts a shadow on the dial plate, the shadow can be calculated as the side opposite the angle created by the sun. The calculation is shown in Figure 11.2.

(Diagram can be found on the following page)

Figure 11.2: Shadow Length Formula

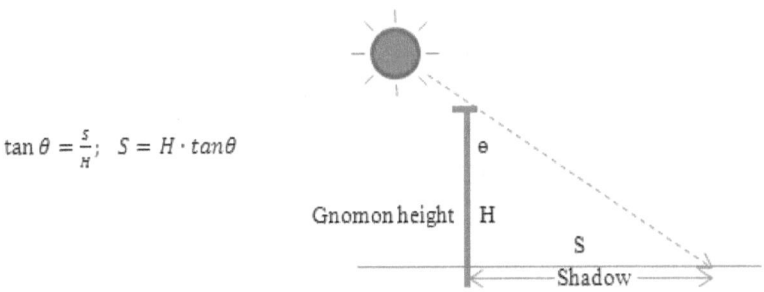

This basic formula is used in many different sundial designs, but as a sundial design becomes more complex, so does the mathematics that determines its functionality. For example, the sundial shown in Figure 11.1 is not very practical because a gnomon of any substantial height would cause the early morning and late afternoon shadows to be so long that it would be impractical to measure them. In fact, a gnomon that is only one foot tall would have to have a dial plate that is nearly 7.5 feet long to indicate the time between the hours of 7:00 a.m. and 5:00 p.m. To provide an extra half of an hour on each end (i.e. the time from 6:30 a.m. and 5:30 p.m.) the dial plate would have to be over 15 feet long. Clearly another design is necessary to create a mathematical function that is more suited to casting a shadow that has both the linear and circular kinds of motions that could be shown on the face of a clock.

Another very common type of sundial that works a little more like a standard circular clock is a horizontal sundial. The dial plate for a horizontal dial is typically circular rather than the oblong board that was illustrated in Figure 11.1. The difference is that a horizontal dial is truly horizontal. That is to say, the dial plate rests horizontally with respect to the surface of the earth in all directions, as opposed to the basic sundial in Figure 11.1 where the dial plate was tilted in one direction to face the sun directly and was oriented to the east and west. The horizontal dial is still composed of the same three pieces (dial plate, gnomon, and style), but rather than using a nail as the gnomon, the horizontal dial normally has a triangular gnomon that sticks up out of the dial plate like a shark fin. The *style* is typically a lesser known piece because it can be part of the gnomon, and is often used interchangeably.

This particular sundial design has three distinct phases of construction: 1) finding the meridian mark, 2) angling the gnomon, and 3) marking the dial plate. Some of these processes were assumed in the illustration of the basic sundial but we need to consider them a bit more carefully here because they are integral to the function of the clock. Again, because we know that shadows are long and point westerly in the morning as the sun rises and long and point easterly in the afternoon as the sun sets, we need a way to make sure the shadow "rotates" as the sun moves over the surface of the earth.

Step 1 – Finding the Meridian Mark: The meridian lines are imaginary lines running along the earth's surface directly between the north and south poles. The meridian line on which an individual might stand is nothing more than an imaginary line from the north to south poles that passes through that particular spot. The time at which the sun is directly overhead (where we do not cast a shadow to the east or west) is called local apparent noon (LAN). Because the apparent movement of the sun is east to west, we can easily locate the meridian without sophisticated technology by following the path an object such as a nail to define shadows of a given length in the morning and again in the afternoon. Concentric circles drawn around the nail can be used to measure the shadow in the morning and afternoon. When the shadows are the same length, but on opposite sides of the noon hour, the amount of time passed must also be the same. For example, the shadows at 10:00 a.m. and 2:00 p.m. must be the same length from the base of the nail. So, if the shadow is measured at the same length in the morning and afternoon, the angle created between the morning shadow mark, the base of the nail, and the afternoon shadow mark can be bisected to find the meridian mark. This is illustrated in Figure 11.3.

Figure 11.3: Finding the Meridian Mark

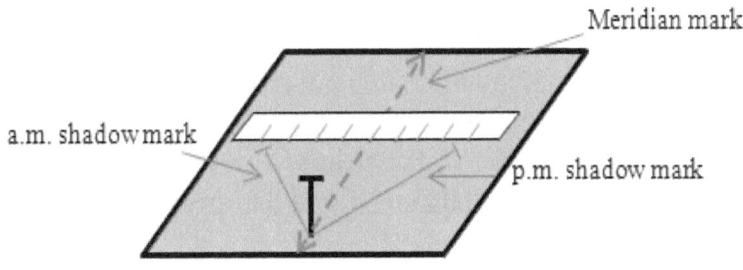

Step 2 – Angling the Gnomon: Now that we have established the meridian mark and have our horizontal dial aimed the right direction, we can calculate the angle of the gnomon. This is similar to the process we used with the basic dial where we made certain the dial plate was facing the sun. With the horizontal sundial, we need to make sure that the dial plate is resting flat on the ground in all directions because the gnomon needs to be angled in such a way that the sun's rays hit the style at a right angle. This means that the gnomon must be angled differently at different latitudes. For example, a gnomon in North Dakota would have to be angled differently than one in southern Texas. Interestingly enough, this means that most commercially produced sundials that you might find in a garden shop will not give the accurate time at most latitudes because the gnomon must correspond to a specific latitude in order to work properly.

Figure 11.4 illustrates how the gnomon must be angled with respect to a horizontal plane tangent to the earth. Again, the base angle of the sundial must reflect the appropriate latitudes so that the sun's rays strike the style at a right angle. As a reminder, latitude is calculated by measuring the elevation of an angle with respect to the equator of the earth given that the angle has a vertex at the center of the earth. One other noteworthy consideration is that the model used here is assumed at equinox. The tilt of the earth changes by seasons with respect to sun. When we suggest that the gnomon angle needs to be perpendicular to the sun's rays, it is also assuming that the gnomon is parallel to the pole of the earth. This will, of course, slightly change the functionality of the sundial as the seasons change.

(Diagram can be found on the following page)

Figure 11.4: Sun's Rays Striking the Gnomon at 90⁰ at Different Latitudes

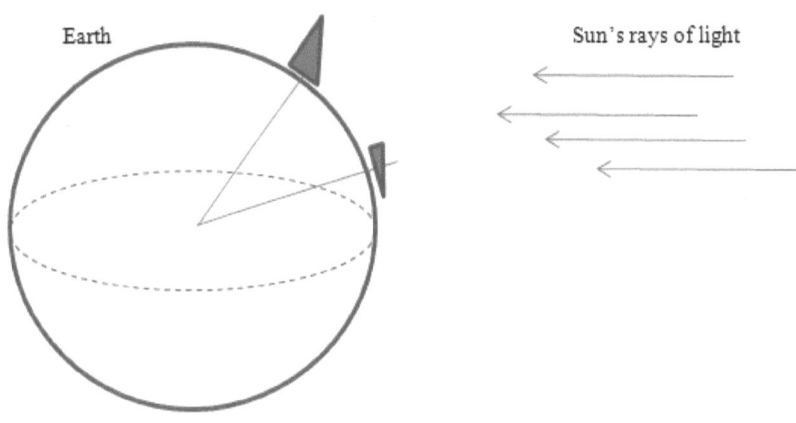

Now using some basic right triangle similarity rules, we can demonstrate that the angle of the gnomon (with respect to the dial plate) must be the same angle as the latitude where the dial is placed. For instance, if the sundial is placed at 30° north latitude, then the base angle of the gnomon must also measure 30°. This keeps the style parallel to the axis of the earth. We can be easily demonstrate this fact by extending an imaginary line from the center of the earth, through an imaginary dial plate and stopping at a point that would be the point of the top of the gnomon. We would then, extend from the top of the gnomon back to the equator. The result is a pair of similar triangles. Figure 11.5 illustrates how these similar triangles can be used to determine the gnomon angle at any given latitude.

Figure 11.5: Similar Triangles Illustrating Gnomon Angle Equal to Latitude Angle

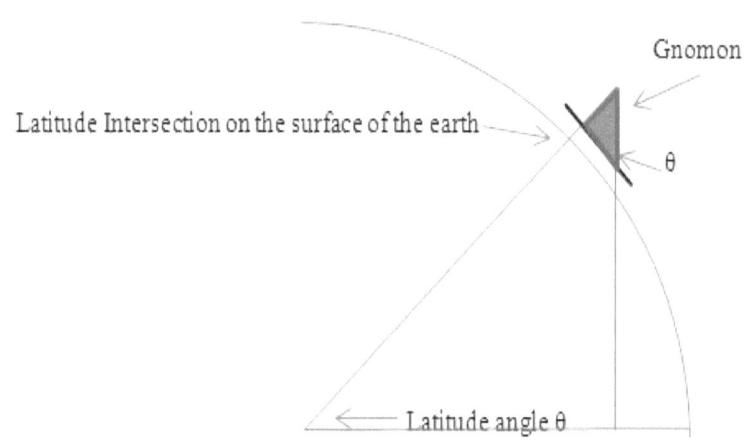

Of course in this example the dial plate is oversized to illustrate the triangle representing the gnomon, but the idea of a horizontal dial is that it rests on the surface of the earth in a horizontal fashion. It should be fairly apparent that the large triangle extending from the center of the earth to the top of the gnomon and then back to the horizontal line representing the equator must be similar to the triangular representing the gnomon. This must be the case because both of the triangles are right triangles and they share the angle at the top of the gnomon. The third angle of each triangle (that representing the latitude angle from the large triangle and that representing the base of the gnomon in the small triangle) must then be congruent.

Step 3 – Angling the Gnomon: This step is the most complex to model mathematically for horizontal sundials because, for the most part, they involve nested trigonometric functions. For example, in this horizontal dial, we are essentially dealing with two perpendicular triangles and trying to determine how the sides of the shadows vary with respect to the sides of the gnomon and the moving sun rays. One of the triangles is, of course, the gnomon (along with the style), which stays constant on all sides during the day. The other triangle is the shadow cast on the dial plate, which is constantly moving and simultaneously changing in two directions at the same time.

Again, because the sun is rotating on an axis through 360 degrees in a 24 hour time period, we can be certain that each hour is defined by a 15 degree arc of the sun's apparent movement over the surface of the earth. This is true at any latitude even though the north/south movement of the shadows will be somewhat different during different seasons based on the relative tilt of the earth.

We now need to look specifically at how to mark the lines on the dial plate that represent the hour marks of our clock. The anchor mark for our dial is the north/south meridian line because it is the 12:00 hour mark. If we create a series of lines on the dial plate that extend from the base of the gnomon and angle outward to the edge of the dial plate, the lines should represent the exact location of the shadow lines created by the style at each hour. Figure 11.6 illustrates the mathematical model used to define the relationship between the gnomon, shadow, and dial plate for our specific model of a horizontal sundial. Note that there are several different derivations for this model. The 3-Dimensional model here incorporates a series of labeled points to define the sides of various triangles, but there are also several coordinate locations that allow the reader to get a better sense of how the diagram might look in three dimensions.

Figure 11.6: Mathematical Model Used for Marking the Dial Plate

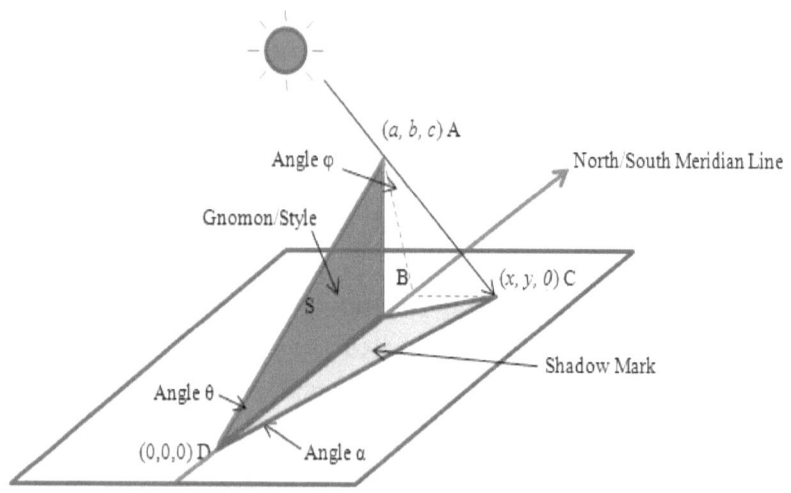

Let us begin with a basic calculation for angle φ that the sun's ray creates with respect to the gnomon at 1:00 in the afternoon. Because we know that the angle at the top of the gnomon moves at 15° per hour, we know that angle φ is 15° at 1:00, 30° at 2:00 and so on if the direction of the sun is only east/west, but there are other angles at play in this equation as well. Suppose that we want to mark the 1:00 hour line on the dial plate. We could elevate the end of the style to any angle and calculate the height of the gnomon as $h = S \cdot \sin\theta$ where the length of the style is S. An adjustable gnomon/style would allow us to have a sundial that worked at any latitude. However, for the purposes of this particular mathematical model, the length of the gnomon/style is actually not necessary. Nevertheless, we are going to define the point at the top of the gnomon as point A at coordinates (a, b, c).

If we assume that we are calculating in a 3D environment, we obtain a complex set of interrelated triangles that will ultimately allow us to calculate the tangent of angle α, which will be the angle of the hour lines on the dial plate with respect to the north/south meridian line and the base of the gnomon. This angle will come from the components on the dial plate that correspond to x and y at the tip of the shadow. Therefore, our derivation is going to come from a series of triangle relations that provide the magnitudes of x and y in terms of a series of points, all of which will be represented as trigonometric ratios based on where the sun is located. The diagram in Figure 11.6 illustrates the various angles and points of the relevant triangles. The following derivation will give us the mathematical model needed to mark the lines on the dial plate.

In Triangle ABD $\qquad \sin \theta = \frac{AB}{DB}$, so $AB = DB \sin \theta$

In Triangle ABC $\qquad \tan \varphi = \frac{BC}{AB}$, so $\tan \varphi = \frac{BC}{DB \sin \theta}$,

which gives us $\qquad BC = \tan \varphi \cdot DB \sin \theta$

In Triangle DBC $\qquad \tan \alpha = \frac{BC}{DB}$, so $\tan \alpha = \frac{\tan \varphi \cdot DB \sin \theta}{DB}$,

Therefore the horizontal
sundial model is as follows: $\quad \tan \alpha = \tan \varphi \cdot \sin \theta$

Now that we know the horizontal sundial formula is defined as the equation: $\tan \alpha = \tan \varphi \cdot \sin \theta$, we can substitute values for our hour marks and the latitude of the sundial. As an exercise, let us mark the 1:00 hour line at 30° north latitude. Remember that each hour is defined as 15° of movement for angle φ. Also, remember that the hour lines are symmetrical on either side of the meridian line. This means that 11:00 a.m. and 1:00 p.m. will have the same angle with respect to the base of the gnomon and the north/south meridian line but will be angling out in opposite directions. The same would be true for sets of numbers that are a.m. versus p.m. and are equally distant from the noon hour.

Assuming a latitude of 30° north of the equator: $\theta = 30°$
At 11:00 and 1:00, angle $\varphi = 15°$
So: angle $\alpha = \arctan(\tan 15 \cdot \sin 30) \approx 7.63°$
At 10:00 and 2:00, angle $\varphi = 30°$
So: angle $\alpha = \arctan(\tan 30 \cdot \sin 30) \approx 16.1°$
Etc.

A vertical dial, meaning one placed on a wall or other upright apparatus, would have a similar derivation but results in a model using cosine. Specifically the mathematical model for a vertical dial would be as follows: $\tan \alpha' = \tan \varphi \cdot \cos \theta$. Additionally, there are a number of unique geometric methods for marking the dial plates based on these models. Figure 11.7 provides a geometric model that only requires the common geometric tools of compass, protractor, and straightedge. Interestingly enough, it is only necessary to construct half of this diagram because the dial is symmetrical with respect to the meridian line.

Figure11.7: Geometric Model for Marking a Horizontal or Vertical Dial Plate

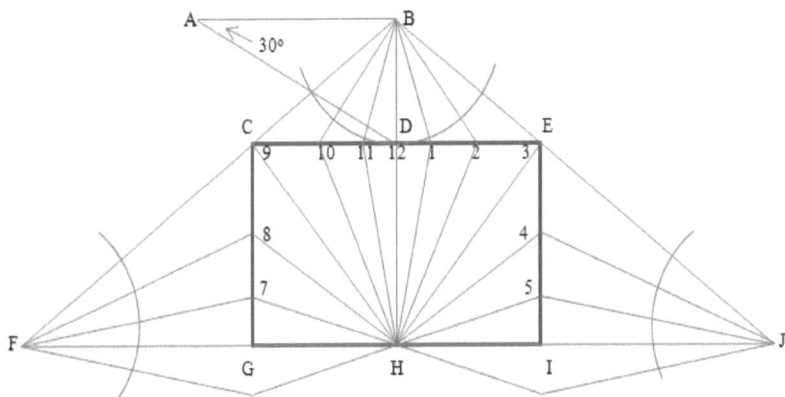

The directions for the geometric layout of the lines on the dial plate shown in Figure 11.7 are as follows:

1. Draw line AB and construct a perpendicular from B that acts as the meridian line for the dial plate
2. At point A, draw segment AD such that angle DAB is equal to your latitude
3. Construct the meridian line such that DH is congruent to AD
4. Connect point B to points F and J
5. Draw FJ through point H at a perpendicular such that FH is congruent to HJ
6. Draw segment CE through point D at a perpendicular to the meridian line and

7. Drop perpendiculars from C and E to points G and I respectively.
8. At points B, F, and J, draw arcs of radius BD
9. Divide the arcs from step 8 into 15° sectors and extend each radius until they intersect the rectangle
10. Extend each of these intersecting points to point H. These are the hour line of the dial.
11. Number the intersections as you would a circular clock.

Every sundial clock has a mathematical model that allows for both algebraic and geometric representations. The horizontal model is fairly straight forward and simple to derive, but some are tremendously complex. It might be surprising but there are a substantial number of unique sundial designs. Some function vertically, some horizontally, some at angles, some by reflections, some by poles, some by arcs, and some by perforations. In fact, the last example, the perforated ring dial, is a loop of solid material (metal or otherwise) that is perforated so that a sliver of sunlight shows through and shines on the interior of the ring. Instead of a shadow indicating the time, a pinpoint of light created by the perforation moves along the interior of the loop and indicates the time as the sun moves.

Other sundial designs such as the *armillary* can be mathematically modeled very easily because the shadow is not cast on a flat plate, but rather, on an arced ring. The reason this is easier to model is that circular motion is not being translated to linear motion as is done with the horizontal and vertical dials. Instead, the circular motion of the sun is simply being modeled as a proportionally smaller version of circular motion. Figure 11.8 illustrates the model used for an armillary.

Figure 11.8: Mathematical Model of an Armillary Sundial (Lateral View)

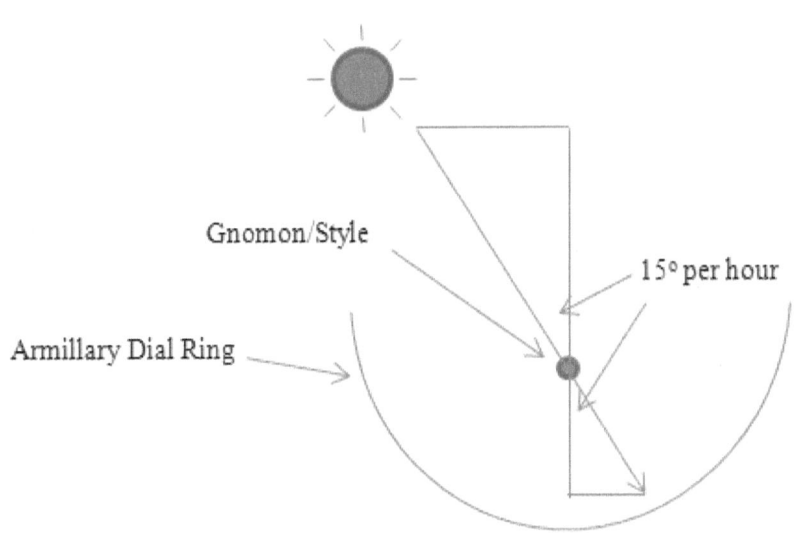

Because the arced path of looped dial on the armillary is in the same general shape as the arced path representing the movement of the sun (only on a much smaller scale), the time can be marked on the armillary loop in even 15° increments. No trigonometry is necessary. This can be seen in the similar triangles in Figure 11.8. Further, the armillary can be tilted to any latitude and also tilted to accommodate for the seasons, which makes it universally functional. Some armillary dial loops can even be rotated 15 degrees to compensate for Daylight Savings Time. For most armillary designs the gnomon is titled so that the sun's rays strike it at a perpendicular, making calculations relative to the movement of the shadow very simple. Having said this, however, it should be noted that no sundial is perfect because the real equation of time is fairly complex and must accommodate a number of variables that we have not yet discussed. The models that have been shown herein are only estimates as they relate to recording time in a predictable mathematical fashion.

The *real equation of time* explains the difference between mean solar time, which is based on an exact 24 hour rotation of the earth and also what would be recorded on a standard analog clock; and apparent solar time, which is the actual time based on the position of the sun with respect to a given shadow-based measurement dial. Real time is affected by two factors. First, the sun moves with a speed, relative to the earth, that varies slightly throughout the year. Because the earth's path around the sun is elliptical, the relative speed of the sun with respect to the surface of the earth is faster during perihelion. This means that the time the sun takes to travel over the surface of the earth varies ever so slightly from one day to the next throughout the seasons.

The second variable that creates a difference in mean solar time and apparent solar time is that the earth is revolving around the earth in an arc and therefore takes longer than one mean solar day to complete a noon to noon rotation. This is illustrated in Figure 11.9.

Figure 11.9: Noon to Noon Rotation of the Earth with Respect to an Arc.

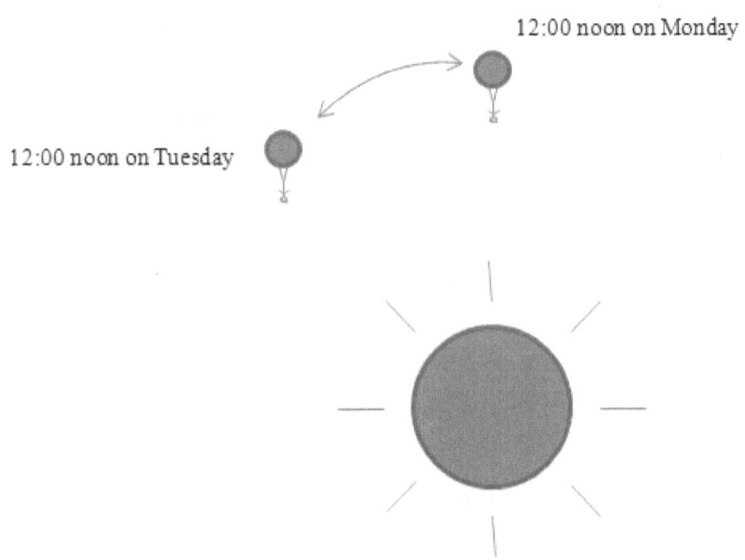

Notice in Figure 11.9 that a complete 360° rotation of the earth from 12:00 noon on Monday to 12:00 noon on Tuesday would not result in the sun being directly overhead for the stick figure. Local apparent noon would have changed because of the arced path of the earth around the sun. Our stick figure would need to rotate a few tenths of a degree more to reach local solar noon. The amount of time that the sundial loses in a given day is small, but it does add up to a complete rotation over the course of a solar year. If we consider only the 360° rotation of the earth, every six months (or 180° of orbit), our clock would be approximately 12 hours slow. Using the diagram in Figure 11.9, this is simple to see because for each complete rotation of the earth, the stick figure would be aimed the same direction. This mathematical model becomes even more complex when we consider that in the winter, when the earth is orbiting around the sun at a rate that is faster than average, the earth requires even more rotational time to complete a solar day.

One other fairly important aspect of sundial construction that has not yet been discussed is the variable of the seasons. It is believed by many sundial enthusiasts that at the time of the ancient Egyptians, people understood that the length of the noon shadow in the summer was shorter than the noon shadow during the winter. This was an important advancement in the mathematical understanding of the sundial because it meant that the seasons could be measured as accurately as the time of the passing day.

The Greeks recognized that the shadow path outlined by the tip of a vertically oriented gnomon traced out the path of a hyperbola during the solstices and traced out a straight path during the equinoxes. By the height of the Roman Empire, more lines were added to the new seasonal dial plate that would show the hours of the day using the direction of the shadows as well as their lengths. It should be noted that the methods used for this seasonal dial plate was an empirical method where shadows were recorded and mapped according to a year-long process of measurement on a dial plate that had already been situated. It was not until the Golden Age that mathematicians and astronomers described the shadows of the seasonal sundial geometrically and analytically. The seasonal dial is known as the *Pelekinon* and can be seen in Figure 11.10.

Figure 11.10: Pelekinon Seasonal Sundial

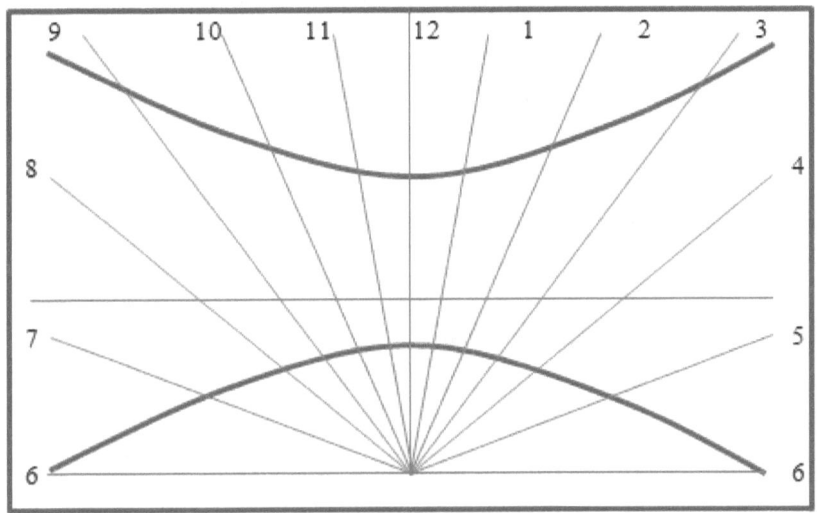

SUMMARY

Sundials really are remarkable machines with a wide range of complexity. There are many books and scholarly articles dedicated to their explanations and functionality. In fact, they have been one of the most widely studied machines throughout history. They also represent, possibly better than any other kind of device, what is meant by mathematical engineering because, as we have discussed, it requires no moving parts. A fairly comprehensive investigation of the number of different sundials that function with unique mathematical models would probably surprise most people. In my research, I discovered nearly 20 different kinds. This is because nearly anything that casts a shadow can be a sundial.

I would encourage anyone wanting to show the direct and meaningful connections of numeric, algebraic, and geometric processes to science and engineering to do some investigation into sundials. The colonial history of sundials is a good place to start because of how they were considered in the development of what would become the United States. Benjamin Franklin was especially fascinated by sundials. In fact, it was because of his influence that the first U.S. coin, the *Fugio Cent*, was minted under the authority of the Continental Congress. It had a sundial on one side and displayed the motto "Mind Your Business."

ADDITIONAL READINGS

Daniel, C.J.H. (2004). Sundials. Shire Publications. Essex: UK

Jones, L.E. (2005). *The Sundial and Geometry, 2nd Ed.* North American Sundial Society.

Lynch, K. (1971). *Sundials and Spheres (A catalog of sundials).* Canterbury Publishing Company: Canterbury CT.

Rovsek, B. (2010). Calibration of a Horizontal Sundial. *The Physics Teacher*. Vol. 48, No 6, pp. 397

Thomson. M. (2010). Sundials. *The Physics Teacher*. Vol. 10, No 3.

Waugh, A. (1973). *Sundials: Their Theory and Construction.* Dover Publications: ISBN 978-0486229478

Wheaton-Smith, S. (2005). *Illustrating Shadows.* Silver City, MN.

SECTION 3: MECHANICAL DEVICES

Nearly every popular product of the past two centuries has gone through some kind of engineering process so that its utility, safety, durability, and efficiency could be optimized. The road to successful product/technology development is fundamentally based on mathematics, and this is where STEM as an integrated set of disciplines really starts to demonstrate its importance. Engineering is often misunderstood within the context of STEM. It is based on the belief that a successful assembling of working parts to achieve a functioning product represents successful engineering. This is not always true. Engineering happens as a process that uses mathematics and science to define a product before anything is ever physically assembled. We can say that Science is applied mathematics, Engineering is applied science, and Technology is applied engineering. To create better technology, we need new and improved mathematical models. To truly engage in an engineering process, we need to understand how to define a product or piece of technology mathematically so that the process of building the product is not an inefficient cobbling together of parts that may or may not work as hoped. Within the process of engineering is the process of experimenting, using mathematical and physical models, and recording results. The mathematical concepts presented in Section 3 are as follows:

Article 12: Sextants, Astrolabes, and Stereographic Projection
Article 13: Reuleaux Polygons and Drilling Square Holes
Article 14: Straight Line Linkages and the Ratio Gauge
Article 15: Pendulums, Gears, and Grandfather Clocks
Article 16: Constructing Robotic Legs

ARTICLE 12: SEXTANTS, ASTROLABES, AND STEREOGRAPHIC PROJECTION

ABSTRACT: Mechanical instruments with moving parts represented an enormous advancement in engineering and technology. Navigation instruments for sea vessels were especially important in advancing transportation, shipping, warfare, and exploration. This article illustrates the idea of how mathematical models were used for developing machines that could calculate locations and movements over a curved surface (the earth) using the sun, moon, stars, and other geometric patterns for navigation.

INTRODUCTION

The word *geometry* literally means "earth measure" and the first formal study of geometry did just that. Applied forms of geometry used what mathematicians had previously discovered to create charts of celestial movements of stars, the sun, and of course, the moon. Although navigation over the surface of the earth is not about measuring the earth, it is about defining points on a sphere based on careful measurements relative to other objects. Early machines such as the *mariner's sextant* and, much earlier, the *astrolabe,* are examples of the innovative thinking and engineering that became very popular during the 18th century and remains so even today. Both of the devices are fairly simple to operate in terms of how the parts move and how the scales are read, but the mathematics and methods of their respective uses are a bit more complex when it comes to locating the position of something like a ship.

The sextant is said to have been invented during the late 17th or early 18th century by Sir Isaac Newton (his invention was something more akin to a double reflection navigation tool), but he apparently never published the work. The first official sextant was made in 1757 by John Bird, who was a mathematical instrument maker (see, mathematical engineering is real!). Other similar devices were developed around the same time such as the octant and Davis Quadrant. The devices are named based on the span of the measurement scale around which they are mounted. For example, the sextant is named based on an arc shaped measurement scale that spans 60°. The name comes from the Latin words *sextans* or *sextantis* meaning *one-sixth*. An octant has a measurement arc of 45° (one-eighth of a circle) while a quadrant (one-fourth of a circle) has a 90° scale.

The astrolabe is only slightly different in that it is a much earlier device that operates like an inclinometer but does not use the reflective properties of the sextant. The word *astrolabe* can be interpreted as *star taker*. The earliest form of the astrolabe is a product of very early engineering efforts, from about 150 BCE. The device is elaborate in that it is not only for measuring the incline of objects, but also as a way to predict the movements of the stars based on spherical astronomy. The astrolabe also influenced the development of the first mechanical clocks because of the rotating disks that could be inserted into some of the designs.

INVESTIGATION AND NOTES

It is worthwhile to note that the sextant and the astrolabe function somewhat differently. Both measure the angles between distant objects, but how they do it is based on some distinct mechanical differences. For instance, the mariner's sextant uses an eyepiece that is pointed directly at the horizon. An integrated mirror system is then used to locate the altitude of the sun or other object by moving an index pendulum (attached to a mirror) along an arc-shaped measurement scale. The astrolabe, on the other hand, assumes that the device is resting on a real horizontal plane and then rotates an eyepiece toward the sun so that the angle of elevation can be measured directly. The result is the same for both devices, that being the altitude of the sun or other target, but the sextant does a better job of creating a real horizontal reference. Figure 12.1 illustrates the basic physical structure used for the mariner's sextant. A double reflection model is used to define the operation mathematically.

Figure 12.1: Mariner's Sextant Model

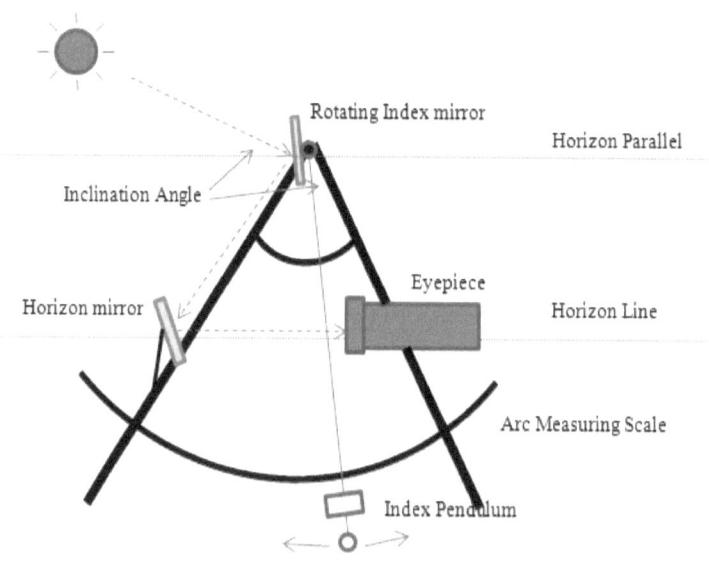

As noted in Figure 12.1, the eyepiece is aimed at the distant horizon to create what is essentially a horizontal reference line. Of course, this line is not exactly horizontal with respect to an actual horizontal tangent line because the eyepiece is few feet above the surface of the earth based on the eye level of the user. However, because we are siting distant objects relative to one another, a certain amount of error is acceptable. By moving the index bar, the index mirror is adjusted to reflect a target object such as the sun into the horizon mirror, which, in turn, reflects the object through the eyepiece. The angle of elevation or inclination of the object is read from the arc measuring scale at the point where the index bar is moved. This scale works like a protractor and reflects the angle of elevation, which can then be translated to latitude by using a numeric table.

The mathematical model used for the reflections in a sextant is from a topic that is often presented in physical science courses. On a reflective flat surface, electromagnetic radiation (light in this case) reflects at an angle equal to that at which it strikes the reflective surface. In short, the angle of incidence is equal to the angle of reflection. For now we will assume the *incidence angle* is the exterior angle rather than the angle on either side of the normal line. This principle must be used to determine how the scale is labeled on the arc of the sextant. Generally the concept is very simple, but it is a bit more complex with this particular tool because there are two mirrors to consider.

Let us suppose we want to force a ray of light to turn a right angle corner using a single mirror. We would simply rotate the mirror with respect to the exterior incidence direction such that 180 − (2 * Exterior Incidence Angle) provides us with the magnitude that we want the light ray to *turn*. In this case we would rotate the mirror such that the incidence angle of the light ray is 45° with respect to the mirror. An incidence angle of 45° means that our reflection angle will also be 45°. This being the case, the interior angle (the angle at which the light turns) will be the remainder of the 180° straight angle along which the light ray was initially travelling. Now suppose that we would like the light ray to turn at an angle of only 60°. In this case, we must remember that this means the angle created *between* the incidence ray and the reflection ray is a 60° turn angle. This means that the mirror would have to be rotated 60° from parallel to the mirror. Figure 12.2 illustrates both cases.

Figure 12.2: Reflection Patterns Base on the Model 180 – 2*(Exterior Incidence Angle)

If we now look at two mirrors used together, a new mathematical model emerges. Suppose we position one mirror, which remains stationary. We will call this a *horizon mirror*. We can use a second mirror, which is also stationary but can rotate freely (we will call this the *index mirror*) to *turn* a light ray into the horizontal mirror. Ultimately we can *turn* or *steer* the light in a number of unique directions, even at an object that is horizontal but offset from the original path.

To demonstrate this idea, let us go back to the examples in Figure 12.2. We defined how light could be *steered* with a single mirror. The path of the light ray described in Figure 12.1 could be aimed any direction within a 180° arc starting from its original path and progressing to a direction immediately back to its source. This could actually be achieved for an entire 360° rotation if we were able to rotate the index mirror in any direction. We used a mathematical model, 180 – 2*Exterior Incidence Angle to define the degree measure of the intended *turn*, therefore it stands to reason that we should also be able to define a given index angle by starting with a target and working backwards. Figure 12.3 illustrates how two mirrors could be used to reflect a light ray onto a path that is removed but parallel to the original direction. Note that the angle between the incidence and reflection angles for each mirror would be 45°.

Figure 12.3: Parallel Reflection Using Two Mirrors

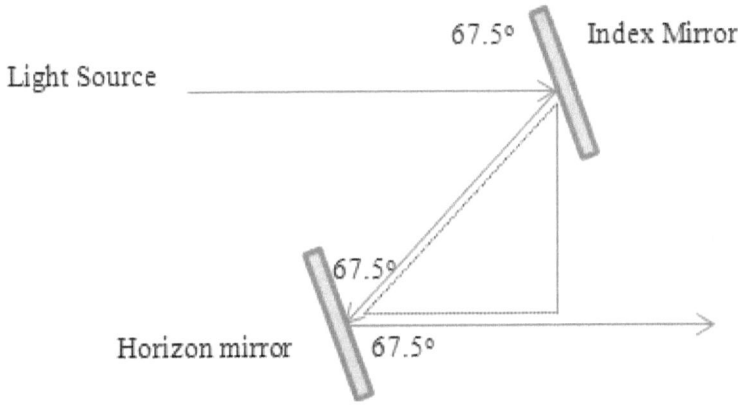

In order to turn the light ray back toward the horizon mirror at a 45° angle, the exterior incidence and reflection angles for each mirror need to be 67.5°. This is true for both mirrors. Note also how the mirrors need to be parallel to make this work. This is true because of a familiar geometry theorem that states parallel lines cut by a transversal have alternate interior angles that are congruent. The alternate interior angles are represented by the reflection angle on the index mirror and the incidence angle on the horizon mirror. Ultimately we find that the index mirror is rotated counterclockwise 22.5° from vertical to make this arrangement work.

Now let us suppose that the inclination of the target object is 30° above the horizon but we still want to focus the resulting light path along the horizon. The index mirror must be rotated so that it reflects the light at the horizon mirror. The horizon mirror must then direct the ray so that it reflects on a horizontal path. What we learn from this is that the horizon mirror must always maintain a 67.5° angle with respect to the horizon because of the 45° fixed arrangement of the mirrors with respect to one another. That is to say, no matter what angle the light source is coming from, the index mirror will reflect the light toward the horizon mirror so that it hits the horizon mirror at a 67.5° angle and reflects at the same angle. This will allow the light to turn at our desired 45°. This will vary from one sextant design to another because they may not all have the same fixed arrangement of mirrors. Figure 12.4 illustrates the mirror angles necessary to reflect a light ray from a 30° inclination through two mirrors back to a horizontal path.

Figure 12.4: Reflection of Light through Two Mirrors from 30° Inclination to a Horizontal Path

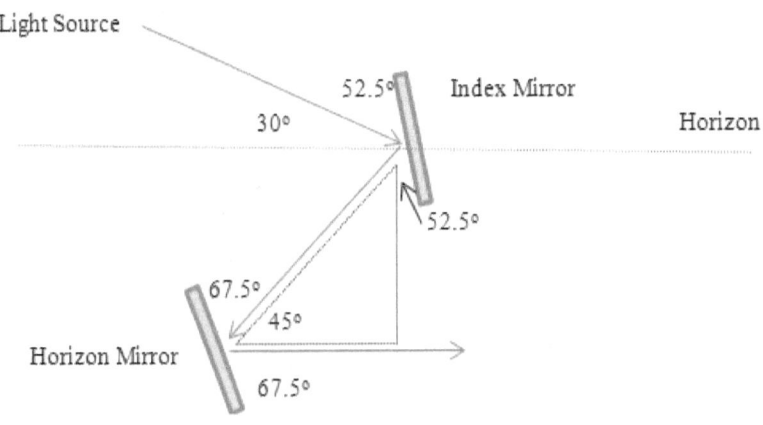

In the example illustrated in Figure 12.4, the *turn* angle of the light source reflected off of the index mirror must be the original 45° associated with the standard horizon angle plus an additional 30° of inclination. The total *turn* angle of the light ray must then be 75° making the exterior incidence and reflection angles 52.5° each. After determining these measurements, we must establish a relationship between the angles of the index mirrors for the two different measurements we have made (remember that the horizon mirror is stationary and is always rotated at a 67.5° angle from the horizontal plane. When the light source was horizontal, the rotation of the index mirror was 22.5° counterclockwise from vertical. When our light source came from 30° above the horizon, our rotation was 7.5° counterclockwise from vertical. The difference between these measurements is 15° or exactly half of the angle of inclination. The halving/doubling factor is due to the fact that we are splitting the additional inclination angle between the incidence and reflection angles when we rotate the index mirror. The measurement shown on the arc of the sextant is always going to read double the actual amount of the rotation angle.

So now what if we are to consider a sextant design that does not arrange the index and horizon mirrors using the 45 degree orientation with respect to one another? A general geometric verification would be helpful to determine an angle of inclination of the target. Figure 12.5 illustrates a more generalized model for a series of mirror angles where the orientation of the index and horizon mirrors is not known. The model demonstrates a generalized case for the sextant.

Figure 12.5: General Geometric Model for a Reflective Sextant Design

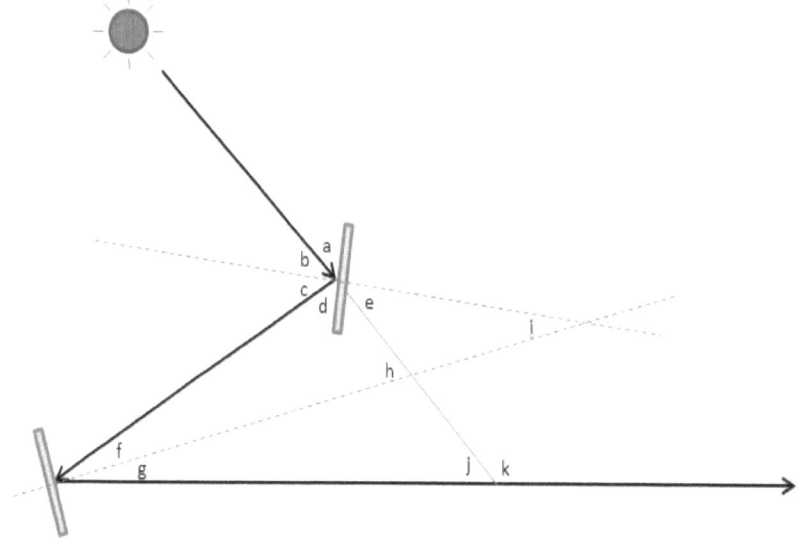

The geometric verification used for this model is based on some very basic angle congruence laws. The most complicated part of the mathematical model is defining a relationship between a given measurement angle and the inclination angle. What we are ultimately trying to illustrate is that the true angle of inclination of the target object (as defined by *angle j*) is twice the angle at the intersection of the normal lines to the mirrors. The normal lines are those that intersect the mirrors at right angles. The normal lines in this model are represented by the dotted lines and the intersection angle of the normal lines is defined by *angle i*. Note that if the mirrors were parallel, the normal lines would also be parallel. As the index mirror is rotated clockwise to follow a target object as it assumes a greater angle of inclination, *angle i* increases accordingly. *Angle i*, however, only increases at half the rate of the actual inclination angle because of the doubling effect of the mirrors that was illustrated in Figure 12.4.

For a general proof, let us assume that the target is the sun as shown in Figure 12.5. The angle of inclination of the sun from the horizon is defined by *angle j*. However, because *angle i* is going to be our reference for determining *angle j*, we will begin by relating *angle i* to angles that are also related to *angle j*. This is needed because the measurement for the angle of inclination of the sun is taken from the rotation of the index mirror instead of a direct line of sight. As we rotate the index mirror, all of the necessary angles come into play and we can define a verification for a sextant of nearly any design.

by the exterior angle theorem, therefore…

$$\angle c = \angle i + \angle f$$

isolating reference *angle i*

$$\angle i = \angle c - \angle f$$

by the exterior angle theorem, therefore…

$$\angle b + \angle c = \angle j + \angle f + \angle g$$

isolating inclination *angle j*

$$\angle j = \angle b + \angle c - \angle f - \angle g$$

define equality of incidence and reflection angles

$$\angle b = \angle c \text{ and } \angle f = \angle g$$

redefine *angle j* by substitution

$$\angle j = \angle c + \angle c - \angle f - \angle f$$

simplify

$$\angle j = 2\angle c - 2\angle f$$

define the doubling factor

$$\angle j = 2(\angle c - \angle f)$$

substitute. QED

$$\angle j = 2\angle i$$

This proof verifies that no matter how the sextant is designed, the same doubling effect from the mirrors is present. That is to say, the mirrors can be arranged in almost any configuration and still provide the appropriate reference angle on the measurement arc. Most sextant designs include an arrangement of two mirrors, which are normally placed in a triangular fashion with respect to the eyepiece at approximately $45°$ as previously discussed. What was not previously discussed is why the sextant uses a process of dual reflection rather than taking a direct siting of the target like a standard inclinometer. The real advantage of this device is that the altitude of an object can be established with respect to the distant horizon rather than with respect to the instrument itself. This ultimately allows for a much more accurate determination of latitude, particularly if one is attempting to measure from a moving platform such as the deck of a ship in rough water.

Finding the angle of inclination of a celestial object is fundamental to establishing the latitude of a moving object such as a ship on the open seas; although, other information is necessary if we are to find an approximate location on the surface of the earth in terms of both latitude and longitude. Typically, detailed charts of the exact elevations, longitude positions, and relative times of the movements of celestial bodies are used to cross reference with the sextant or astrolabe measurements to determine the latitude and longitude from where the measurements are taken.

The Astrolabe and Stereographic Projection: A much earlier device for finding latitude is our next topic of investigation. The astrolabe is a *direct siting* device similar to an inclinometer where the altitude of the target object is taken relative to the device rather than relative to the horizon (as is the case of the sextant). The device was invented much earlier than the sextant but included a set of disks that could be placed in a circular middle section and rotated to complete various calculations. Plates with different patterns, particularly celestial patterns, would be inserted into a circular indentation and rotated to a given position to reflect the information needed for desired calculation. For example, the first mechanical clocks were influenced by the design of the astrolabe because a rotating plate in the center of the device could be used to keep track of the positions of the moon, stars, and even the elevation of the sun. The plates would essentially be a map of the stars in the night sky during a given time frame and for a given region. Plates could easily be removed and replaced with different versions to accommodate different seasons or locations.

The disk of an astrolabe is called the *Mater* (mother), which is a hollowed out circular section that would hold plates called *tympans*. A tympan would typically be designed for specific latitudes and be engraved with a stereographic projection of circles, ellipses, and other markings that would define the elevation and azimuth of a partial sphere above the visible horizon. The rim of the *mater* would be marked in degrees or hours. Depending on the design, a freely rotating arm (called the rule) would help define measurements. On the reverse side of the mater, there were often a number of scales that would help with conversions related to locating celestial bodies based on the time in the month or hours in the day. Figure 12.6 (the Hartmann astrolabe at Yale University) shows the complexity of markings on a common astrolabe.

Figure 12.6: The Hartmann Astrolabe (Circa 1532)

The key to understanding all of the complex markings on the astrolabe is to understand the idea of stereographic projection. This topic was mentioned briefly in Article 1 but was not described in any detail. A stereographic projection is a way to project points from a sphere onto a plane, which results in a circular graph. The process is a geometric way to flatten a sphere while maintaining the integrity and orientation of all of the circles and angles from the original sphere. To help describe this process, imagine looking down at the earth from the North Pole and slicing the earth into five different latitudes. If we looked only at the circles created by the surface of the earth from each latitude slice, we would see what looked like a series of five concentric circles, one from each slice; however, if we discount depth perception, we would see these circles on a single plane. If we then moved away from the North Pole and described the relationship of the circles to one another, they would appear as ellipses because we would be looking at them from an angle. This is largely what the elliptical markings on the astrolabe represent.

To demonstrate this idea in a bit more detail, we will explore the mathematical model of stereographic projection. One of the simplest ways to think of the stereographic projection is to imagine a light source at the North or South Poles that shines through the sphere and marks every point on a flat plane on the opposite side of the sphere. Figure 12.7 illustrates this concept with a few lines. Note how the lines originating at the North Pole (N) follow a straight path through the sphere and plot points *a* and *b* from the sphere as *a'* and *b'* on the plane E, which represents the equatorial plane of the sphere. The same process could be done from the South Pole.

(Diagram can be found on the following page)

Figure 12.7: Stereographic Projection

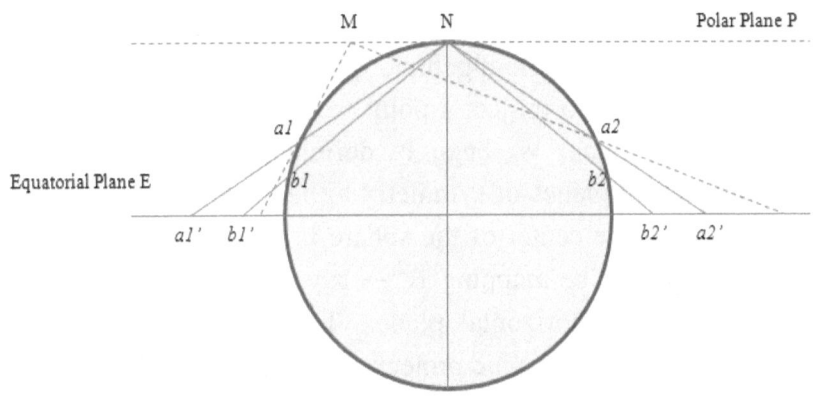

Note that all points at the latitudes where *a1, a2, b1* and *b2* rest would project as concentric circles on Equatorial Plane E. Also, the spherical points closest to the equator are graphed on the equatorial plane as the smallest circles. In some sense, the projection is inverted but this depends on one's perspective. Now imagine that the light source is moved within a Polar Plane P from point N to point M. The projection would change slightly to represent concentric ellipses as noted by the new projections of *a1* and *a2* from the dotted lines.

The question that emerges from this projective system is how do we identify the planar points (u,v) coming from a three dimensional system that defines a sphere? If we reexamine the projection, we can see that any point on a Cartesian sphere with the center at the origin can be defined by the equation of a sphere $x^2 + y^2 + z^2 = 1$. This being the case, we also know that a point on the sphere can be defined as (x,y,z). Given that any lateral slice of a sphere creates a circle, we know that the projection of (x,y,z) on a plane will result in a circle containing points in the form (u,v) such that $u^2 + v^2 = r^2$. These relationships are fairly common within proofs of stereographic projection equations. There are, however, many different forms of proofs and derivations for the formulas for the projections, and nearly all of them are much more complicated than they need to be.

A simple geometric-algebraic derivation is as follows. Let us suppose we want to project a point from the surface of a sphere onto a lateral x,y plane. We begin by defining any one of an infinite number of vertical planes of symmetry to be the x,z plane. We will also assume that the center of the sphere is located at the origin of R^3 and that we will be mapping $R^2 \rightarrow x,y$, which for our purposes will always be the horizontal plane. Figure 12.8 illustrates the derivation of the stereographic projection formula.

Figure 12.8: Derivation of Stereographic Projection Formulas

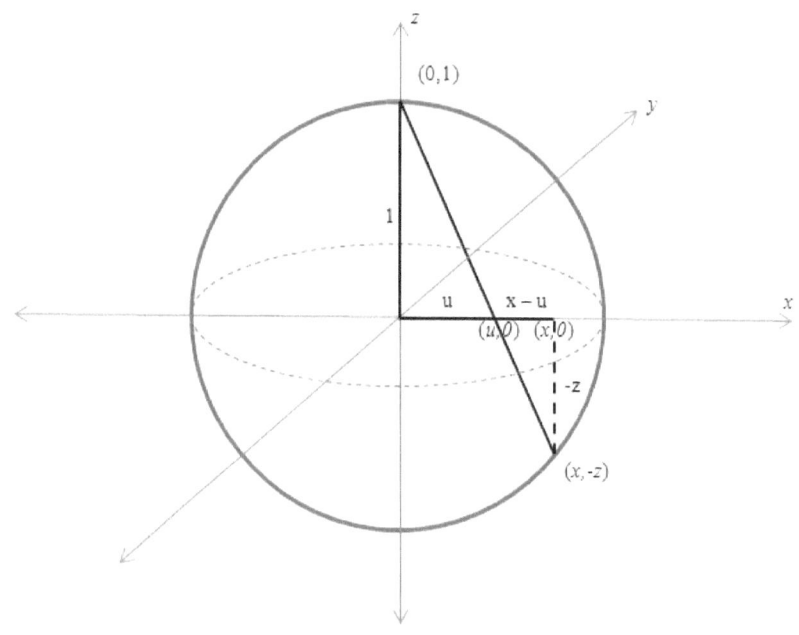

The projection of (x,-z) onto the x,y-plane will happen where the x-value is defined by u. The y-value would follow the same derivation process but be defined by v. Thus, the planar projection point is defined by (u,v) even though we are only deriving u in this example. We will use a simple relationship between similar triangles to complete the derivation. If we are projecting the point (x,-z) from polar north of a unit sphere, we can relate similar triangles as follows: the ratio of the short side of the large triangle to the short side of the small triangle is equal to the ratio of the long side of the large triangle to the long side of the small triangle.

$$\frac{u}{x-u} = \frac{1}{-z}$$

$$-uz = x - u$$

$$u - uz = x$$

$$u(1-z) = x$$

$$u = \frac{x}{1-z} \quad \text{and thus ...} \quad v = \frac{y}{1-z}$$

What this tell us is that every planar point (u,v) can be mapped using the ordered pair, $\left(\frac{x}{1-z}, \frac{y}{1-z}\right)$.

The projection formulas continue to get more complex but the previous derivation does provide a basis for mapping the point from a sphere onto a plane. The formulas can then be reversed to expand the planar map to the three dimensional system that represents something akin to the positions of the stars, planets, and sun. The astrolabe uses this projective mapping technique to make all sorts of calculations such as the time at a given location based on the positions of celestial bodies. Again, like the sextant, the astrolabe requires the use of celestial data to make these calculations, but in more of a geometric form. Where the sextant used tables of the locations of celestial bodies during certain times for a specific latitude and longitude, the astrolabe used the geometrically inscribed tympans.

SUMMARY

Although these two devices came from different time periods, they are both mechanical devices that were designed for the same purposes. They may even be thought of as early computers. Certainly they were influenced by other devices such as the *Antikythera* computer, which has a unique history in and of itself. The bottom line is that these kinds of devices are great examples of early mechanical engineering, which was a direct extension of mathematical engineering. The devices have also stood the test of time in that they are still used in various forms even today. Of course, Global Positioning technology has made navigation using mechanical devices unnecessary for the most part but the mathematical models responsible for navigation based on celestial patterns transfers easily to other kinds of mathematical engineering solutions, and particularly to those elements of geometry that involve parts that move systematically and relative to one another. This geometric interplay between moving parts will become fundamental to understanding the tools described in subsequent articles.

ADDITIONIAL READINGS

Bauer, B. (1995). *The Sextant Handbook*. International Marine/Ragged Mountain Press. 2nd Ed.: Camden, Maine. ISBN: 978-0070052192.

Blewitt, M. (1994). *Celestial Navigation for Yachtsmen*. International Marine/Ragged Mountain Press: Camden, Maine. ISBN: 978-0070059283.

Morris, W.J. (2010). *The Nautical Sextant*. Paradise Cay Publications, Inc. ASIN: B008PYM5QK

Morrison, J.E. (2007). *The Astrolabe*. Janus Publications: United Kingdom. ISBN: 978-0939320301

ARTICLE 13: REULEAUX POLYGONS AND DRILLING SQUARE HOLES

ABSTRACT: The following article on the geometry of drilling square holes is primarily a visual exploration of an engineering application for a geometric figure known as a Reuleaux Triangle. This article explores how the overlapping intersections of three or more circles form a series of Vesica Piscis figures (introduced in Article 1), which make the Reuleaux triangle and other Reuleaux polygons possible. The uniform elliptical motion associated with the construction of the Reuleaux curves allow the figures to outline a square or other regular polygon, depending on the shape of the original Reuleaux figure. The equations needed to calculate the area of the Reuleaux triangle and to define the square outline are discussed herein.

INTRODUCTION

Perhaps you remember the classic idiom about not being able to put a square peg in a round hole? Of course, the saying has generally come to describe a contradiction in logic about the way things fit together (or, more commonly, do not fit together), but a little bit of imagination with some basic geometric principles not only allows you to conceptualize a square peg in a round hole, it guarantees the possibility. Putting the proverbial square peg in a round hole has been the basis of a popular woodworking tool for nearly a century, and not in a figurative sense. If you have ever watched television programming involving finish carpentry, you may have seen a power drill that can drill a square hole in a board.

That is to say, the *circular* motion associated with drilling a circular hole can be manipulated to create a *square* hole if the right kind of drill bit and the right kind of rotation is used. The phenomenon is fairly counterintuitive even as you watch it happen, and that is largely what makes the engineering process so interesting and fun. It also illustrates how necessary it is to thoroughly understand basic geometric principles and how they can be used creatively in the engineering process.

These square holes, or *mortises* as they are called in the woodworking business, have been popular in furniture building for many years from both the decorative and the practicality standpoints of woodworking. We most often see square *mortis and tenon* joints in handmade furniture; particularly where strong right angle joints are needed without having the advantages of fastening hardware such as nails or screws. Most people can guess that the device used to make these square mortises involves a special kind of drill bit, which is correct and also which most people instinctively understand. However, to consider a single drill bit, having no straight edges of any kind, and that drills square holes is especially unique. The tool involves some clever manipulations of both circles and ellipses, and this particular kind of functionality is probably beyond what most people consider when it comes to drilling holes simply because they cannot imagine how circular motion can create a square outline.

The development of this special bit is an excellent example of how a unique knowledge of mathematics, (coordinate geometry, trigonometry, and parametric equations in particular) is a critical ingredient for engineering innovations. The shape of the drill bit in question is known as a *Reuleaux triangle* and it can be better understood by revisiting some of the topics presented in Articles One, Two, and Four. The fact that this roughly triangular region can be rotated to create a shape that is virtually square is the basis for the drill bit application.

The device was invented by Henry Watt, patented in 1917, and was known as the Watt square drill bit. Both the shape of the bit and the motion of the drilling frame contribute to the square outline of the holes it produces. The drill bit, however, is only the most familiar application of the Reuleaux figure described here. There are many other applications as well and they are related to Reuleaux polygons in general. Reuleaux polygons can have any number of sides, but ironically none of the sides of the drill bit are straight. In this sense, it is a bit of a misnomer to call the figures polygons, but we can get away with it because the edges, though curved, are all separated by distinct vertices. Most Reuleaux figures are considered regular polygons as well, particularly in their practical engineering, artistic, and architectural applications.

A special characteristic of the Reuleaux figures is that they are *curves of uniform width*. What this tells us is that the figures can be rolled between two parallel lines and remain tangent to both lines as they roll, even though they are not circular. Basically this means that there are a number of unique engineering and other practical applications for the figures, which most people, for lack of exposure, have never been able to consider (the square drill bit being only one such example). For instance, a manhole cover is typically circular because it is one of the only shapes that cannot fall through the hole it covers. Obviously a shape such as a square being used as a lid could be oriented so that it would fall through the hole it covered because the length of the diagonal of a square hole would be longer than the side of the square cover. However, Reuleaux figures, being uniformly wide, could also be used as a cover for a manhole because no Reuleaux figure will fall through the hole it covers.

The Reuleaux figures have an interesting history, at least over the past century, because of their many applications to mechanical engineering, art, and architecture. Some countries have coins that are Reuleaux shaped (the Reuleaux heptagons are particularly strange looking coins). Occasionally you will find the Reuleaux triangle in architectural designs for windows and doors, mostly on cathedrals and other Renaissance era buildings. It is also the shape used for the emblem of the Colorado School of Mines and the U.S. Parks Service's National Trails System. You will often find other more obscure but interesting applications as well, such as guitar picks and even some pencil designs. Reuleaux triangular pencils, interestingly enough, are less likely to roll off of a table than an octagonal or circular pencil because the center of gravity must move up and down as the pencil rolls even though it has a constant width. For our purposes, we will explore a number of connections between mathematics and engineering design that are dependent specifically on the Reuleaux triangle.

INVESTIGATION AND NOTES

It should be noted prior to any ongoing investigation that the *mortis* (hole) the Watt square drill bit produces is only *mostly* square. The corners of the outlined square hole are ever so slightly rounded. In fact, the drill-bit carves out about .9877… of the area of a square hole. This will become more apparent as we explore the geometry behind the design.

The Reuleaux triangle is an interesting looking figure and can be best conceptualized by revisiting a topic from *Article One: Circles and Segments*. One of the main ideas considered in Article One, as you may recall, was the overlapping region known as the Vesica Piscis.

The Vesica regions are fundamental to the development of all Reuleaux figures but we must use three or more overlapping circles instead of only two in order to create a Reuleaux polygon.

We would need three circles to form a Reuleaux triangle, five to create a pentagon and so on. The Reuleaux figures can be generalized to regular polygons with an odd number of sides.

Figure 13.1 illustrates the highlighted Reuleaux center region created by three overlapping circles. Note that each of the three circles passes through the centers of the others. The sides of the Reuleaux triangle are then created by three separate circular arcs, each being one-sixth of the edge of the original circles. This allows the triangle to be equilateral, or *regular*.

(Diagram can be found on the following page)

Figure 13.1: Reuleaux Triangle Created by 3-Circle Vesica Piscis

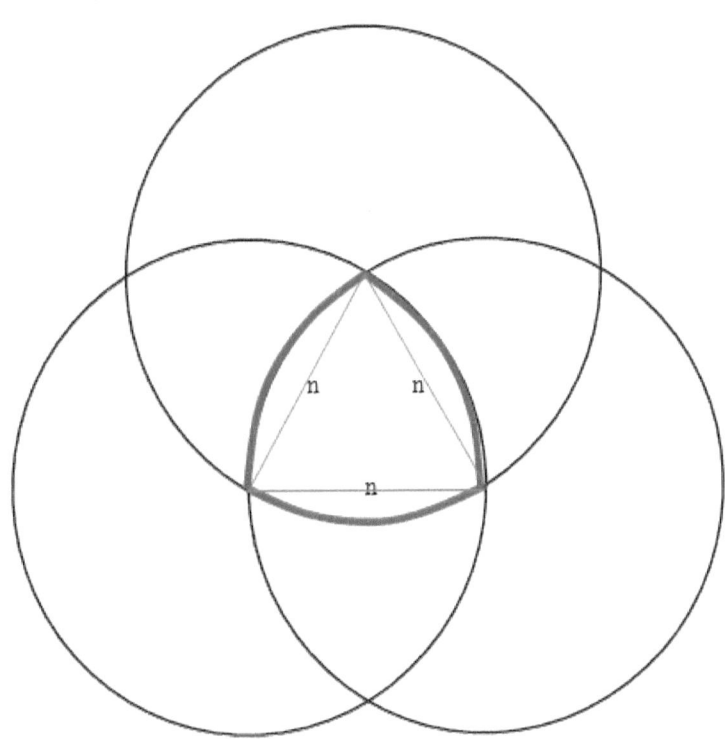

    The equilateral triangle in the center of the figure helps to define the nature of the Reuleaux triangle. Notice that the sides of the Reuleaux region are defined by 60° arcs of a circle, which makes the area formula for the Reuleaux triangle a fairly simple derivation. Let us assume that the radius of each of the overlapping circles is n units, as shown in Figure 13.1. The triangle in the center would have a base of n units and a height of $(\sqrt{3}/2)n$. The resulting area of the center triangle is then $(\sqrt{3}/4)n^2$, which comes from the standard area formula for a triangle. Now, given that the sectors (from one of the vertices to the opposite arc) each represent one-sixth of a circle, the area of a sector must be $\left(\frac{\pi n^2}{6}\right)$. It follows then that each *segment* (the area of the region between a chord and the arc of a circle) must be the difference between the sector and the triangle. The area formula for a Reuleaux triangle can then be calculated as follows beginning with the formula for calculating the area of a segment:

Area of a Segment:

$$A_{segment} = A_{sector} - A_{triangle}$$

$$A_{segment} = \frac{\pi n^2}{6} - \frac{\sqrt{3}n^2}{4}$$

$$A_{segment} = \left(\frac{4\pi - 6\sqrt{3}}{24}\right)n^2$$

$$A_{segment} = \left(\frac{2\pi - 3\sqrt{3}}{12}\right)n^2$$

Using the formula representing the area of a segment, we can now derive a formula for finding the area of a Reuleaux triangle based on the sum of the triangular area (defined by the center points of the three circles) and of the area of three segment regions (defined by the arcs of the circles and the sides of the triangle).

Reuleaux Triangle Area:

$$A_{Reuleaux\ Triangle} = A_{triangle} + 3 \cdot A_{segment}$$

$$A_{RT} = \frac{\sqrt{3}n^2}{4} + 3\left(\frac{2\pi - 3\sqrt{3}}{12}\right)n^2$$

$$A_{RT} = \frac{\sqrt{3}n^2}{4} + \left(\frac{2\pi - 3\sqrt{3}}{4}\right)n^2$$

$$A_{RT} = \frac{\sqrt{3}n^2}{4} + \frac{2\pi n^2}{4} - \frac{3\sqrt{3}n^2}{4}$$

$$A_{RT} = \frac{2\pi n^2}{4} - \frac{2\sqrt{3}n^2}{4}$$

$$A_{RT} = \left(\frac{\pi}{2} - \frac{\sqrt{3}}{2}\right)n^2 \ \ or \ \ A_{RT} = (\pi - \sqrt{3})\frac{n^2}{2}$$

Based on our derivation, we can see that the area of the Reuleaux triangle is easily calculated to any reasonable degree of accuracy with a hand calculator because the radius of the original circle is the only variable used in the formula. The coefficient involving the parenthetic expression and division by 2 can be approximated to 0.70477092301, which can then be multiplied by the square of the radius of our original circles. The radius of the circles also happens to be the straight line distance between any two vertices. The area formulae for all Reuleaux polygons are derived in similar ways.

There are in infinite number of polygons of constant width (not all of them Reuleaux polygons), but the proofs involved with verifying their widths at different points is fairly complex and not commonly applied in the engineering process, so that particular process will not be described in this article. Demonstrating a Reuleaux triangle's uniform width, however, is fairly intuitive if you are willing to accept a visual model for verification. To that end, we will create one.

Let us suppose that a circle of radius n is rolling along a straight line. The center of the circle remains at a constant distance from the line in the same way that the center of a tire remains at the same height with respect to a smooth road upon which it rolls. Knowing that the sides of the Reuleaux triangle are arcs of a circle centered at the opposite vertex, the distance from any point on an arc (side of the Reuleaux triangle) to the opposite vertex must be the radial constant, just as it would be for a circle. Also, the straight line distance between any two vertices of the Reuleaux triangle, as we know, is also the length of the radius of the circle from which it is generated. If we roll the Reuleaux triangle between two straight lines it becomes clear that as an arc rolls along one of the lines, the opposite vertex slides along the opposite line at a uniform height. When the rolling triangle comes to the end of the arc of one side, a vertex is momentarily in contact with the lines on both sides and it alternates to a rolling arc on the opposite line. The process is shown in Figure 13.2. Observe how point A moves along the top line as the arc on the bottom rolls clockwise to the next vertex B. As we continue to roll the triangle between the lines, vertex B then slides and the arc rolls along the top line.

Figure 13.2: Constant Width of Reuleaux Triangle

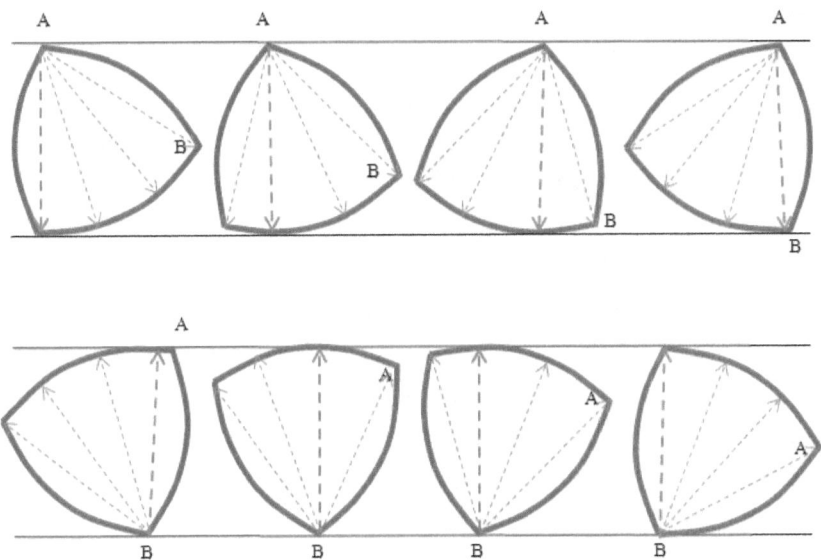

The constant width of the Reuleaux triangle is, of course, uniform in all directions, which makes the Watt square drill bit possible. The illustrations in Figure 13.2 clearly demonstrate how the Reuleaux triangle is constantly spaced evenly between two horizontal, parallel lines as it rolls (or as it would *rotate* in the case of a drill bit) regardless of its orientation. It is, therefore, reasonable to assume that it would also roll or rotate evenly between a pair of vertical, parallel lines whose distance of separation is the same as for the horizontal lines. In fact, the Reuleaux triangle rotating simultaneously between two sets of evenly spaced parallel lines is the foundation of the Watt square drill bit because the figure is essentially spinning within a square outline. We do not, however, know how far into the corners it will reach so another illustration is necessary if we want to explore the drill bit application further.

What is not obvious from the illustrations in Figure 13.2 is that the center point of the Reuleaux triangle is not equidistant to the horizontal lines as it rotates. This tells us that designing a drill bit around the Reuleaux polygon concept will require a moving axis; one that both rotates and revolves in circular fashions.

Figure 13.3 illustrates how the Reuleaux triangle fits between both vertical and horizontal pairs of parallel lines, those that outline a square region. However, the diagonals of the square shown in Figure 13.3 compared with the diagonals that define the center of the inscribed Reuleaux triangle also demonstrate that the center of the square is not necessarily the center of the triangle. The center of the Reuleaux triangle oscillates slightly as it rotates, fascinatingly enough, causing both the *geometric centroid* and the corners to follow the paths of parts of an ellipse. Note that to find the center of the Reuleaux triangle, we simply find the intersection of the segments that bisect the arcs and opposite vertices.

(Diagram can be found on the following page)

Figure 13.3: Reuleaux Triangle Inscribed in a Square

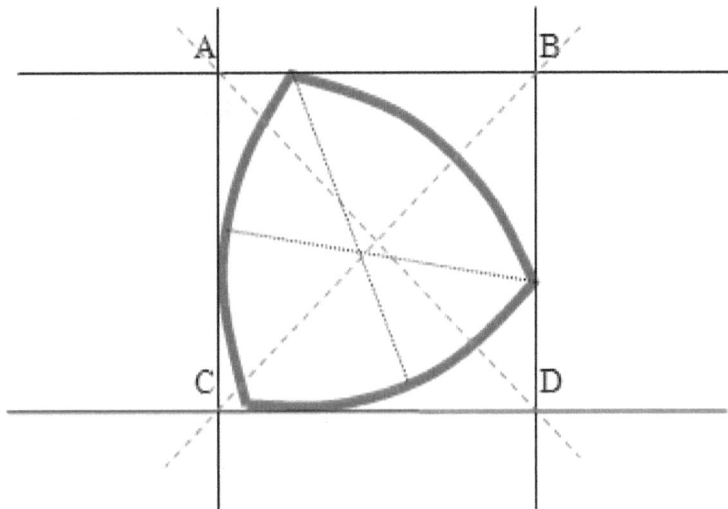

The intersecting diagonals of square ABCD shown in Figure 13.3 clearly do not coincide with the center of the Reuleaux triangle, which falls at the intersection of the segments extending between the vertices and the center points of the opposite arcs. It turns out that because of the issues of radial symmetry, we can predict the location and motion of the center of the triangle as it rotates within the square. You may have guessed that it revolves in a circular fashion, but this is incorrect. The path of the geometric centroid is not circular as the triangle rotates. It is formed from a path of four independent arcs of various ellipses.

If we intend to use the Reuleaux triangle as a drill bit, we will need to look at how far the triangle will reach into the corners of the square. Figure 13.4 shows the Reuleaux triangle oriented such that the corners of the triangle and square are aligned with the diagonal of the square. The path of the end of an ellipse is as close as the Reuleaux triangle can get to cutting out the corners of a square. In Figure 13.4, observe how the ellipse defines the corner cut by the Reuleaux triangle.

Figure 13.4: Elliptical Path of the Corners of a Reuleaux Triangle

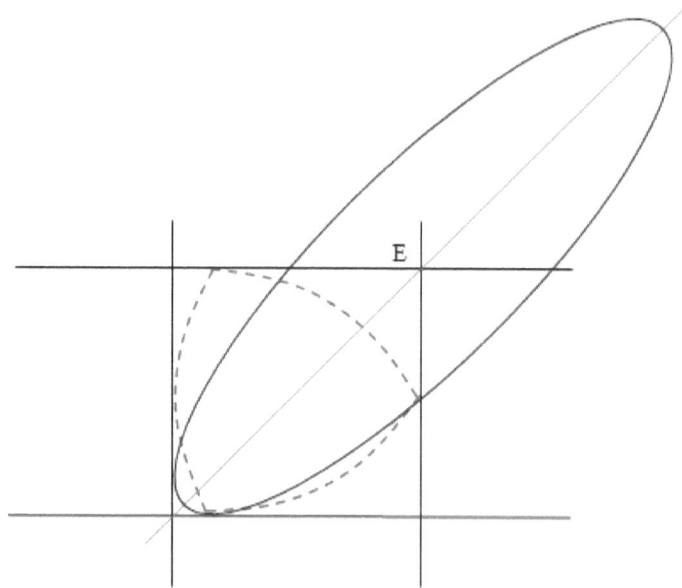

As we can see from the illustration in Figure 13.4, there comes a point where a given vertex loses it tangency with the side of the square and swings in an elliptical arc until it becomes tangent with the adjacent side of the square and temporarily begins to move in a straight line again. The path that the vertex follows during this time is outlined by the focal ends of an ellipse along the major axis. It leaves an untouched corner inside the square but outside the Reuleaux triangle. The area of this region is relatively small and can be calculated by determining the eccentricity of the ellipse and finding the exact points of tangency.

As we continue to explore this idea, it becomes more apparent that the centroid of the Reuleaux triangle does not move in a perfectly circular fashion either. This is because the motion of any given vertex is not uniform along an arc of a circle when the triangle rotates. The vertices follow an elliptical path as they move around the corners of the square between the points of tangency, both to and from the horizontal and vertical sides of the square envelope that contains it. Essentially this means that the centroid of the triangle, with its fixed distance to any vertex of the triangle must move in a similar fashion; that is to say, that the motion of a vertex is more horizontal or vertical as it slides through the path of the long side of the square and more curved as the it follows the short elliptical path around the corners. The centroid point follows this same kind of motion, though on a much smaller scale and with less drastic direction changes than the motion of the vertices at the corners.

As we draw to a close, it is appropriate to indicate that there are a number of machining options for the family of Reuleaux polygons that were not discussed in this article. Additional investigations will show how some of the functions allow for the Reuleaux triangle drill bit to create types of holes other than squares. For example, if a larger hole is cut in the middle of the Reuleaux triangle and the triangle is then allowed to revolve around a smaller circular central post, the bit will produce a rectangle with curved ends. At this point, the function of Reuleaux triangle drill bit and chuck design begins to take on properties of the epicycloid and hypocycloid functions presented in Article Four.

SUMMARY

Part of the reason Reuleaux triangles are considered so important in engineering is because a circular cross section is probably one of the most frequently used figures in engineering design, and Reuleaux triangles have three distinct circular sections of interest. Training in mechanical engineering, in particular, devotes a great deal of time to describing how to translate circular motion into other kinds of motion so the cross-sections of shapes such as the Reuleaux triangle are critical for innovative designs and process improvement in all sorts of manufacturing. In fact, some engine designs even use Reuleaux triangles as a basis for their functioning. In manufacturing, in general, it is certainly not an exaggeration to suggest that machining forms that deviate from true roundness are probably the most challenging because we rely so heavily on ideas such as conserving energy through rotational inertia. This would certainly be a difficult task without the advantages of a circle. So now we know... there are some great alternatives to circles for the imaginative engineer or machinist.

The Reuleaux triangle presented in this article is also unique because it is the shape with the least area of any curve of a constant width. The idea of constant width can be extended into three dimensions as well, which creates a Reuleaux tetrahedron. The solid figure can be created from the intersections of four spheres of the same radius. Oddly enough, the Reuleaux tetrahedron does not create a solid surface of constant width, but it can be modified so that it works as one. The resulting shape is called a *Meissner body* or *Meissner tetrahedron* and could virtually replace an object such as a ball bearing because it would roll evenly no matter how the Meissner body was oriented. Of course, the three dimensional versions of surfaces of constant width are a bit more complex than their two dimensional Reuleaux counterparts. At any rate, the

Reuleaux polygons create a somewhat unique perspective when it comes to engineering design.

We rely on the interaction of moving parts for all kinds of machines and devices. To improve these devices in terms of sustainability, reliability, or even in reducing the necessary materials needed for production could simply be a clever use of some common geometric principle that no one has yet applied; and really only because we have become so accustomed to re-designing that which we are already familiar.

The family of Reuleaux polygons, and in particular the Reuleaux triangle is named after a German engineer named Franz Reuleaux (1829-1905), but the Reuleaux figures can be seen in the writings of earlier mathematicians dating as far back as Leonard Euler in 1778, which is testimony that engineering in some sense is as old as mathematics itself.

ADDITIONAL READINGS

Artobolevsky, I. I. (1976). Mechanisms in Modern Engineering Design. Moscow: MIR.

Bryant, J, & Sangwin, C. (2008). *How Round is Your Circle*. Princeton University Press, Princeton, N.J. ISBN 978-0-691-13118-4

Cole, D.E. (1972). The Wankle engine. *Scientific American*. Vol. 227 No. 2, 14-23.

Kearsley, M.J. (1952). Curves of a constant diameter. *The Mathematical Gazette*. Vol. 36(317). 176-179.

Nash, D.H. (1977). Rotary engine geometry. *Mathematics Magazine*. Vol. 50(2). 87-89.

ARTICLE 14: STRAIGHT LINE LINKAGES

AND THE RATIO GAUGE

ABSTRACT: The following article on straight line linkages describes a number of simple mechanical devices that use a series of connected links to create straight line and approximate straight line motion. In particular, the Watt linkage, Chebyshev linkage, Peaucellier-Lipkin linkage, and Hoekens linkage are illustrated. Additionally, the manuscript provides details for creating other simple linkages and describes the geometric principles behind the construction of a homemade *ratio gauge*.

INTRODUCTION

Linkage mechanisms have been an integral part of simple mechanics and mechanical engineering design for several hundred years. A linkage, for our purposes, can be thought of as a series of hinged, rigid segments that are fastened to a stationary frame and that move together as a single functioning device. They typically work as a system and vary in complexity from very simple to very complex.

For the most part, the study of straight line linkages is about defining methods for turning rotational motion into straight line and approximate straight line motion. Throughout recent history, a number of notable mathematicians, scientists, and engineers have explored the world of linkage mechanisms in order to learn about transforming systems of motion, mostly to capture rotational energy sources and to design machines to do various jobs. Mechanical linkages have been a critical factor in large scale automation, and for many of the other conveniences we enjoy on a daily basis.

In the late 17th century, prior to the development of milling machinery, it was very difficult to machine parts for devices needing straight edges because very little attention was given to how *straightness* was really achieved. We see this, even today, in the assumptions of straight line measurements. For example, the *straight edges* of a straight edge measurement device such as a ruler seems self-consistent and, therefore, beyond the need to consider. However, the first *straight edged* rulers contained anything but straight edges. In fact, the assumptions of *straightness* were quickly dispelled when experimental machines failed to function properly because the parts that had been presumed to be straight, were not. Ultimately, the mechanics needed for the straight line motion of the pistons of a steam engine provided the context for James Watt to establish a basis for the mechanical linkages we will be exploring herein.

There are a number of linkages that have applications in mechanical engineering contexts such as the pistons of an engine and the rear suspensions of automobiles, but not all of the linkage applications are found in cars. There are also much simpler applications that are still used today, which involve scaled drawings, extension gates, robotic limbs, and even some kinds of door hinges. Linkages that transform rotational motion into straight line motion are also critical for providing mechanical advantages in the spirit of lever/fulcrum arrangements.

INVESTIGATION AND NOTES

Most straight line linkages involve three components. They are *segments* (note that these are sometimes referred to as rods, bars, or links), *fixed* (stationary) *hinges*, and *non-fixed* (floating) *hinges*. The segments can vary in length and will typically move with respect to one another based on how they are connected. The non-fixed hinges connect the rods together but can move freely with respect to the frame to which they are attached. The fixed hinges attach the linkage mechanism to a stationary frame or surface. As simple as the components of a linkage appear to be, they are highly adaptive and useful in many different applied settings. Only a few of the most basic and simple mechanisms are described here, but be assured that the world of linkages is vast.

It is a bit surprising to see just how many unique behaviors can be achieved using such simple devices. Some of the more interesting devices are used in a branch of mechanics called *biomimicry*. In this field, linkages are used to do things such as emulating the walking behavior of animals and insects. For example, a useful linkage device would be one that could lift the end of a link from the ground, place it a specified distance from the original position and then draw the entire device to the new position. This is essentially what happens when we walk. Repeating this motion is, of course, what provides many living things mobility, but we are getting ahead of ourselves.

Let us begin our investigation with the simplest linkage example possible, one with a single segment and a single fixed hinge. As you may have already guessed, the only behavior of a device such as this is for the link to rotate with respect to the frame to which it is attached. The result is one of the *simple machines* discussed in physical science courses; more to the point, a *lever*.

Figure 14.1 illustrates two lever arrangements, both showing the relative motion of the ends of the segment and the mechanical advantaged achieved by moving the fixed hinge closer to one end of the device. Note that in the following diagrams, a hinge representing where the device would be anchored to a fixed point on a frame is represented by a black circle, while a floating hinge connecting two or more segments is shown as a white circle. No floating hinges are needed for the device shown in Figure 14.1.

Figure 14.1: Single Segment Linkage with a Fixed Hinge

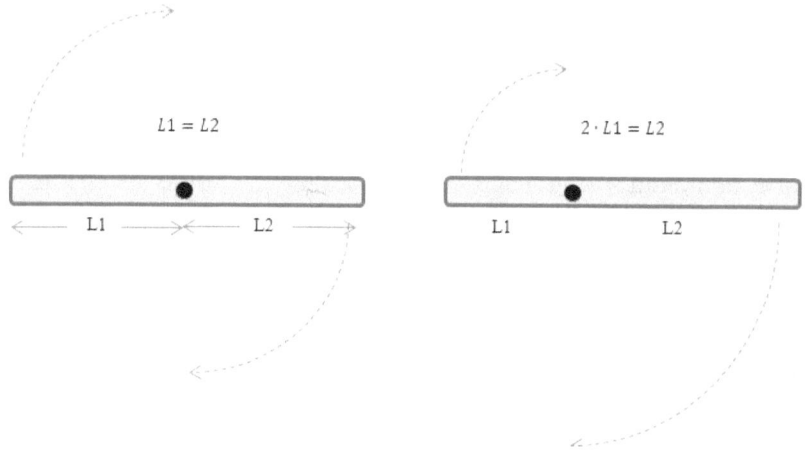

Figure 14.1 shows two segments. The segment on the left has a fixed hinge in the middle of the device separating two spans of equal length. As the device rotates, the path of a point on each end of the linkage must sweep out congruent arcs because the distances from the fixed hinges to each end point create radii of equal lengths. This device also offers no particular mechanical advantage when used as a lever. That is to say that a mass of 1 unit placed at one end of the segment (L1) would be balanced by an equivalent mass placed at the opposite end of segment L2. We are able to determine

this fact based on the Mass/Lever arm relationship. The quantity obtained by a mass multiplied by the length of lever arm on one side of a lever must be equal to a mass multiplied by the length of the lever arm on the opposite side. For example, the segment on the right has the fixed hinge placed such that the length of lever arm one (L1) is half of the length of the lever arm on the opposite side (L2). In order to maintain a balance using two masses placed on opposing sides of the device, we must have two factors of the given mass on the left and one on the right. Note also that the arc of an endpoint of L1 sweeps out only half the distance of its counterpoint placed at the end of L2 as the device is rotated. This can be verified mathematically by using the fixed hinge as the center point of each of two circles, where each respective circumference is defined by the length of the lever arms representing each radius.

As we investigate more complex linkage devices, it is important to note that the placement of various hinges is an important element for controlling the function of any linkage mechanism. For example, a single free floating hinge will not move if placed between two fixed hinges. Further, a free floating hinge attaching a segment to a device without another fixed hinge to anchor it, or another free floating hinge to work in conjunction with it, would result in a mechanism with very little control. There are a few practical exceptions to this rule, such as a trebuchet.

Our next linkage mechanism is a three bar linkage known as *Watt's Linkage*. It is a simple arrangement of components that allows for a very practical application in automotive mechanics. It was also one of the first devices that could define a virtually straight line. The device has two fixed hinges and two floating hinges connecting one short segment between two longer segments. The device is illustrated in Figure 14.2.

Figure 14.2: Watt's 3-Bar Linkage

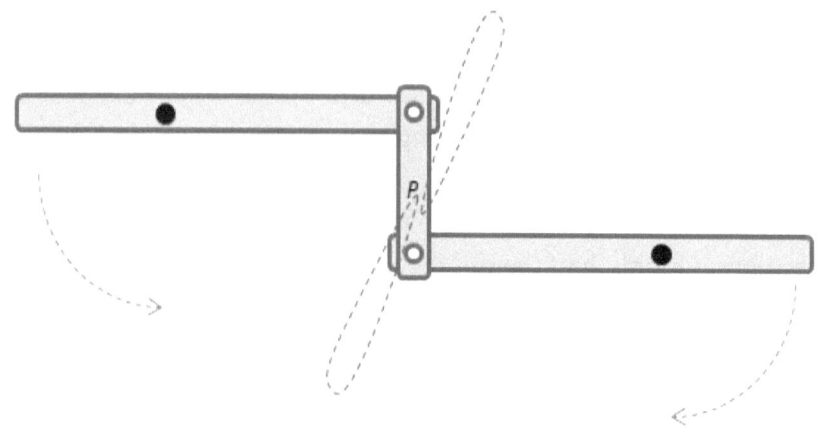

Notice that the outer ends of the mechanism rotate in the same direction as the device functions. As the rotation begins in the direction indicated by the arrows, the center bar slowly moves up and rotates in a counterclockwise direction until it forces the rotation of the outer links to change direction and complete the cycle in the opposite direction. Following the path of point P on the center bar of the device, we can see that a figure 8 path is created with two relatively straight intervals. Several good animations of the functioning Watt's Linkage are available online.

One of the primary applications of Watt's Linkage is in automobile suspensions. Imagine the ends of the linkage in Figure 14.2 being attached to shock absorbers. The fixed hinges represent where the mechanism would be attached to the frame of the vehicle. As the vehicle encounters bumps, the linkage mechanism transfers the force of the impact on either one of the shocks so it is shared evenly with the other. Because the mechanism is designed to be nearly symmetrical across the suspension of the vehicle the outer endpoints of the linkage sweep out the same arc and in the same direction, which causes the wear on the shocks to be virtually identical. This makes for a more stable, safer ride as the vehicle moves.

Another linkage similar to Watt's linkage is known as a Chebyshev linkage. This mechanism is named after the Russian mathematician Pafnuty Chebyshev. Like Watt's linkage, Chebyshev's linkage also uses three segments, two fixed hinges, and two floating hinges, but it uses a slightly different configuration of the segments to define an approximate straight line path at point P. As a result of the configuration, there are some potential limitations in how the device can move. Figure 14.3 illustrates the crossing arrangement of the Chebyshev linkage.

(Diagram can be found on the following page)

Figure 14.3: Chebyshev Linkage

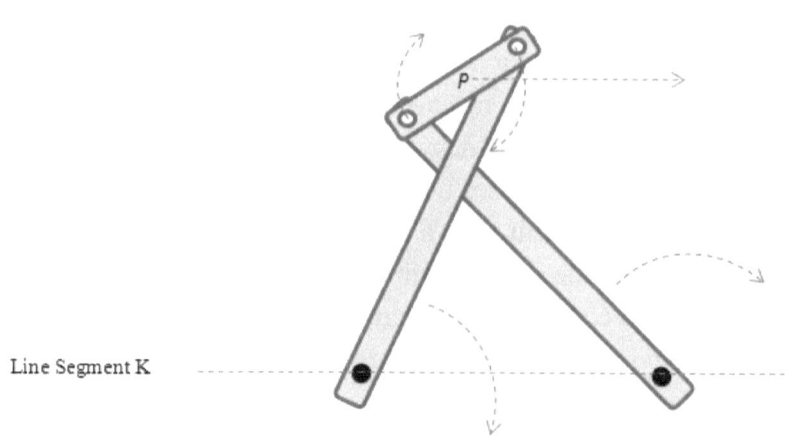

As the two longer segments rotate clockwise, as shown in Figure 14.3, the short segment suspended between them rotates in a tight clockwise direction as well. The middle of the short segment at Point P follows an approximately straight path perpendicular to the line segment connecting the fixed hinges. Using simple triangle calculations, we can mathematically verify that the distance of Point P to line segment K varies slightly as the long segments rotate but is fairly straight.

In learning a bit more about how the linkage mechanisms operate, we begin to understand how difficult it is to create exact straight line motion from circular motion. Linkages moving in a circular motion have floating hinges where the position of the hinges is predictable based on trigonometric functions. Inserting new segments within such a mechanism, one that has floating hinges or points that follow a straight path, (based on the movement of other independent segments) is a real challenge. However, such devices do exist.

One such device is the Peaucellier-Lipkin linkage (sometimes called the Peaucellier-Lipkin *Inversor*). This device is slightly more complex than the previous mechanisms, but it is simple enough to understand. This is a seven segment linkage with two fixed hinges and four floating linkages. It was invented in 1864 and was the first planar device that could transform circular motion into exact straight line motion. This was a critical breakthrough in the evolution of machining technology for no reason other than the ability to machine a straight edge. Figure 14.4 illustrates configuration of the segments and the basic operational parameters of the device.

Figure 14.4: Peaucellier-Lipkin Linkage

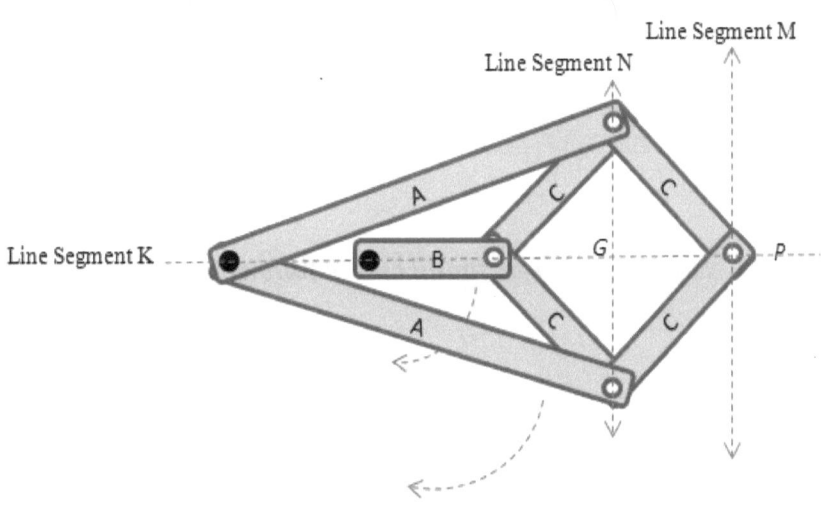

Because the Peaucellier-Lipkin linkage claims to produce an exact straight line path at Point P on vertical segment M, we will verify the algebraic relationship that allows this to happen. First, we need to look at the device conceptually. Note that the four hinges along the horizontal line segment K (Figure 14.4) are arranged to be collinear. Additionally, the rods are labeled A, B, or C to represent rods of equal length. As the device rotates in either direction around the fixed black hinges, Point P follows the vertical path indicated by line segment M. Finally, Rod B is centered on the fixed hinge such that the distance from the fixed hinge on Rod B to the floating hinge at the corner of the rhombus is equal to the distance of the two fixed hinges.

As the device rotates around the fixed hinges, the rhombus created by the four Rods labeled C elongates such that Point P stays on segment M. For this to happen, the diagonal span connecting the opposing floating hinges at the end of Rod B and at Point P must expand by an amount equivalent to the distance from the edge of the circle created by Bar B and Line Segment M. You may notice that we can verify this relationship using some familiar triangle geometry. Figure 14.5 illustrates a simple repositioning.

(Diagram can be found on the following page)

Figure 14.5: Peaucellier-Lipkin Linkage Repositioned

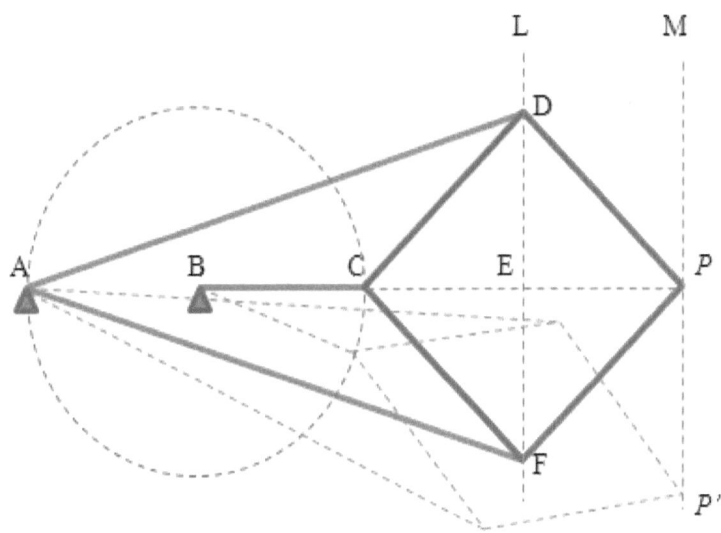

As the mechanism rotates, the short bar labeled BC turns on a tighter axis than the AD and AF bars, causing the rhombus to elongate. Figure 14.5 illustrates a generalized version of the device moving, which shows how Point P would be represented at a new location P' on the same vertical line M. The simplest way to verify a single case of the movement is to superimpose the device over a coordinate plane and choose convenient points so that basic triangle relationships can be used, but this only provides evidence in a single case. For a more generalized verification, we will examine how a product relationship can be described as a constant based on the Pythagorean Theorem.

The links are designed such that AD = AF and CD = DP = FP = CF. Let us establish our triangle relationships using points from Figure 14.5.

Pythagorean Theorem Equation 1

$$(AE)^2 + (ED)^2 = (AD)^2$$

Pythagorean Theorem Equation 2

$$(EP)^2 + (ED)^2 = (DP)^2$$

Difference of Equation 1 and Equation 2

$$(AE)^2 + (ED)^2 - ((EP)^2 + (ED)^2) = (AD)^2 - (DP)^2$$

Simplified to a difference of squares

$$(AE)^2 - (EP)^2 = (AD)^2 - (DP)^2$$

Rewritten as a product

$$(AE - EP)(AE + EP) = (AD - DP)(AD + DP)$$

Substitution of actual segment values

$$(AC)(AP) = (AD - DP)(AD + DP)$$

We now know that AC·AP must be a constant because if we examine the equality, we can see that the values of AD and DP never change. Therefore, we know that AC·AP must be a constant. To simplify the remainder of the verification, we will assign AC·AP value of j^2, a constant. For the second part of the verification, we must examine the device based on some arbitrary movement away from its original, horizontal position. Figure 14.6 illustrates the new position arbitrarily selected at 30 degrees.

Figure 14.6: Peaucellier-Lipkin Linkage Rotated 30 Degrees

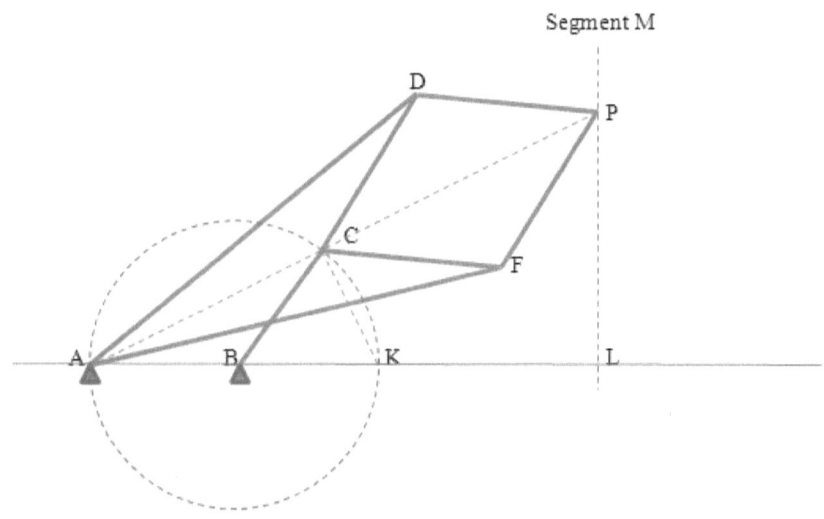

j^2 as a constant from the previous section

$$AC \cdot AP = j^2$$

Establishing a ratio for segment AP

$$AP = \frac{j^2}{AC}$$

Establishing a ratio of sides in similar triangles. Remember that AB = BC = BK

$$\frac{AL}{AP} = \frac{AC}{AK}$$

Solving for AL as a ratio of two constants

$$AL = \frac{(AC)(AP)}{AK}$$

j^2 and AK are both established as constants

$$AL = \frac{j^2}{AK}$$

Because we now know that AL is a constant as point P moves, the motion of P must be a straight line that is perpendicular to the line segment M as shown in Figure 14.6, and thus, we have verified a straight line motion. There are additional verifications and proofs for the Peaucellier-Lipkin linkage that incorporate trigonometry and other geometric proportions, but for the more basic verifications, simply locating points on a coordinate plane and calculating distances works well enough to convince most people that the line is going to be straight.

The last linkage to be formally illustrated in this article is known as Hoeken's linkage. Hoeken's linkage is a three bar linkage that, once again, only approximates a straight line path at a given end point, but it is organized a bit differently than those linkages previously presented. It also has a number of different applications than the previous linkages because of its shape and unique arrangement of segments.

The rotation of a single short bar in this mechanism results in a combination of approximate straight line motion coupled with elliptical motion. Because of the kind of motion the linkage creates, it is ideal for applications such as robotic legs. Figure 14.7 illustrates the arrangement of bars and shows the outline of the path of a point P, which is located at the end of the longest segment. In particular, the ratio of the segments is critical for defining the exact motion needed for certain applications.

(Diagram can be found on the following page)

Figure 14.7: Hoeken's Linkage

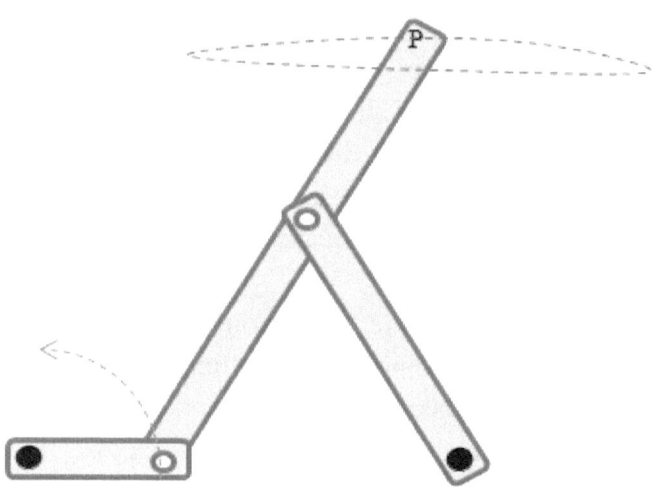

As we have already discussed, the process of assembling segments into linkage mechanisms is tremendously useful in mechanics and mechanical engineering. In fact, many of the linkages we have explored have been adapted in one form or another to operate as fundamental systems in many of the machines we use on a daily basis. However, that does not necessarily mean that a linkage needs to be complicated in order to be useful. For example very simple linkage mechanism can expand a simple geometric idea into a device that is highly popular such as a baby gate. A baby gate expands between two walls by employing a series of floating hinges on two sets of parallel segments. It is repurposing this idea that allows us to build a homemade ratio gauge.

A ratio gauge uses some very simple geometry rules, triangle similarities in particular, to create an adjustable linkage mechanism that holds a constant ratio. For our purposes, we will illustrate the concept based on constructing the device with some basic yardsticks and bolts. Also, because this device is mobile, there are no fixed hinges. Instead we will drill holes in our yardsticks at fixed intervals and create four movable floating hinges. Figure 14.8 illustrates the basic principles of the mechanism using triangle similarities.

Figure 14.8: Triangle Similarities within a Ratio Gauge Mechanism

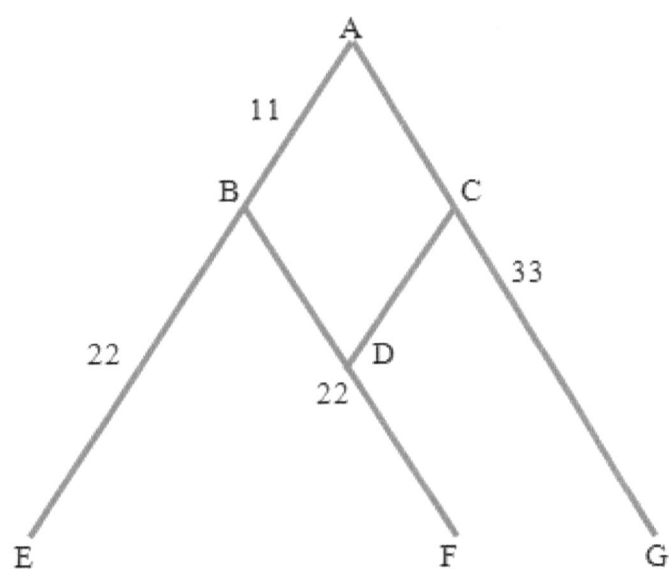

Let us suppose, for the sake of argument, that segments AE and AG measure 33 units, and segments BE and BF measure 22 units. We arrange the segments such that we create two similar, isosceles triangles EAG and EBF. Further, BF and AG are arranged to be parallel and held parallel by the segment CD. If floating hinges attach the mechanism at points A, B, C, and D, we have created a linkage mechanism that will hold a constant 2:1 ratio between the points E and F versus F and G. This is valuable because the distance between endpoints E and G can be increased or reduced while the device maintains a constant 2:1 ratio.

The triangle similarities that allow this to happen are very simple. Because all corresponding parts of similar triangles are similar, all proportions between the triangles' parts must also be constant. Side AE of triangle AEG is 33 units. Side BE of triangle BEF (a similar triangle) is 22 units. The ratio of 33/22 (or 3/2) must be constant in all corresponding parts of the two triangles. This includes the ratio of EG to EF (the bases of the triangles) regardless of how far the device is expanded or collapsed. By default, the ratio between the endpoints EF and FG must then be 2:1.

Building the actual ratio gauge device (should a person decide to construct one) is particularly fun because the floating hinges can be moved very easily to create different ratios. For example, if we wanted to create a 3:1 ratio between endpoints E, F, and G, we would create floating hinges on a yardstick such that BE = 24 units and AB = 8 units. This would mean drilling holes on the yardstick at 24 inches and 32 inches. Note that the segment CD only needs to hold segments BF and AG parallel to one another. This means that segment CD must be attached at the same interval as the length of segment AB. The process will work even if the rulers are not cut to the specific length needed to hold a given ratio. What normally works best is three full length yardsticks to act as segments AE, AG, and BF, and one half-length yardstick to act as segment CD. We will leave some overlap at points B and D but it will also allow us to create a gauge that can create many different ratios with the same four rulers.

Of course the ratio gauge, in and of itself, is limited in its application so it is nice to think about how the linkage concept was leveraged from more historically relevant applications. For example the ratio gauge can be set to represent any ratio while remaining moveable, but it can also be anchored to a frame at a single point if desired. If one of the points E, F, or G is fixed to a frame, the other two points will still move within a plane at the same ratio as the arrangement of segments demands. An application that functions from the same basic design is the Pantograph.

The pantograph is a mechanism that has been adapted for many different uses over the years, but the original pantograph was designed for reproducing scaled drawings. It was invented by a 16th century priest named Christoph Scheiner. Scheiner, was also a physicist and astronomer. In 1603, he invented the pantograph, which looked very much like the ratio gauge we have been exploring. Figure 14.9 shows Scheiner's original pantograph design.

(Diagram can be found on the following page)

Figure 14.9: Christoph Scheiner's Pantograph Design (1603)

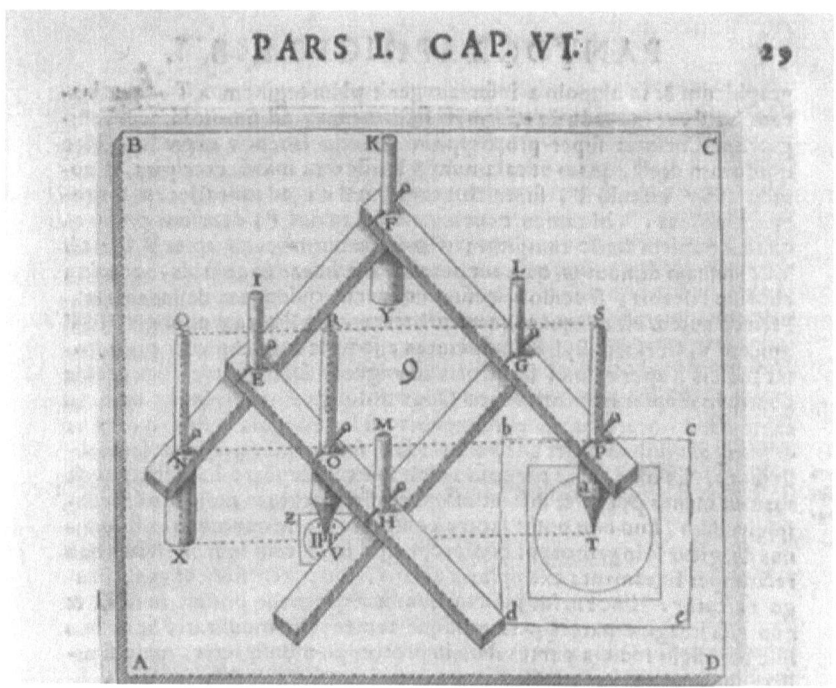

SUMMARY

There are many additional linkage mechanisms that were not explored herein. For the most part, this article has been an introduction to how linkages translate circular motion into straight line motion but there is a nearly endless supply of other linkages that have other purposes as well. In fact, it is simply not possible for the human mind to reasonably consider all possible curves, lines, and systems of motion that can result from the endless configurations of bars and hinges. An engineer named Meccano Sylvester summarized this idea as follows, "It is quite conceivable that the whole universe may constitute one great linkage, that, a system of points bound to maintain invariable distances, certain of them from others, and that the law of gravitation and similar physical rules for reading off natural phenomena may be the consequences of this condition of things. If the cosmic linkage is of the kind I have called complete, then determinism is the law of nature; but, if there be more than one degree of liberty in the system, there will be room reserved for the play of free-will."

Linkages have been a critical part of the advancement of nations, particularly during the Industrial Revolution(s). Many countries experienced rapid industrial growth throughout the 19th century because of the improvement of steam engine technology. Large scale production became much more commonplace as inventors like James Watt and Francis Thompson developed the mechanical technology that allowed large powerful engines to work more reliably. James Watt, in fact, gained such popularity in his work developing linkages as to have a unit of power named after him.

Other straight line linkages are worth investigating as well, such as those invented by Richard Roberts, Pierre Sarrus, Harry Hart, Scott Russell, and James White. All of these inventors made unique contributions to the field of mechanical engineering.

ADDITIONAL READINGS

Artobolevsky, I. I. (1976). Mechanisms in Modern Engineering Design. Moscow: MIR.

Bryant, J, & Sangwin, C. (2008). *How Round is Your Circle*. Princeton University Press, Princeton, N.J. ISBN 978-0-691-13118-4

Ferguson, E.S. (2008). *Kinematics of Mechanisms from the Time of Watt.* The Gutenberg Ebook Project.
www.gutenberg.org/files/27106/27106-h/27106-h.htm

Hartenberg, R.S., & Denavit, J. (1964). Kinematic Synthesis of Linkages. New York: McGraw-Hill. ISBN: 978-0070269101

Uicker, J.J., Pennock, G.R., & Shigley, J. (2003). Theory of Machines and Mechanisms. Oxford University Press ISBN: 978-81203-2901-0

ARTICLE 15: PENDULUMS, GEARS, AND GRANDFATHER CLOCKS

ABSTRACT: The *Pendulums, Gears, and Grandfather Clocks* manuscript illustrates how gear ratios and interconnected moving parts, such as linkages, can be arranged into a mechanical device that keeps time. Specifically the mathematics of pendulums and the related rates associated with translating rotational speeds of interconnected gear mechanisms will be presented.

INTRODUCTION

As human beings, we have been fascinated with the keeping of time... probably since the dawn of time. The reasoning is circular, I know, but the point is that as our societies progressed through the enlightened ages and advanced scientifically, the desire to keep time has never waned. The sundial, as presented in Article 11, was our first real expression of mathematical engineering and our first real tangible device for recording time consistently, but it certainly had its limitations. Exploring sundial mechanisms gave us a clear look at the mathematics of cycles and this was an important concept for engineering in general. The problems with the sundial, however, are that it is far from mobile, it only works on sunny days, and it only allows clear delineations of time that are accurate to increments of about an hour.

What early scientists and inventors really wanted were ways to mechanically recreate the cycles associated with the revolution of the earth relative to the sun, but in a much more precise way than had previously been possible. There were several reasons they believed this was important. First, time divisions such as the hour could be clearly seen on a sundial, but counting off minutes and seconds was simply not possible using a device like the sundial. More precise and reliable equipment was needed, especially for scientific investigations. Minutes and seconds were becoming increasingly important to scientists and engineers because the *time* variable was becoming increasingly more important in many scientific investigations. Time, conceived as a scientific variable, became an important and common unifying factor in many early scientific experiments, and remains so. We see this routinely in calculus, even now, particularly in related rate problems. Rates were compared or unified through the *time* variable almost as a matter of habit, so what was needed were innovative ways to develop devices that could reliably collect these necessary time measurements.

The development of mechanical clocks began in a rather unusual place, and that was with a power source. The first conceivable power source for a clock was naturally the sun; not in terms of solar-electric power as we know it but rather as the movement of a shadow on a marked surface; hence the need for mathematical engineering to be defined. So, the power source considered for the newer mechanical clocks of the time was not solar radiation but came from a source that was equally familiar, that being gravity. Gravity could affect moving parts for long periods of time, and thus, a naturally renewing power source was defined.

The first mechanical clocks that stored energy (via gravity) and claimed a relatively high degree of accuracy for the era were pendulum clocks. The energy used to keep the pendulum moving was typically a substantial mass that applied pressure to a drive cylinder, which supplied an amount of energy necessary to restore what was lost from friction within the gear mechanisms as a pendulum swung back and forth. As the clock devices became smaller, coiled springs were used to store energy in much the same way that weights were used for the larger pendulum clocks. These smaller clocks, which ultimately became wrist watches, could use a small key or pin to rewind the spring mechanism in much the same way that winding a grandfather clock would re-coil the cable holding the weight.

Today the idea of a mechanical clock is still enticing, even if only for decorative purposes. Grandfather clocks that use weights to store gravitational potential energy and drive the clock movement are still very common. In fact, some are very accurate.

INVESTIGATION AND NOTES

Because we know the story of the mechanical clock begins with the pendulum, we are going to begin this investigation by examining the mathematics of the pendulum. Of course, with any clock designed to function on its own, we must manage the issue of keeping the pendulum swinging. We have already introduced the idea of using weight as an energy source, and this is very common with pendulum clocks. The idea behind using a weight, which slowly unravels from a cylinder, is to store enough gravitational potential energy to keep the clock operating on its own for a given amount of time. Many pendulum clocks can operate for time intervals as long as a week before they need to be rewound. The weight being used to drive the clock is an energy storage device that slowly transfers gravitational potential energy through the gears and ultimately back to the pendulum. The difficulty comes when we try to control the rate of release (spin) of the drive cylinder.

Suppose we want to create a drive cylinder that completes exactly one rotation per minute. This is a more complex task than it initially appears. First, a mechanism needs to be in place that consistently slows and regulates the rotation of the drive cylinder. If such a mechanism was not used, the drive cylinder would not only spin freely under the force of a counter weight, it would also accelerate as it spun. A free-spinning cylinder would render the power source useless because too much of the gravitational potential energy would be transformed into kinetic energy too quickly. Under these circumstances, the power mechanism would not pass gravitational potential energy back into the system needed to power the device for more than just a few seconds. A pendulum was ultimately used for the purpose of regulating the speed of the drive cylinder.

Christiaan Huygens is credited with the conception of using a pendulum and a special gear as regulating mechanisms for the spinning cylinder. As we are about to discover, pendulums have a unique and mathematically powerful property. The period of a pendulum, which is the time it takes to complete one back and forth cycle, is related to two factors. The first factor is the force of gravity and the second is length of the pendulum. Because gravity applies a constant force to masses, we can use the gravity variable as a constant instead of an unknown in the calculation of a period. Therefore, the only real factor contributing to the time of a single period for a pendulum is the length of the pendulum itself. Even the arc length through which the pendulum swings is an insignificant factor for the time of a period. This property was briefly described in the Brachistochrone article. It is what also makes the pendulum the perfect device for regulating the speed of the drive cylinder. By appropriately adjusting only the length of the pendulum, we can create a period of exactly one second based on the gravitational acceleration here on earth. Also, the counter weight on the cylinder can be designed to restore nearly the exact amount of energy lost through friction as the pendulum swings.

As simple as the motion of a pendulum appears to be, there are still several forces and angles to be considered; and of course, the forces being applied to the weight at the end of the pendulum are constantly changing as the pendulum swings because the path of the mass at the end of a pendulum is an arc of a circle. In short, the position of the weight at the end of the pendulum with respect to the arc through which it swings determines the various forces at any given point in its path. Figure 15.1 illustrates the forces affecting the periodic motion of a simple pendulum.

Figure 15.1: Pendulum Motion Forces

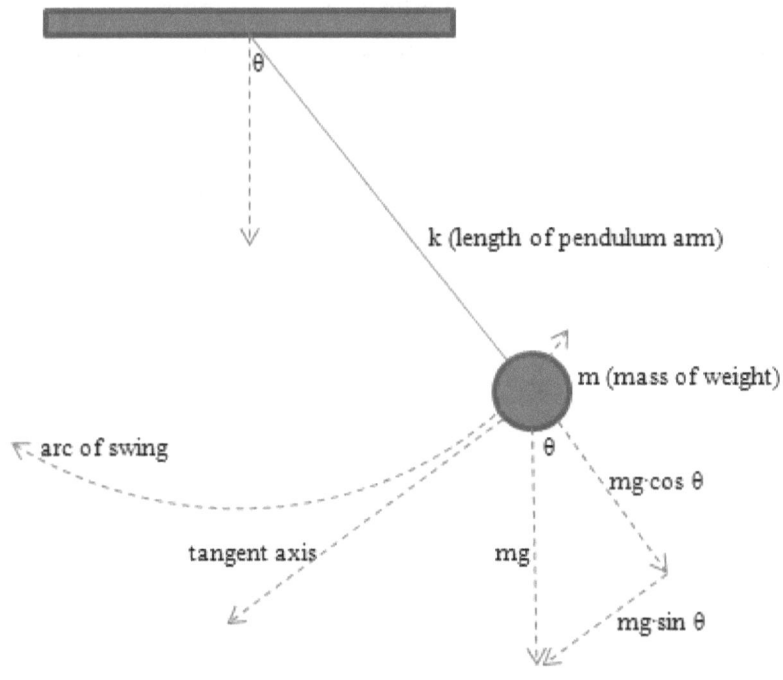

Having a picture of how the forces are being applied to the mass of pendulum allows us to derive the differential equation that represents its motion. The path the pendulum follows is an arc of a circle with radius k but we can examine the instantaneous forces using a tangent line to the arc. The angle θ will be measured in radians and the instantaneous velocity of the mass at the end of the pendulum will be the line tangent to the arc and perpendicular to the pendulum line. The most common derivation of this equation is to first consider Newton's equation $F = ma$ where F is the sum of all forces acting on the mass. In this derivation, we are interested in changes in the speed of the mass as it applies to the tangential axis. We can define the force associated with the tangential axis thusly: *a=-g·sinθ* where g is acceleration due to gravity. If we then substitute our acceleration value back into Newton's original force equation, we arrive at $F = -mg \cdot \sin\theta$. We are now ready to derive the differential equation:

s is the arc length based on the pendulum length, k

$$s = k\theta$$

velocity defined as the change in position over change in time

$$v = \frac{ds}{dt}$$

position equation differentiated implicitly

$$\frac{ds}{dt} = k\frac{d\theta}{dt}$$

determine acceleration by differentiating velocity

$$a = \frac{d^2s}{dt^2}$$

velocity equation differentiated implicitly

$$\frac{d^2s}{dt^2} = k\frac{d^2\theta}{dt^2}$$

substitution into the acceleration equation for the tangent axis. Thus:

$$\frac{d^2\theta}{dt^2} = -\frac{g}{k} \cdot \sin\theta$$

Though we can now define the forces associated with a known angle of displacement and pendulum length, we cannot yet define the time of a single period without an additional formula derivation. For our purposes, we are going to forego this derivation and assume that we can create a period of any given increment of time. The result of this derivation is a time equation associated with approximating the period based on the length of the pendulum: $T = 2\pi\sqrt{k/g}$ where k is the length of the pendulum and g is acceleration due to gravity.

Our next task is to discover how the pendulum is used to regulate the rotation of the drive cylinder powered by the counter weight. This is typically done with an *escapement* mechanism. An escapement is a device specially designed to engage a gear connected to the pendulum's drive cylinder. The escapement is so named because it works by allowing one tooth of the escapement gear to "escape" for each swing of the pendulum. It also provides an extra pulse of energy to maintain the kinetic energy in the system and keep the pendulum moving with the same angular displacement.

Now, if we were to create the pendulum cylinder gear that had 60 teeth and arranged the pendulum to swing once each second, we would have created a clock that has a second hand that would turn once per minute. We could make accuracy corrections for our second hand very easily by making minute adjustments to the length of the pendulum. Figure 15.2 provides an illustration of how the mechanism described would function. Notice that the drive cylinder with the counter weight is attached directly to the escapement gear. Normally this would not be the case because it would require frequent rewinding. This is, however, an easy problem to solve and will be described in the following section.

Figure 15.2: Drive Cylinder/Escapement Mechanism

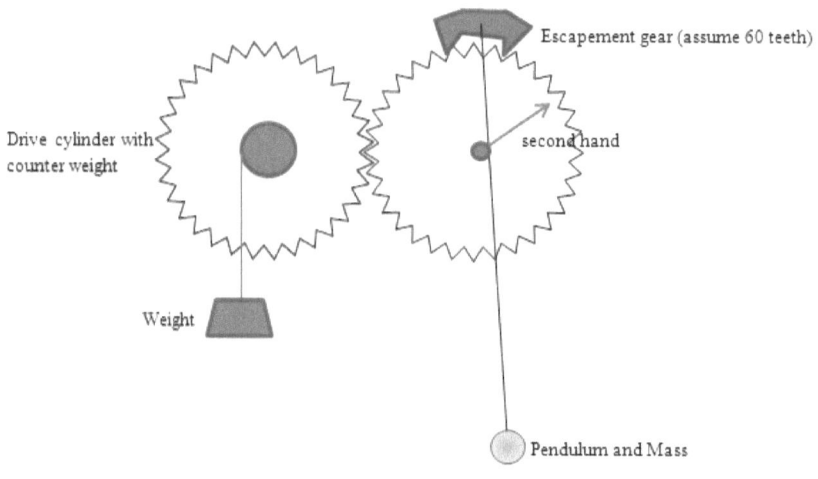

As we can see in Figure 15.2, a single turn of the drive cylinder results in a single turn of the escapement gear, which controls the second hand. If the pendulum length is designed for one period per second and the gears each have 60 teeth, we will have created a reasonably accurate *seconds* hand. As previously mentioned, this design is impractical because the clock would need to be rewound so frequently. To overcome this problem, we would need more gears sequenced such a way that the drive cylinder would turn only once for numerous turns of the escapement gear. Our investigation, must now be directed toward describing the mathematics of gear ratios.

Gear Ratios: We can understand gear ratios by examining related rates based on either the size of the connected gears, the number of teeth, or the angular velocity of the connected gears. It stands to reason that gear ratios can be calculated based on the circumference of each gear in the gear train or by their related angular speeds, but the calculated ratios are not the same for each calculation.

Let us begin with a very simple example. Suppose our gear train contains only two gears. The first gear (gear A) will have a radius of 2 units and the second gear (gear B) will have a radius of 1 unit. Recall that our gears are circular so each gear in our train will have a circumference that is described by the formula $C = 2\pi r$. Assume also that the teeth of the gears mesh perfectly so as to eliminate slippage. If gear A is our drive gear it will have a circumference of 4π units while gear B will have a circumference of 2π units. In this instance, the gear ratio based on radius of A:B is 2:1. However, it should be noted that the gear ratio is inversely proportional to the angular speed ratio. That is to say, if the ratio of the radii is 2:1 the speed ratio of A to B is actually 1:2. This makes sense because one full revolution of the larger gear would cause two complete revolutions of the smaller gear because the larger gear has twice the circumference. Figure 15.3 illustrates the relationship of the gear and speed ratios described above. Note also that a larger drive gear and a smaller driven gear generates a mechanical advantage (gains or loses based on the relative size of the gears) in a way similar to how a lever does. A large drive gear affecting a smaller driven gear loses power but gains distance.

Figure 15.3: Gear and Speed Ratios for Gear Train A and B

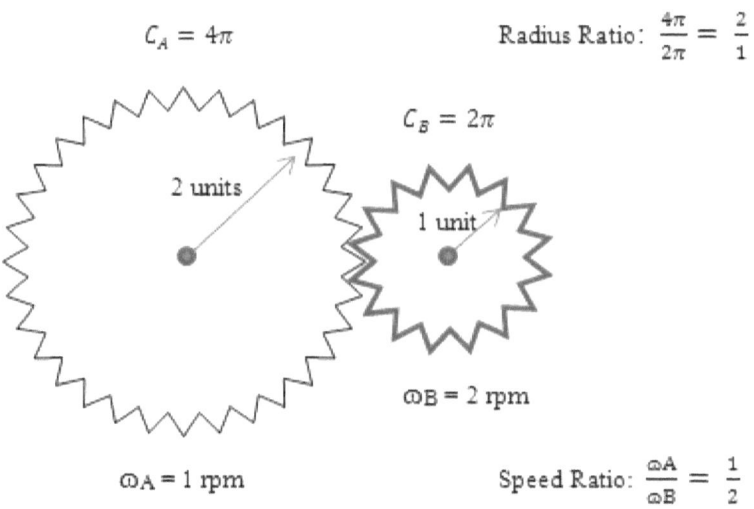

Examining this concept using related rates notation from calculus allows us to make calculations for drive trains with additional gears. Again, we can compare the relative radii, number of teeth, speed, torque, or even find needed gear sizes based on how we want our final gear train to function. Suppose, for example, that we want the drive cylinder to turn a transforming gear, which then turns the escapement gear. Each of the three gears can be any size, but for convenience, let us assume that we want a speed ratio of 1:60 between the drive gear and the escapement gear. This arrangement would allow our clock to work for perhaps something closer to a day rather than for only a few minutes. Because we want our escapement gear to turn 60 times for each turn of the drive gear, we need some arrangement of three gears that allows the ratios to work out correctly. It should be noted that there are a number of correct ways to accomplish this task.

Figure 15.4 illustrates an example of a gear train involving three gears. The speed ratio between gear x and gear z is calculated by multiplying a series of related rates. Our final speed ratio should be 1:6. That is to say, one rotation of the drive gear should result in 6 rotations of the escapement gear.

Figure 15.4: Gear Train for a 1:6 Speed Ratio

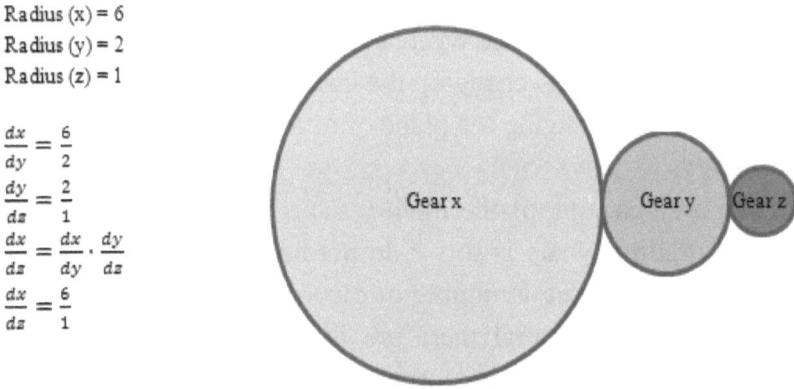

Radius (x) = 6
Radius (y) = 2
Radius (z) = 1

$$\frac{dx}{dy} = \frac{6}{2}$$

$$\frac{dy}{dz} = \frac{2}{1}$$

$$\frac{dx}{dz} = \frac{dx}{dy} \cdot \frac{dy}{dz}$$

$$\frac{dx}{dz} = \frac{6}{1}$$

Recall that the radius ratio and the speed ratio of a gear train are inverses of one another. The related rates described in Figure 15.4 are actually calculated using radii of the respective gears. The radius ratio is 6:1 meaning that the speed ratio is 1:6. This makes sense when we examine the function of the gear train from a conceptual standpoint. If gear x has a radius of 6 units and gear y has a radius of 2 units, then the circumference of gear x must be three times that of gear y. Therefore, gear y must make three complete revolutions for each revolution of gear x. The same principle is used when relating gear y and gear z. For each revolution of gear y, gear z will revolve twice.

By establishing the rates at which gears spin relative to one another, we can calculate the speed of any gear within a gear train relative to any other gear. The related rates method works for variables such as torque as well. In the last example, you might be asking why we did not simply use two gears to create a direct 1:6 ratio, thereby saving ourselves an additional gear. Though this is certainly possible, the goal of the example was to illustrate how radius, torque and speed calculations can be done for gear trains with multiple gears. It is worth noting, that an additional gear is sometimes desirable based on how we want the gear train to function. For example if we wanted to use the intermediate gear for another purpose such as changing the direction of the rotation of the last gear, or even changing the plane of rotation, an extra gear would be necessary.

In a clock, one of the main reasons we would want a gear train with multiple gears is so we do not have to constantly rewind our clock, but there are a number of other reasons for creating gear trains. In fact, in general there are four main reasons for using various gear trains: 1) to transform angular speed, 2) to increase or decrease torque, 3) to change the plane of rotation, and 4) to change the direction of rotation. All of these gear uses are needed for a complex mechanical clock. Figure 15.5 illustrates a sample gear arrangement where we can observe a change in mechanical advantage and rotational speed.

Figure 15.5: Gear Train Transforming Mechanical Advantage, Rotational Speed, Direction, and Plane of Rotation:

Gear A: Radius = 1 foot
Gear B: Radius = 5 feet
Gear C: Radius = 3 feet

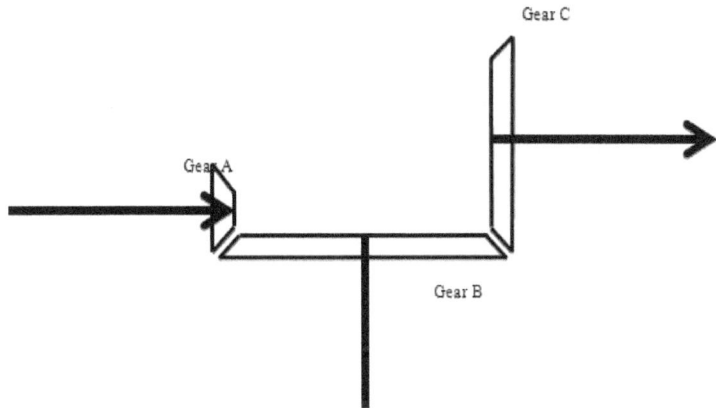

Let us suppose that we want to increase mechanical advantage in a gear train and transform that advantage to a perpendicular plane. Because mechanical advantage for gears is calculated in much the same way it is for levers, we can determine the mechanical advantage based on the radius of the gears involved in the system. Recall that balance can be attained for a straight lever system if the force being applied to one side of the lever multiplied by the length of the lever arm on the same side of the fulcrum is equal to the force being applied to the opposite side multiplied by the length of the lever arm on the opposite side of the fulcrum.

Simply put, a 1 lb. mass placed 10 feet from the fulcrum of the lever on one side of the fulcrum must balance with a 2 lb. mass placed 5 feet from the fulcrum on the opposite side. The same is generally true for gears. If a drive gear has a 1 foot radius and the driven gear also has a one foot radius, there is no mechanical advantage. However, if the drive gear has a one foot radius and the driven gear has a two foot radius, we have created a 2:1 mechanical advantage. As with any mechanical advantage, when we gain a torque advantage, we sacrifice distance. In other words, even though we have gained a 2:1 mechanical advantage, we have to turn the drive gear twice to in order to complete one rotation of the driven gear.

If we look carefully at the gear train in Figure 15.5, we can see that gear A has a radius of 1 unit while gear B has a radius of 5 units. This means that as gear A rotates, it gains a 5:1 mechanical advantage (discounting friction, etc.). However, it must rotate five times for each revolution of gear B so the mechanical advantaged gained by the smaller size of gear A means that we sacrifice distance. In other words, we have a mechanical advantage on gear B but we only turn gear B 1/5 of a rotation in the process of gaining this advantage. Examining the relationship between gear B and gear C, we discover that we have a 3:5 mechanical advantage. Using related rates notation once again, we can calculate the overall ratios for rotational speed and mechanical advantage.

This rate represents the radius ratio while the inverse 5:1 represents the speed ratio and mechanical advantage.

$$\frac{da}{db} = \frac{1}{5}$$

This rate represents the radius ratio while the inverse 3:5 represents the speed ratio and mechanical advantage.

$$\frac{db}{dc} = \frac{5}{3}$$

The final radius ratio must be 1:3 based on the related rates notation so the system must have a 3:1 speed ratio and mechanical advantage

$$\frac{da}{db} \cdot \frac{db}{dc} = \frac{da}{dc}$$

Again, examining this gear train contextually, we can see that gear A must make five complete rotations for each rotation of gear B. Each rotation of gear B, then, results in 5/3 rotations of gear C. We can say by extension that five complete rotations of gear A must result in 5/3 rotations of gear C. Therefore, a single rotation of gear A must result in 1/3 of a rotation of gear C. We use the inverse ratios to establish speed and mechanical advantage. This gear train must have a 3:1 angular speed ratio and mechanical advantage.

The gear train shown in Figure 15.5 is not particularly complex, but it does represent all four uses of gear trains. Because each of the three gears varies in size, the gear train is automatically translating rotational speed and torque all along the gear train. Notice that the arrangement of the gears is also translating the planes of rotation and the direction of rotation for each gear. Finally, it should be noted that mechanical advantage becomes a bit more difficult to calculate if more than one gear is attached to an axis of rotation. It turns out that this mechanical arrangement is important to understand because it is fairly common to see multiple gears attached to a single axis of rotation in mechanical devices. Many grandfather clocks, for example, simultaneously drive a second hand, a minute hand, and an hour hand around the same axis of rotation. This is normally done by running a series of hollow axes through one another as shown in Figure 15.6.

We have now established the basic mathematical functions of both pendulums and gears. All we have left to do is to look at how all of the parts can all be arranged to make a functioning grandfather clock. The design of the *movement* of a grandfather clock is fairly complex, so an extremely abbreviated version will be shown here in Figure 15.6. The key points of the diagram focus on how a gear train can be arranged to manage three different hands while using a pendulum and an escapement to regulate the speed of the drive gear and driven gears. Figure 15.6 provides a basic side view configuration of gears that allow the clock to function with three different hands.

(Diagram can be found on the following page)

Figure 15.6: Abbreviated Mechanical Configuration of a Grandfather Clock

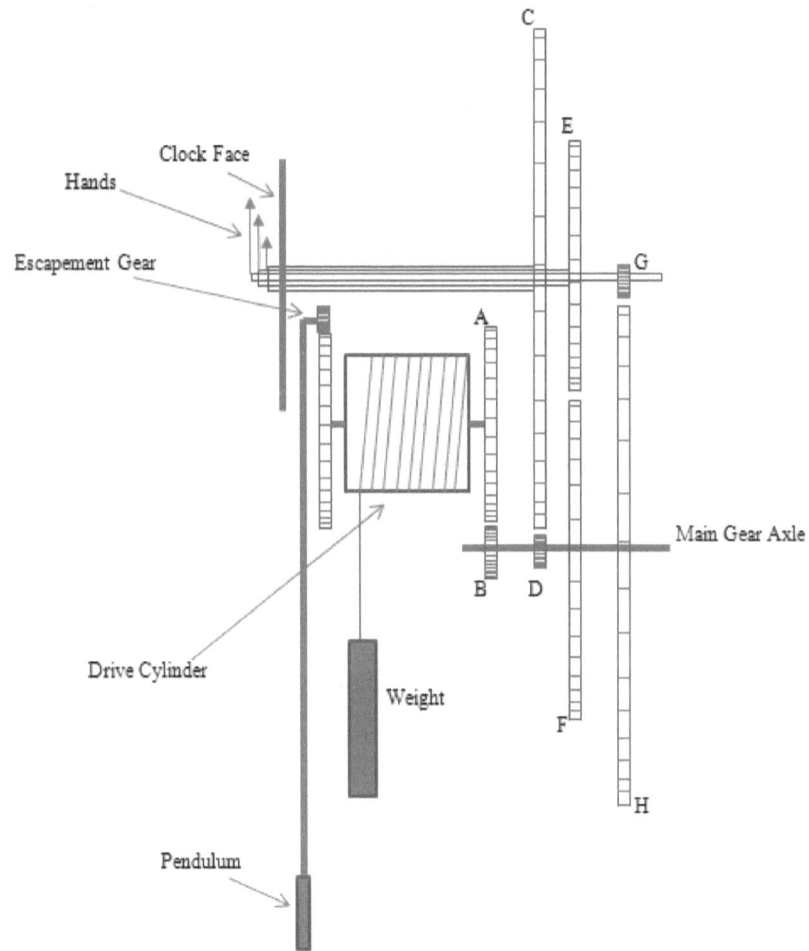

It is important to understand that the diagram used in Figure 15.6 is not drawn to scale nor is it a replica of an actual working clock movement. It is designed to present the basic concepts of how clock gears can be arranged to regulate the operation of three independent time units, namely seconds, minutes, and hours. That being said, this model illustrates the interactivity of a pendulum and escapement gear, which is driven by a cylinder, which is, in turn, powered by a weight. The gears are named A-H and vary in size to accommodate the angular speed translations needed for the hands showing seconds, minutes, and hours. The diagram represents what would essentially be the working parts of the clock known as the *movement*, but it has been substantially simplified from how an actual clock movement would be designed.

We begin by looking at the drive cylinder. This is typically a spool shaped device. A weight is attached to the spool and wrapped around the drive cylinder, usually with a thin metal cable. On the front of the drive cylinder, as we face the clock, is the escapement gear and pendulum. As the weight turns the drive cylinder, the escapement and pendulum regulate the amount the cylinder turns. The length of the pendulum determines the period of each "tic." Directly attached to the back side of the drive cylinder is gear A. This gear engages gear B to turn the main gear axle. The main gear axle turns three other gears, each of which acts as a drive gear for the *seconds* hand gear, the *minutes* hand gear, and the *hour*s hand gears. Note the relative sizes of the pairs of engaged gears. Gears D, F, and H all turn with a constant angular speed.

As the drive gear turns the main gear axle, gear D being very small, must make many revolutions to turn the very large gear C just one time. This pair of gears controls the hour hand of our clock. Gear C turns a wide hollow shaft one time per hour and this is the axle to which the hour hand is directly attached.

Gear F is a medium sized gear that engages gear E. The medium sized pair of gears E and F is designed to turn the minute hand axle one time per minute. Note that the minute hand axle is attached directly to gear E and runs directly through the inside of the hollow shaft of the hour hand.

The final gear arrangement is the pair G and H. Note that gear H is very large and as such turns very quickly relative to the *hours* hand and minute hand gears. Gear H engages a very small gear G which creates the rapidly turning gear we use as the *seconds* hand. Again, gear G turns a very small axle that runs directly through the middle of the *minutes* hand axle.

The design of this clock is fairly simple but once we have created an escapement-pendulum mechanism that provides the power necessary to overcome the friction inherent in the device, we have a nice mechanical timepiece that will operate independently for a reasonable period of time.

SUMMARY

The grandfather clock (or longcase clock as it is technically named) like so many other mechanical devices, has an interesting history. One of the most important improvements made to the longcase clock was to the type of escapement device. The original escapement device was called a *verge escapement*, which required fairly broad pendulum swings of somewhere between $80°$ and $100°$. For a long pendulum, this made the task of fitting the clock into a *long case* virtually impossible. The pendulum needed to be short, which caused it to have a very short period. As improvements to the escapement mechanism were made, a new device called the *anchor escapement* was the result. The swings of the pendulum using this new escapement could be both controlled and reliable at somewhere around $5°$. This meant that the pendulum could be much longer and ultimately have a longer period.

The original longcase clocks were designed to have two different kinds of movements, an eight-day and a 30-hour. The eight-day movement is still common today and only needs to be rewound (typically by turning a key) approximately once a week.

As functions were added to the clock (e.g. the chimes and a moon-phase dials), more gears and weights were added to the device. Most of the 30-hour clock designs used a single weight to drive all of the functional mechanisms, often including the three hands and the chime mechanism. Even though the 30-hour design is simpler and cheaper, it eventually lost popularity to a larger clock that could be rewound once per week and otherwise enjoyed.

There are several stories about how the longcase clock came to be named the grandfather clock. The most common story is based on a pair of brothers who, as the story goes, owned a hotel, which was a popular stop in Piercebridge, North Yorkshire, England. In the lobby of this hotel was a longcase clock that kept unusually accurate time for a mechanical clock. On the day that one of the brothers unexpectedly died, the clock suddenly began losing time, when previously it had been very accurate. Several clocksmiths were brought in to repair the clock but all were unsuccessful. When the second brother finally died, the clock stopped working entirely. The new manager of the hotel gave up trying to have it repaired and left the clock standing in the corner with the time displayed that the second brother had passed. In the mid-1870s an American songwriter named Henry Clay Work happened to be staying at the hotel and was told the story of the clock. Work eventually composed a song about the device titled "My Grandfather's Clock" and the rest, as they say, is history.

ADDITIONAL READINGS

Bridgewater, A., & Bridgewater, G. (2012). *Building Wooden Machines: Gears and Gadgets for the Adventurous Woodworker*. Popular Woodworking Books. ISBN: 978-1440322228

Brown, H.T. (2005). *507 Mechanical Movements: Mechanisms and Devices*. Dover Publications: New York. ISBN: 978-0486443607

Bureau of Naval Personnel. (1971). *Basic Machines and How They Work*. Dover Publications: New York. ISBN: 0-486-21709-4

Jones, F.D., & Ryffel, H.H. (1961). *Gear Design Simplified*. Industrial Press Inc. ISBN: 978-0831102098

Law, I. (1987). *Gears and Gear Cutting*. Trans-Atlantic Publications Inc. ISBN: 978-0852429112

Sclater, N. (2011). *Mechanisms and Mechanical Devices Sourcebook, 5th Ed.* McGraw-Hill Professional. ISBN: 978-0071704427

Williams, G. (1980). *Designing and Building a Grandfather Clock*. A.S. Barnes & Co. ISBN: 978-0498022098

ARTICLE 16: CONSTRUCTING ROBOTIC LEGS

ABSTRACT: The article contained hereafter deviates somewhat from the format of previous articles. The primary goal of the *Constructing Robotic Legs* manuscript is to provide additional concrete applications for plane geometry concepts and straight line linkages. The mathematical formula derivations and calculations are deemphasized in this article to the extent that the presentation is largely focused on diagrams that provide the steps needed for constructing three kinds of working mechanical legs. The plans for a *walking* robot are presented.

INTRODUCTION

Some of the most challenging engineering research being conducted in robotics during this modern age is that which provides basic bipedal locomotion and humanlike balance. For some reason, the experimental robots that impress us the most tend to be the kinds that look like we do. Popular movie culture has conditioned us to think of robots as largely humanoid even though most of the contemporary educational robotic platforms are much smaller and are designed around the functionality of a car. Based on information provided in some of the previous articles, the reason for this should be fairly apparent. The circular motion of a wheel is natural while the adapted approximate straight line motion of taking steps must be translated in some rather complex ways. The notion of service robots that look and move like humans is one that will probably stay popular because the human form is one we understand. Yet, to create working models of robots that are humanlike is still a fairly difficult process; although, research engineers and scientists are making impressive progress.

If we look at the most basic forms of leg movement used for transportation, we must recognize that humans *learn* the balance required to walk. Our first efficient form of locomotion is actually to move by crawling on our hands and knees. In fact, moving on four *legs* instead of two seems like a natural place to start moving our robotic mechanisms.

For our purposes, we will not be creating a robot in the purest sense, but rather, a mechanical device that will transport itself by taking steps. To do this, we must grapple with engineering concepts such as balance and translating circular motion into adapted, approximate straight line motion. It should be noted that for the balance issue, humans adopt a diagonal stepping process when learning how to crawl on all fours. The weight of a human, as it crawls, is placed on diagonally opposing limbs. That is to say, as we learn to crawl, it is natural to alternately place weight on one front limb and the opposing back limb. This process keeps the center of gravity of a moving body more consistently balanced. This seems very natural, but if you look at other animal species, it is not always the case. Giraffes, for example, move both legs on one side of their bodies simultaneously, much like a file of humans marching in step. This is an important factor to consider because as we look more closely at robotic locomotion, we can solve many of our original design challenges by creating horizontal, vertical and diagonal symmetries. To create the geometric model for a machine that operates in a similar way to that of a crawling human child will be our quest.

INVESTIGATION AND NOTES

We will explore three specific leg designs in the following pages. The first design is very simple and is based on an *approximate straight line linkage* known as the Hoekens linkage. This linkage is used because it has a near constant velocity at the end point (foot) as circular motion is translated from a drive segment to the link acting as the leg. The formal mechanical engineering resources refer to the Hoekens linkage as a 4-bar linkage, but it is technically made from only three segments, two fixed hinges, and two floating hinges.

The second leg design comes from a modern Dutch artist and inventor named Theo Jansen. Jansen is most widely known for his mechanical creatures called strandbeests. The strandbeest leg, although much more complicated than a Hoekens linkage, has a motion and shape that is more interesting and, in some sense, more human. The third mechanism uses the same basic principles as the Ratio Gauge presented in Article 14 but introduces a fixed hinge and a rotating drive segment. All three mechanisms have some unique characteristics.

We will begin by examining the motion of the Hoekens linkage and then present the measurements and arrangement of hinges for a working leg model. Figure 16.1 provides the basic motion of the Hoekens linkage.

Figure 16.1: Hoekens Linkage

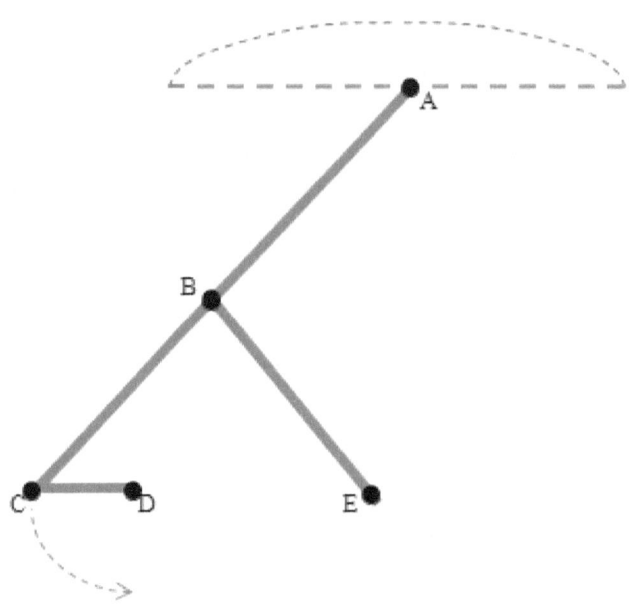

In this linkage, points D and E represent fixed hinges. That is to say that they are fixed to a frame and will not move relative to one another other than rotating. Hinges B and C are floating hinges and move relative to other points in the linkage. Point A follows the path outlined by the dotted lines above the linkage. The drive linkage is represented by segment CD. As point C rotates around point D, point A follows the dotted path. The motion is fairly simple but is ideal for a robotic step because it involves both an approximate straight line path and an elliptical path. This is not too different than what happens when a leg takes a step. The straight line path may represent the body moving relative to the ground while the elliptical part of the path could represent the leg lifting the foot and moving it forward so that it is prepared to take the next step. All we really need to do is to invert the device and establish a body to which we can attach the leg so we can observe the movement.

To some extent, the path outline by point A will depend on the measurement of the various segments, so as we establish the measurements, one step may look different than another even though the linkage design is not changing. For our leg design, we will invert the image and fix points D and E on a horizontal frame at a distance of 10 inches. Segment AC will be cut to a length of 17 inches while the distance between floating hinges at points B and C will be 9 inches. The drive segment, which rotates around point D and is turned by some external source (typically a motor), will connect hinges at points D and C at a distance of 4 inches. Finally, triangle BCE is isosceles making the distance from point B to point E also 9 inches. Figure 16.2 illustrates the inverted device but using the same points and labels as those defined in Figure 16.1. Note also that the measurements given are distances between hinges and could vary substantially depending on the design specifications of the device. In order to construct the device, we would need to cut the segments slightly longer than the measurements shown so that holes could be drilled to connect the segments.

(Diagram can be found on the following page)

Figure 16.2: Hoekens Linkage used as a Leg

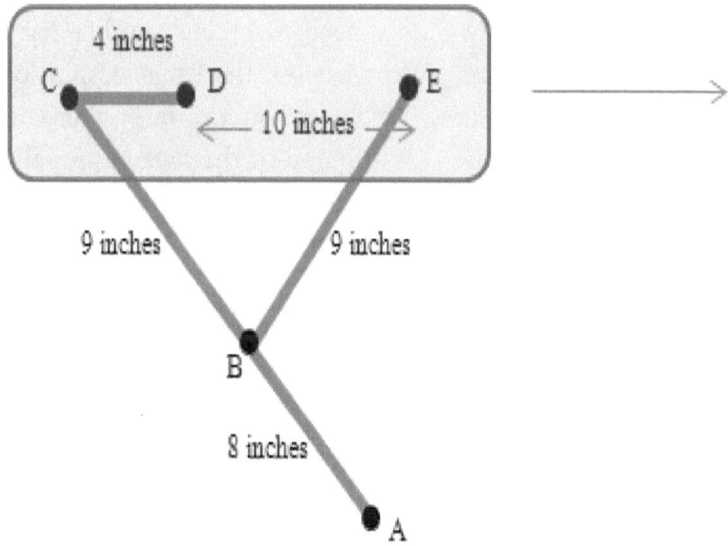

The device is attached to a frame (the body of the mechanical creature) at points D and E. Later on we will need to make the body longer to accommodate two legs, but for now we simply want to define the motion of the linkage through a single, complete step. As point C turns counterclockwise, the motion at point A creates a path similar to a step. This is important since we need to somehow propel our creature forward in increments. Point C rotating counterclockwise from its current location in the diagram pushes point A down and forward until it contacts the walking surface. As point C revolves below point D, point A begins to move in the opposite direction propelling the creature forward. Finally, as point C approaches the line between points D and E, it lifts point A at a diagonal off of the walking surface and begins to bring the foot forward.

This seems to be a leg design that will work because of the appropriate type of stepping motion that results, but our challenge is really just beginning. We now need to create another leg on the same side of the creature. We must use the same design, one that not only uses the same drive segment but alternates the stepping/propelling motion. While one of the legs is propelling the creature forward, the other leg should be lifting and moving forward in an elliptical motion. Ultimately this will be reversed on the opposite side of the device.

The best way to do this seems to be to connect the drive segment to the long segments of each separate Hoekens linkage such that they are at $180°$ differences in their cycles. This can be accomplished by adding only two more segments to our mechanism. The two legs will operate independently but will share a drive segment. The linkages will be connected and share a floating hinge at point C. This arrangement, as we will discover shortly, has some significant flaws which will require modification. For now, we will attempt to verify how the stepping cycles of the two linkage mechanism complement each other. Figure 16.3 illustrates the mechanism with both legs at opposite ends of the rotational cycle.

Figure 16.3: Two Mechanical Legs Working in Unison

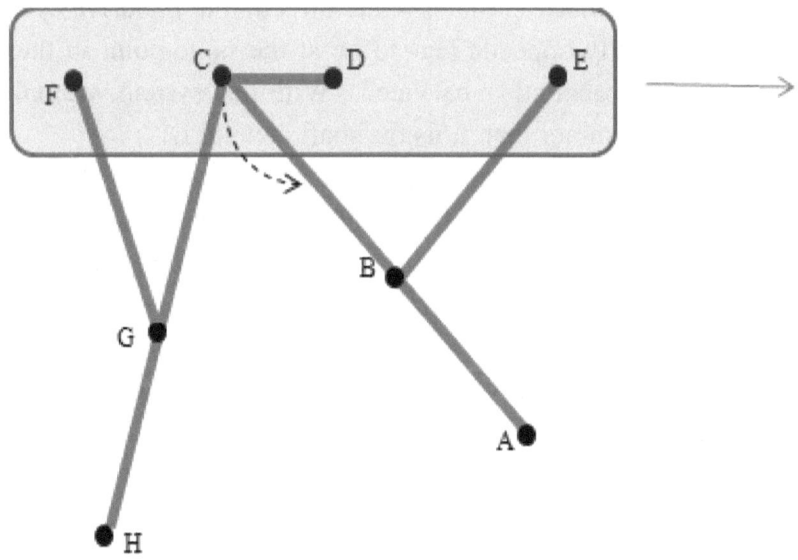

To stay consistent, the points of the original linkage (A-E) have been labeled as they previously were. This part of the mechanism is on the right hand side of Figure 16.3 and will act as the front leg. Points F, G, and H make up the linkages of the second (rear) leg. Notice that the two linkages share a floating hinge at point C, which rotates counterclockwise around the fixed point D. In this position the front leg is in the process of moving forward to place point A at the new step location. The rear leg is pushing the mechanism forward and closing in on the end of its step cycle.

It appears that the apparatus we have developed will create two similar, alternating step cycles. To complete a robotic type mechanism that will move smoothly, we need two more legs on the opposite side. The same arrangement of linkages on the opposite side of our robot will not only drive the robot, it will also balance the robot as long as the cycle of our drive linkage at point C is oriented in the opposite direction on opposite sides of the device. Having the legs extended in the opposite direction in the drive cycle allows for diagonally opposite legs to be at the same point in their step cycles so the robot stays balanced. With this system, we only need a single drive motor that turns the shaft at point D.

The steps our robotic device takes using this linkage arrangement will make for a fairly awkward gait. The motion achieved using four legs typically results in a repeated belly flop. The reason is that at some point in the cycles of the legs, they are all half way retracted at the same time. If we adjust the leg cycles on either side to be $90°$ different in their step cycles instead of $180°$, the robot will be out of balance either diagonally or front to back.

To make the walking motion a little bit smoother, we can add more pairs of legs and adjust the drive linkage by a desired number of degrees so that there are always two pairs of balancing feet on the ground while the other pairs of feet are retracted. This also helps stabilize the device from falling forward or backwards. The easiest way to do this is to divide the $360°$ turn cycle by the number of pairs of legs on the device. For example, if we have two pairs of legs, the two DC segments would be set at $180°$ from one another on the drive linkage. If we have four pairs of legs, the four DC segments would be set at $90°$ increments within the step cycle. In a side-by-side arrangement of the legs, all of the legs can operate from the same drive linkage so that only one motor is needed. If we use two pairs of legs in tandem on each side of the device, we would either need two motors or a more sophisticated drive mechanism that could be driven by a single motor. For our robotic device, the drive hinge has been located at point D, so our last step would be to include a power source such as a motor and battery. It would need to be mounted in such a way that it could turn a shaft attached to the hinge at point D.

Our next robotic leg model is quite a bit more sophisticated than the Hoekens linkage mechanism shown in Figure 16.3 but provides a more interesting and humanlike stepping motion. There are many adaptations of the next linkage mechanism but they all function in similar ways. The most significant factor affecting the overall movement is the relative lengths of the interacting segments. The design shown here was invented by a Dutch artist and inventor named Theo Jansen. Jansen calls the working device a *strandbeest*, which roughly means "beach creature." Different variations of the strandbeest mechanisms can be seen online.

The leg linkage mechanism consists of 11 segments, two fixed hinges, and six floating hinges. The key to its successful operation is the careful assembly of the various segments using exact measurements. Again, this linkage mechanism is driven by a single short rotating linkage for both the front and back legs. The simplest way to illustrate how the mechanism works is to show the construction of three unique components of the leg. This will be done in Figures 16.4 and 16.5. Figure 16.4 shows the flexible square/rhombus mechanism around which the linkage functions. Figure 16.5 completes the device by illustrating how three triangular structures of the device can be assembled around the square and attached to a single drive linkage.

Figure 16.4: Assembled Jansen Linkage (Step 1 – Square/Rhombus)

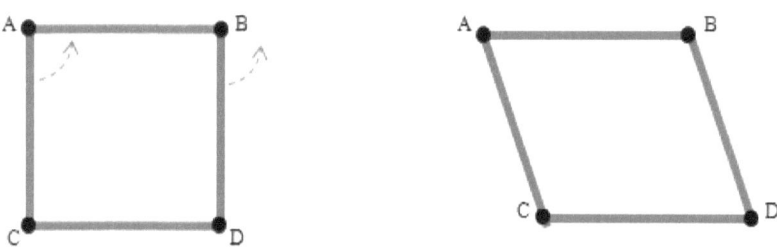

The first part of the linkage (shown in Figure 16.4) contains four segments and three floating hinges at points A, C, and D. Although it cannot be seen in the diagram above, the hinge at point B is fixed in the final mechanism. Figure 16.5 illustrates step two of the design where triangles are added to the top and bottom of the original square/rhombus mechanism. The bottom triangle represents the leg structure and foot while the triangle on the top acts a kind of hip joint. The purposes of the independent parts are much easier to see when the device is moving. The top triangle is isosceles and includes a perpendicular leg that is the same length as the sides of the original square. The lower triangle uses the base of the original square as one of its sides and extends the longest side past the bottom vertex of the triangle. This extra length on the bottom triangle is what is used as the "foot" of the device.

Figure 16.5: Assembled Jansen Linkage (Step 2 – Triangles and Drive Segment)

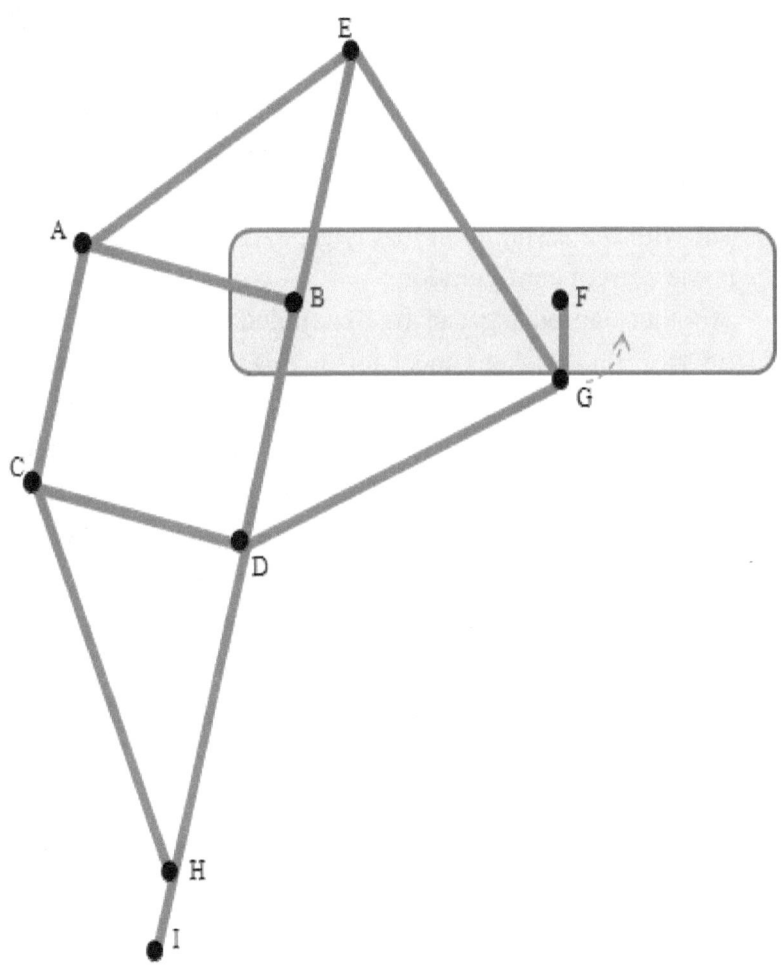

Notice that the entire leg mechanism needs to be angled slightly prior to attaching it to the drive linkage so that the necessary stepping motion can be achieved. That is to say that the vertical sides of the original square are angled approximately 15° from a vertical orientation. Note that in Figure 16.5, three triangles have been attached to adjacent sides of the original square/rhombus mechanism. All of the new segments are 1.75 times as long as the original square with the exception of segment AE and the drive segment FG. Segment AE being the hypotenuse of triangle EAB is simply 1.41 times the length of the side of the square. The drive linkage FG is approximately one third of the length of the side of the square. The mechanism is then fixed to a frame at points B and F. The drive linkage FG then rotates around point F. The device is assembled with the assumption that angles ABE and CDH are right angles in the current configuration.

Another Jansen leg can be assembled and reversed just as was done with the Hoekens mechanism in Figure 16.3 so that the same drive segment turns both leg mechanisms through the stepping cycle but at a 180° phase shift. This will cause one leg to be in contact with the ground while the other leg is retracted and moving forward to take its next step. Figure 16.6 illustrates how the Jansen legs might look at opposite ends of the stepping cycle. Just as was the case with the Hoekens arrangement, more legs tend to make for a smoother gait for the overall Jansen mechanism.

(Diagram can be found on the following page)

Figure 16.6: Pair of Jansen Robotic Legs Working in Unison

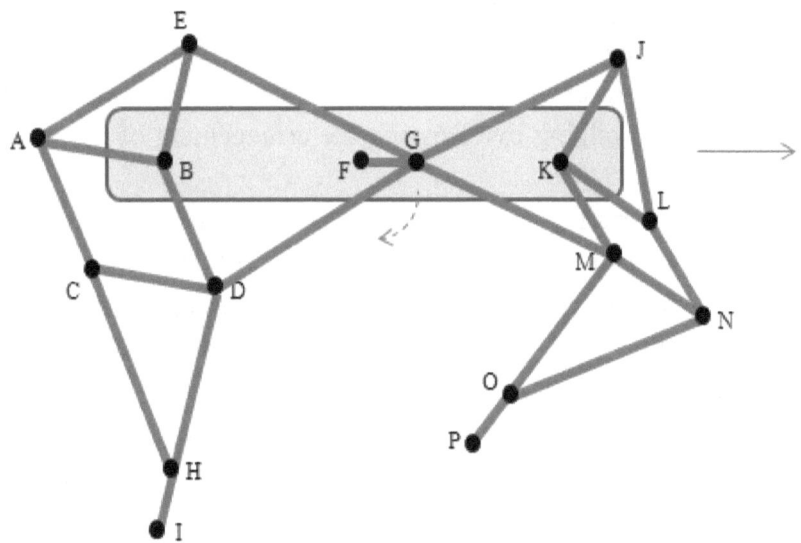

As the drive segment FG rotates clockwise, the robot moves toward the right. In particular, Figure 16.6 illustrates how the square/rhombus linkage alternately collapses and expands to create the stepping motion of the strandbeest. The Jansen legs are a bit more efficient than the Hoekens legs in that a shorter drive shaft is used, which allows for a lower torque to be used to move the device.

The final mechanism is one that varies somewhat in from the first two leg designs. The inspiration for the device presented in the following paragraphs comes from the Ratio Gauge as described in Article 14. In some sense, the ratio gauge format provides a leg that operates a little more like a spider leg in that the knee is situated more toward the top of the leg like an elbow. The other difference with this leg design is that when the two legs are assembled on a single drive segment, the legs are both on the ground at virtually the same time as the drive segment rotates simply because of the kind of motion being used. In some cases, this can be very effective in terms of smoothing out the gait if many pairs of legs are used. The final motion of such a device looks more like a gallop than a walk. The mechanism can be adapted to a cycle that alternates steps in a way that mimics walking by changing the arrangement of the drive mechanism.

The Hoekens leg and the Jansen leg are both designed to use symmetrical pairs of legs that are attached to the same point of a rotating drive segment. The way these legs are designed allows the drive segment to define opposite ends of the stepping cycle for the pairs of legs. In order for this to happen with our new device, we need to attach each leg to opposite ends of the drive segment such that the drive segment spins from the middle rather than from one end. Figure 16.7 illustrates the design of a single leg while Figure 16.8 shows how the mechanism can be set up to create a smooth step cycle.

(Diagram can be found on the following page)

Figure 16.7: Robotic Leg Design Based on Ratio Gauge

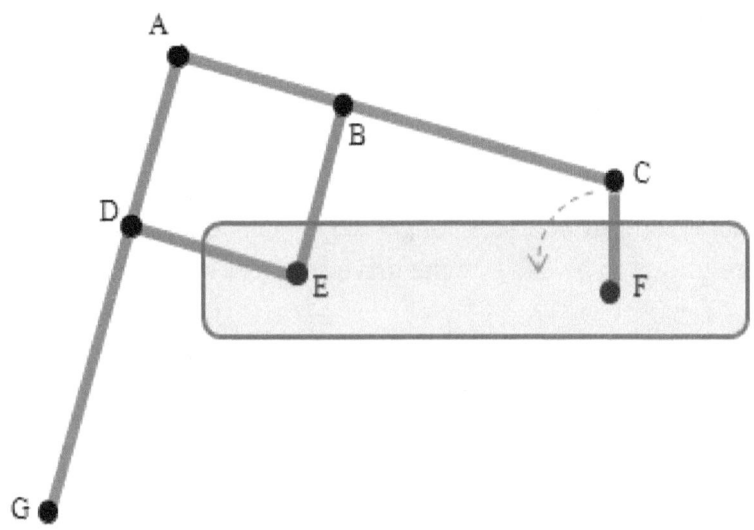

In closely examining Figure 16.7, we can see that the ratio gauge leg device works with only one fixed hinge, located at point E; and, of course, an additional fixed hinge for the drive segment located at point F. As point C rotates counterclockwise around point F, point C and the fixed point at E are forced closer together, which draws the foot at point G closer to the rotating point C as well. As point C continues to rotate, it moves downward thus lifting the leg as the entire mechanism pivots around point E. As point C moves downward, point G must move upward. As point C moves back toward its original position, point G extends outward, loops back downward, and contacts the ground completing the step cycle.

The simplicity of this design makes it highly attractive from a utility standpoint. With only four segments (not including the drive segment), it is only slightly more complex than the Hoekens linkage and much less than the Jansen linkage. The fact that the device has very few joints creates a low overall coefficient of friction and the step cycle can be more easily controlled by changing the length of the drive segment CF than in the other two devices. Further, the length of the strides can be more easily manipulated by setting the desired ratio between segments AC and AG. For example, a long drive segment (CF), a short driven segment (AC), and a longer leg segment (AG) will result in very broad sweeping movements, and of course a longer step. This does require quite a bit more torque to be used on the drive segment in order to carry the device.

Alternately, a short drive segment, a long driven segment, and a short leg results in shorter, more stilted steps, but can function with minimal torque. To some extent, we can manipulate the step cycles of the other linkages as well but their designs limit how they move, so the drive linkages must operate within a much smaller range than the ratio gauge linkage. Again, by duplicating the leg mechanism and attaching a mirror image of it to the same drive segment, we have created a device that will take steps. The device as shown in Figure 16.8, however, creates step cycles on the opposing legs that put the feet on the ground at almost the same time. In order to create a more even stepping cycle, we need to attach the opposing legs to opposite ends of the drive segment. Figures 16.8 and 16.9 illustrate the changes that must be made in order to create an even step cycle for two opposing legs.

Figure 16.8: Ratio Gauge Robotic Legs Working in Unison (Drive Segment Design 1)

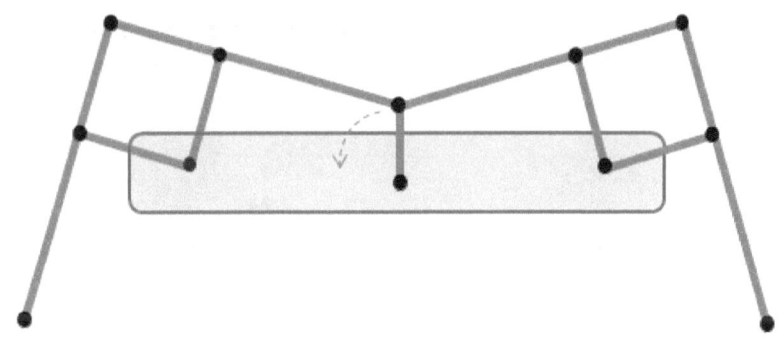

As we can see, the same basic leg symmetry exists within the ratio gauge mechanism as with the Hoekens and Jansen mechanisms. The difference is in what determines the endpoints of the stepping cycle. In the Jansen mechanism, the fixed hinge is attached to the top of the square/rhombus linkage and the leg swings in a sweeping motion based on the opening and collapsing of the square/rhombus. This creates a step cycle that starts and stops based on opposing ends of the drive segment for each leg. In the ratio gauge mechanism, the fixed hinge is attached to the bottom of the square/rhombus linkage and the leg moves by rotating the entire mechanism around the fixed hinge, so as the drive segment becomes vertical at the top, the legs continue to move as if they are marching in step, which puts both feet on the ground at virtually the same time. In order to fix this, we need a new design for our drive segment. Figure 16.9 illustrates a drive segment design that defines a better stepping cycle for the mechanism. As we can see, attaching the driven segment of each leg to the opposite ends of the drive segment, we create what can also be considered opposite ends of the step cycle.

Figure 16.9: Ratio Gauge Robotic Legs Working in Unison (Drive Segment Design 2)

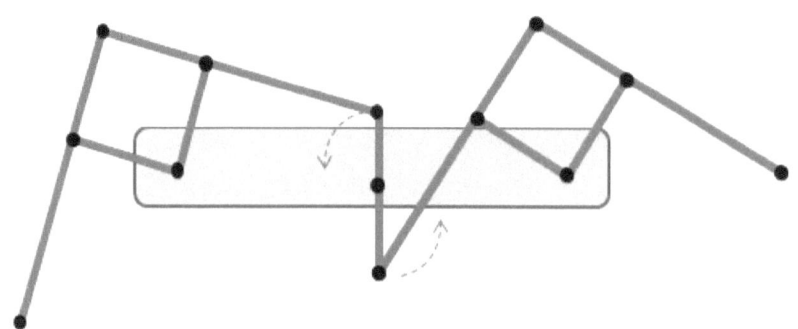

One of the most interesting revelations that come from modifying existing designs is that we occasionally stumble on to some very productive unintended designs. There are many examples throughout the history of engineering where substantial mistakes transformed into some very useful products. With our ratio gauge leg model for example, a little experimenting shows us that the ratio gauge design can be inverted and still function as a pair of legs. In fact it is actually a design that has a smoother step cycle when it is upside down. Figure 16.9 illustrates how the ratio gauge design works when directly applied, but notice that the elbows at the top of the device have a similar stepping cycle to the legs at the bottom. The cycle is simply smaller because of the way the mechanism is attached to the frame.

Figure 16.10 shows a more plausible leg design that begins to mimic the Jansen mechanism. To make the ratio gauge device function as a pair of legs, we simply invert the existing device and then remove the superfluous segments. The segments we need to remove are the legs of the device when it is right side up.

Figure 16.10: Inverted Ratio Gauge Leg Mechanism

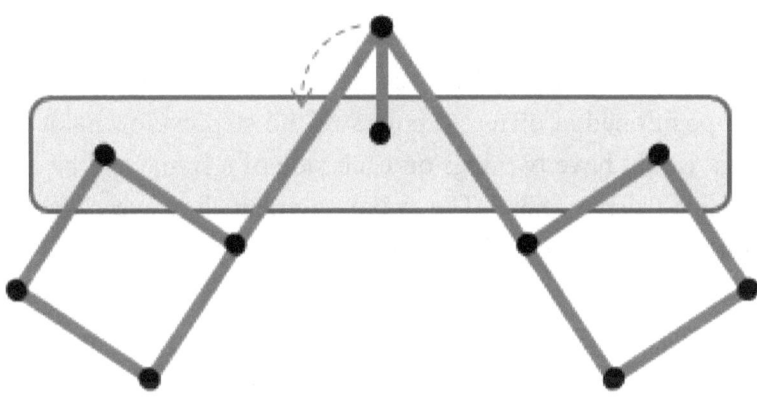

As the drive segment of the model in Figure 16.10 spins, the square/rhombus linkages of each leg elongate along the diagonals, which creates the steps. The difference is that the motion of each step is more subdued because the original model was designed to have more animated movements at the opposite end of the legs. This is analogous to a lever that has a fulcrum closer to one end. The movement of the end of a lever where the fulcrum is close is proportionally smaller than the movement at the opposite end. In this case, the fixed hinge in Figure 16.9 is closer to the elbow of the device making the stepping cycle motion of the elbow much smaller than the opposite ends, which represent the legs. Using the elbow ends of the device in Figure 16.9 as the legs provides greater support and strength for the overall mechanism in much the same way it does with the Jansen model. Note specifically that the model in Figure 16.10 once again has the same symmetry and opposite step cycles using only one end of the drive segment. This device is one of the simplest and most smooth walking devices that can be created by novices.

If we were to build this device, we would need at least four sets of legs to smooth out the gait and balance the device properly as it processes each step cycle. Figure 16.11 illustrates a basic design as a top view of the model to show how the four sets of legs would need to be positioned. Each set of legs would include four leg devices positioned at different points of the step cycle. Each set of four legs would have two legs on each side of a frame and be driven by the same drive axis. The drive segment, however, would be positioned on opposite ends of the step cycle.

(Diagram can be found on the following page)

Figure 16.11: Top View of Inverted Ratio Gauge Model with Four Sets of Legs

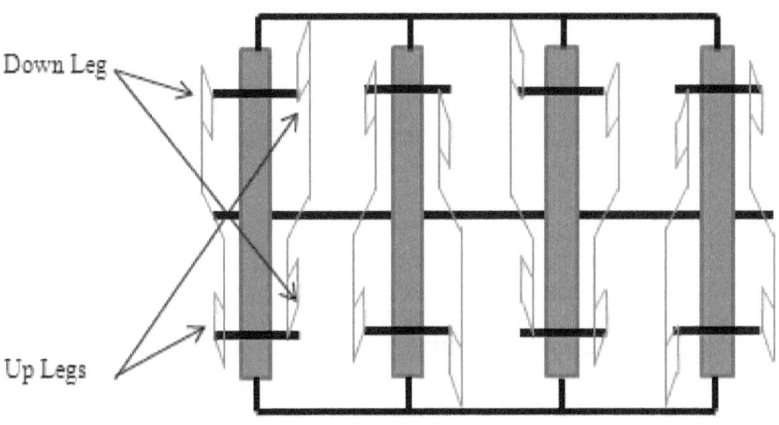

Note that the entire device consists of four connected columns, each having two pairs of legs. On each column, the up and down legs are diagonally at the same place in their respective step cycles. We know that the center of gravity for each column remains at the center of that column since diagonally opposing legs are on the ground at the same time. This is true for all of the individual columns. The two outside columns will have the same step cycles, as will the two inside columns; however, the inside columns and the outside columns will be positioned at 90° from each other within the step cycle. This looks a bit awkward but creates a smoother, more balanced locomotion for the entire mechanism. Generally, the more sets of legs included on the mechanism, the smoother the gait will be.

SUMMARY

There are many more straight line linkage mechanisms that could easily be adapted to fit the purpose of a robotic leg. The mechanisms shown here can also be adapted for a more three dimensional frame of movement that will give us working arms as well. The nature of the linkages presented here are such that they all illustrate a translation away from a circular form of motion to a more human stepping motion. Because they only need to represent a periodic stepping cycle in their final movement, there are literally hundreds of ways to adapt, change, and modify these devices by experimenting with a few very basic linkages. The study of robotic linkages is really central to success in careers in mechanical engineering, and more than anything, the modifications are about seeing potential for solving certain types of problems. For example, the last linkage (Figure 16.9) using the adaptation of the ratio gauge can also be used upside down since the elbows at the top of the mechanism have basically the same movement throughout the step cycle as the feet at the bottom. The cycle is simply smaller and supported in a different way. This kind of modification could potentially allow us to adapt a very similar leg style to solve a new problem. Indeed, there are many more modifications that could be made to the same linkage to create new kinds of legs. In some sense, experimenting with linkages to create robotic appendages is as much about imagination as it is about pure geometric knowledge. It is through this revelation that we will really being to understand why mathematics needs to be applied in a much more integrated fashion and in a much more routine way.

ADDITIONAL READINGS

Brown, H. T. (2005). *507 Mechanical Movements Mechanisms and Devices*. Dover Publications. ISBN: 978-0486443607

Cook, D. (2010). *Robot Building for Beginners (Technology in Action)*. 2nd Ed. Apress. ISBN: 978-1430227489

Craig, J. (2004). *Introduction to Robotics: Mechanics and Control*. 3rd Ed. Prentice Hall. ISBN: 978-0201543612

Roberts, D. (2010). *Making Things Move DIY Mechanics for Inventors, Hobbyists, and Artists*. McGraw-Hill/TAB Electronics. ISBN: 978-0071741675

Williams, K. (2004). *Build Your Own Humanoid Robots: 6 Amazing and Affordable Projects*. McGraw Hill/TAB Electronics. ISBN: 978-0071422741

SECTION 4: PHYSICS AND MATH

The fit between Physics and mathematics is very natural. Physics is often taught as applied mathematics, and yet there still seems to be a fair amount of reticence among mathematics teachers to engage students in physics based applications that incorporate experimentation as a way to verify calculation and measurement. The study of physics is a natural way to connect the modeling done in geometry to the physical design heuristics of engineering. Without physics applications, students often miss the critical connections that make the engineering process efficient and successful. Physics stems from the mathematical principles of natural philosophy so aptly presented by Isaac Newton. Physics, after all, is the lynchpin that connects mathematics to the natural and designed worlds. The mathematical concepts presented in Section 4 are as follows:

Article 17: Using a Multi-Meter Electrical Measurements
Article 18: Optics and the Geometry of Light
Article 19: Engineering Mechanics (Explorations in Statics)
Article 20: Using Calculus in Product Design

ARTICLE 17: USING A MULTI-METER FOR ELECTRICAL MEASUREMENTS

ABSTRACT: This article illustrates the basic operations of a volt-ohm meter (also referred to as a multi-meter or VOM) in measuring resistance, current, and voltage. Basic concepts of electricity are presented. Applied examples of using a multi-meter for both traditional and non-traditional *resistors* are given in order to better establish the framework for how the resistance variable is conceived in electronic circuits. Although the manuscript focuses primarily on using a volt meter to measure electrical resistance, voltage and current relations are also briefly explored and integrated into the examples.

INTRODUCTION

Nearly all of the trade and construction careers use measurement as a way to justify, verify, calculate, design, or test the success of certain tasks they need to complete. Measurement, in fact, is a critical skill for technicians and design engineers in nearly every aspect of the design process, and in nearly every creative design field. In short, the ability to measure is a helpful skill for anyone to have whether they need it for their career or not. Individuals make measurements all the time without really thinking about it. For example, when we hang a picture, dress appropriately for the seasons, or check the tires on our car, we are using a ruler, checking the thermometer, or looking at a tire gauge.

Measurement is a skill that is best learned by doing, but for the most part it is still taught as a didactic textbook skill in school classrooms rather than as an applied process skill with real results and usable data. Many mathematics texts provide illustrations of how to use devices such as rulers and protractors, but students are too infrequently required to apply their learning in meaningful ways. Part of the reason for this is that there are many ways to measure things and many different devices to master in the process of learning to measure. Schools are often bound by curriculum parameters that simply do not allow the time needed for applications. Or perhaps they lack the funds needed to provide the necessary equipment to their students. Because of this, students are often not exposed to some helpful practices that are useful both in home situations and in future careers. For example, you may be amazed at the number of high school science curriculums that omit measurements related to electricity and electronics despite the fact that chapters on Electricity and Magnetism are in nearly every physics book, and using a volt-ohm meter is one of the most practical skills a person can have for diagnosing problems within their houses, in their cars, with their electronics equipment, and even with their hobbies. Knowing the basics of a volt-ohm meter and the diagnostic information it provides can be extremely helpful even with a very limited knowledge of electricity.

  The first device that was designed for detecting electric current was engineered around a moving pointer mechanism called a galvanometer. It was invented in 1820 and was used to measure voltage and resistance. About a hundred years later, the multi-meter (what we call the volt-ohm meter) was invented by Donald Macadie who was a British postal engineer. He used it as a way to troubleshoot early telecommunications circuits. Though aspects of the volt-ohm meter have changed, the principles of how it works are basically the same as they were a hundred years ago.

INVESTIGATION AND NOTES

In the following pages, we will explore some very basic (and fundamental) ideas related to electricity and electronics. In fact, a good place to start this investigation is to define the difference between *electric* and *electronic* devices. Electric devices are those that use electric current to transform electricity into other forms of energy. For example, a light bulb is an electric component that transforms electricity into light and heat. In some cases, electricity is transformed into motion by turning devices such as a fan. *Electronic* components differ somewhat in that they manipulate electricity into doing things that are useful in ways other than transforming energy. For example, a volt-ohm meter is considered an electronic device because it allows us to take measurements related to various forms of energy by reading the properties of electricity. Even a simple diode can be considered an electronic device because it limits the flow of electricity in a circuit to one direction.

Despite all of the inherent complexities in the design of the electrical devices we routinely encounter, they all use electricity in basically the same way. Admittedly, these electrical devices can be pretty intimidating if we look at the circuits inside them. Of course, it is really no more necessary to understand the science behind the actual components when using an electronic device than it is to understand the internal combustion engine when driving a car. Still, troubleshooting problems is important in many career fields and this includes the development and repair of electrically powered equipment.

Part of the process of troubleshooting with electricity is isolating the system or systems where problems may exist. One great way to do this is by taking measurements to be sure that the functioning systems are operating within acceptable ranges based on their specifications. Nowhere is this more important than in functioning systems that have parts that change due to other operational parameters. With electricity, for example, this may happen when batteries are low or a short circuit may have occurred. Certainly it is helpful to have some device that can narrow where we should look for trouble. The volt-ohm meter is ideal for this kind of troubleshooting.

A standard volt-ohm meter, or multi-meter as it is often called, measures three basic electrical scales; voltage, current, and resistance. For the purposes of this article, we will be measuring voltage and resistance to illustrate how the multi-meter is used. I have selected those particular scales because they tend to be safer kinds of measurements. Electricity, as you may know, can be harmful to both people and equipment if it is not treated with respect, so there will be periodic references to the safety aspects of using the multi-meter throughout this manuscript.

Before we begin measuring with the multi-meter, it will be helpful to have some basic understanding of the interplay of the forces inherent in what we call electricity. A common analogy used to help describe the electrical components of *voltage*, *current*, and *resistance* is that of a garden hose. If we have a small garden hose, and we turn on a faucet, we can feel the pressure of the water pushing against anything we might use to stop its flow, say, our thumb. Voltage is analogous to pressure. When we measure the voltage of a battery, we are in essence measuring the *potential pressure* of that battery. We call it *potential* pressure because the electricity does not actually need to be flowing to measure the pressure, just as the water does not actually need to be moving through the hose to measure the pressure of the water. If you have blocked the end of the hose with your thumb, for example, you can feel the pressure of the water even though the water is not moving.

Now let us suppose we want to measure current. Electrical current is much like the volume of the water passing through a hose.

If we compare a small hose and a large hose, the volume can be very different if even if the pressure of the hoses is the same. Because the current of electricity is analogous to the volume of water flowing, electricity needs to be flowing for us to actually measure it, just as we would need to measure the volume of water by filling a bucket in a given amount of time. Electrical power is then calculated by multiplying voltage (pressure) by current (volume). Many people fear high voltage output but if the volume (current) is extremely low, a very high voltage would not necessarily hurt a person. Likewise, high current is not necessarily dangerous if the voltage is extremely low. The bottom line is that we do not need to be so concerned with high voltage or high current, but rather, high electrical *power*, which is measured in Watts.

Electrical *resistance* is efficiently described as a material's opposition to the flow of current. If, for example, we consider current the volume of flow of water in a hose, we can reduce the volume in a given amount of time by reducing the diameter of the hose. In some sense, the idea of electrical resistance is analogous to the mechanical notion of kinetic friction.

Based on the way these three electrical scales have been described, it is now possible to see how they are critically interrelated. Figure 17.1 illustrates how any one of the measurements can be described as a ratio of the remaining two. The formulas below provide the relationships where R is defined as resistance (measured in *ohms*), V is defined as voltage (measured in Volts), and I is defined as current (measured in *amperes*). The diagram in Figure 17.1 graphically represents the relationship of the three scales by Ohm's Law.

Figure 17.1: Ohm's Law Described by Formula and Graphically

Resistance: $R = \dfrac{V}{I}$

Voltage: $V = I \cdot R$

Current: $I = \dfrac{V}{R}$

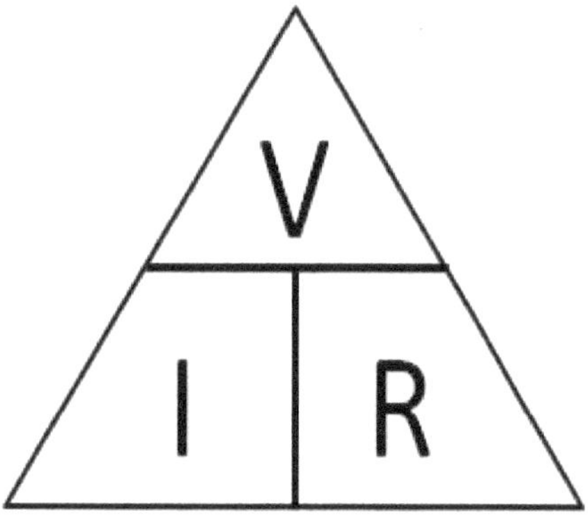

The triangle in the diagram of Ohm's Law shows the relationship of the three scales graphically. If we are calculating current, we select the variable *I* and establish the relationships based on the position of the other two variables in the triangle. In this case we can see that I must be equal to the voltage divided by the resistance because if we cover the *I*, the relative positions of the variables in the triangle show *V* over *R*. If, instead, we are calculating voltage, we select the voltage variable by covering it and look at the relative positions of the remaining two variables. In the case of calculating voltage, the relative side-by-side positions of *I* and *R* indicate that the variables would be multiplied.

Now that we have developed a better sense of what each scale represents, we can think about using a measurement device that will put some numeric values in perspective and allows us to verify the formulas given above. Our next task is to look specifically at the multi-meter and provide some information about how it operates.

Volt-Ohm meters or multi-meters come in a variety of forms but most of them now have a digital output screen (normally LCD) with an analog dial that allows us to select the scale and magnitude of what we want to measure. Most multi-meters also have options to measure both alternating current and direct current, although some will automatically select based on the input that is being sensed by the meter. This kind of automation in a meter helps keep the equipment from being damaged if a user inadvertently selects an improper setting. As a rule of thumb, alternating current, or AC current, is what comes out of a wall outlet in your home, while direct current, or DC current, is what comes from a battery.

A decent, reliable multi-meter with a digital display can cost as little as $5-$10. This kind of device will be satisfactory for most home diagnostic needs. A dial in the center of the device allows the user to select the scale being measured (i.e. AC/DC voltage, current, or resistance). Electrical data is collected in the meter using two sharp probes, one red representing the positive lead and the other black representing the negative lead. The blunt ends of the probes are plugged into sockets at the bottom of the device and these are used to feed information into the meter. The sharp ends of the probes are then touched gently to the devices, such as batteries or resistors. Figure 17.2 shows the meter and the plug-in points for the probes. Note that in this figure, the meter is in the OFF position so there is no readout visible on the LCD screen.

Figure 17.2: Multi-meter with Leads

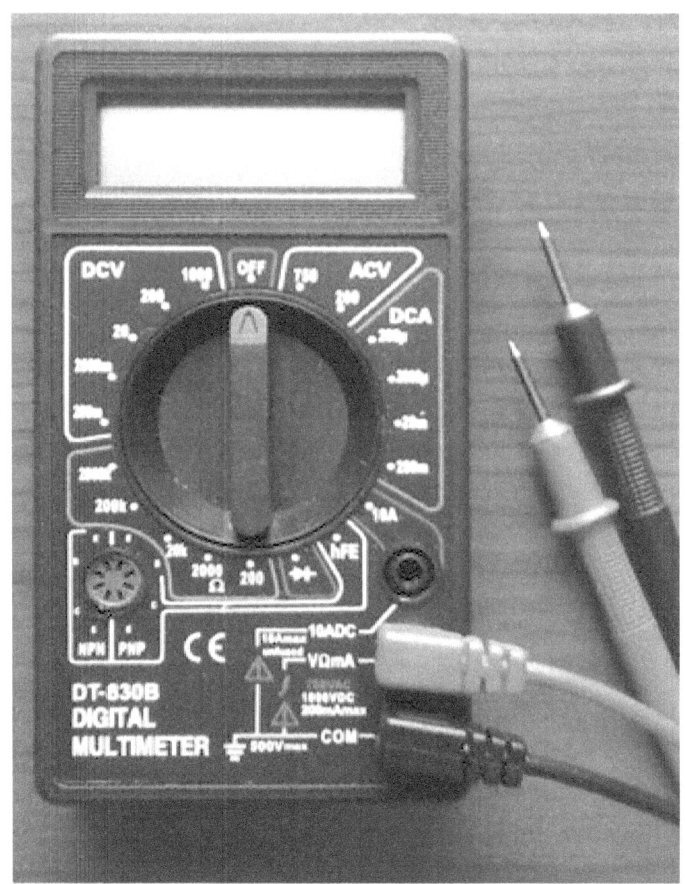

With this simple multi-meter, we can see that the scale for measuring DC voltage is contained in the DCV band in the upper left rotation of the dial. The scale for measuring AC voltage is in the narrow band just to the right of the OFF position. The band labeled DCA is a DC current measurement scale. The band in the lower left range of the dial is used to measure resistance. It is, again, important to remember that if you are going to be measuring high AC/DC voltages to first set the switch to the highest range and then slowly increment down as needed to avoid damaging the meter. As a point of information, the multi-meter shown here will do select measurements on transistors and diodes, but we will not be exploring those options in this article. Finally, shown in Figure 17.2 are the positions of the leads that are plugged into the appropriate jacks. Notice that the positive (Red) lead is plugged into the VΩmA, the center of the three jacks and the negative (Black) lead is plugged into the COM jack. This is a fairly standard arrangement for measuring small voltages and resistance values, so it is suitable for our purposes. If you intend to use the multi-meter for other purposes such as measuring voltages above 240 volts or currents in excess of 200mA, consult the Operator's Instruction Manual included with your multi-meter.

Once the battery has been installed and the leads plugged into the appropriate jacks on the multi-meter, we can do a quick check of the device by rotating the dial two places either direction to a common voltage setting. We should see a 00.0 value appear on the LCD screen. If we turn only one position to the left or right, we will see a small "HV" and a set of random numbers that slowly settle to 000. Occasionally we may see a flashing negative sign as well. This is normal for the model used in the demonstrations hereafter.

When a measurement scale is selected and a range is established we can turn the dial to the appropriate position on the multi-meter, connect the red lead to the positive end of our subject and the black to the negative end. The value we are attempting to measure should appear on the LCD screen. Figure 17.3 shows how the meter can be used to measure the voltage of a new 9-volt battery.

Figure 17.3: Meter in Test Mode and Measuring a 9-volt Battery

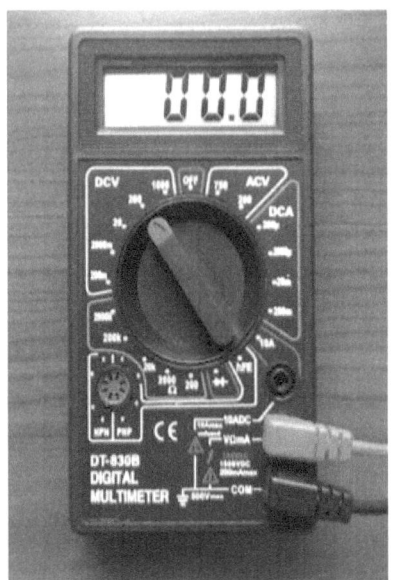 

Notice that when we turn the dial two positions to the left, where the setting is 200, what we are doing is preparing the meter to read a value that ranges anywhere from 0 to 200 DC volts. In the photo on the right, we have turned the switch three places to the left. By doing this, we have prepared the meter to measure up to 20 volts. This is appropriate because we expect a value of approximately 9 volts. As you can see in the photo, touching the red lead to the positive pole on the 9-volt battery (the solid circular lead) and the black lead to the negative pole of the battery (the perforated hexagonal socket), we get a reading of 9.26 volts.

We can now experiment a bit by attempting to verify that connecting batteries in series adds the voltage values. When we connect batteries in series, it is basically like arranging the batteries end-to-end, such that the negative pole of one battery touches the positive pole of the next. All batteries would be facing the same direction so that the "pressures" accumulate. Figure 17.4 illustrates how two 9-volt batteries can be connected in series by using an alligator clip to connect the positive pole of one battery to the negative pole of the next. We then connect the red lead of the multimeter to the positive lead of the first battery and the negative lead of the second. As we can see, the reading does indeed indicate that the values of the two batteries accumulate to a total of 18.50 volts. The equation defining this is as follows: $V_t = V_1 + V_2 + \cdots V_k$

Figure 17.4: Voltage Accumulation Resulting from 9-volt Batteries Connected in Series

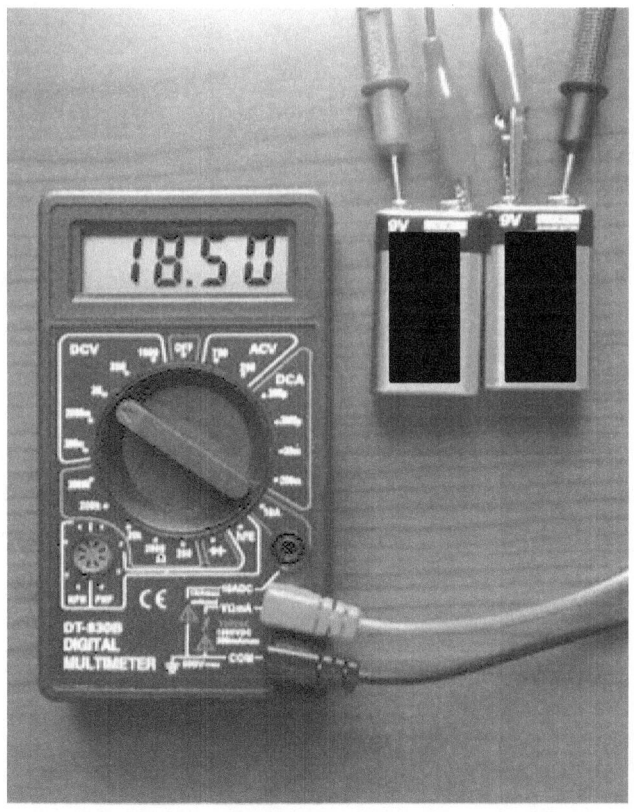

If we were to connect a third battery in this series, we would need to remember to change the setting on our multi-meter one position to the right because we would expect to exceed a voltage measurement of 20 volts. In doing so, we lose a position behind the decimal from our measurement. For example, if we connected three 9-volt batteries in series that had an exact voltage of 27.76 volts, our meter would read 27.8 volts since the meter would now need to round the value. There are a number of other experiments we can do with measuring voltage as well, but for now, we will move on to measuring resistance.

Resistance, as previously described, is analogous to friction for a sliding object. If we have an object that slides easily over a surface, that surface would probably have a fairly low coefficient of kinetic friction. As friction increases, the object becomes more difficult to slide; hence, we might say there is more *resistance* in sliding the object. The same is true with electrical resistance. Most physical mediums or devices cause *friction* for electricity. In fact, the electrical components we call resistors are not the only electrical components that resist the flow of electricity. Every electronic component provides resistance of some kind. Even the wires through which electricity flows impose a resistance component.

For proper resistors, meaning an electronic device deliberately designed for manipulating resistance, the resistance values can be measured by connecting the leads of the multi-meter to the ends of the resistor. We can also determine resistance by examining a color code on the resistor itself. Most common resistor components have a 4, 5, or 6-bar color code that provides the resistance value information and the tolerances of the component. Figure 17.5 illustrates a color code table for evaluating resistance.

Figure 17.5: Resistor Color Code Chart

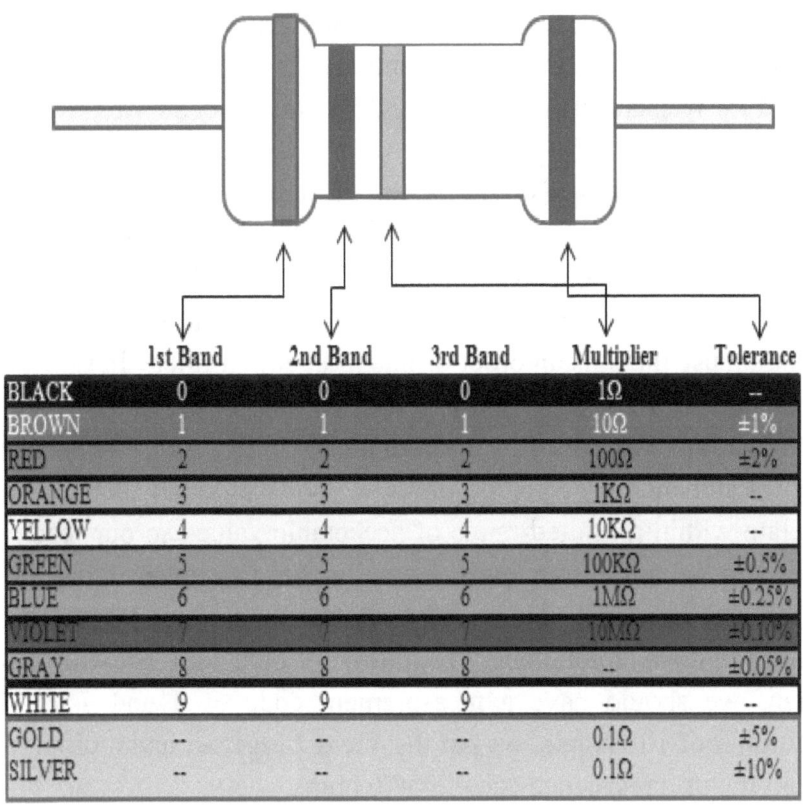

	1st Band	2nd Band	3rd Band	Multiplier	Tolerance
BLACK	0	0	0	1Ω	--
BROWN	1	1	1	10Ω	±1%
RED	2	2	2	100Ω	±2%
ORANGE	3	3	3	1KΩ	--
YELLOW	4	4	4	10KΩ	--
GREEN	5	5	5	100KΩ	±0.5%
BLUE	6	6	6	1MΩ	±0.25%
VIOLET	7	7	7	10MΩ	±0.10%
GRAY	8	8	8	--	±0.05%
WHITE	9	9	9	--	--
GOLD	--	--	--	0.1Ω	±5%
SILVER	--	--	--	0.1Ω	±10%

If we are only interested in measuring simple resistance with our multi-meter, the tolerance band on the right end of the resistor is of little consequence to us. That is to say, the resistor is not going to be incorporated into a circuit so we don't really care about the tolerance as long as we can get a fairly accurate reading from our multi-meter.

The example shown in Figure 17.5 has been placed such that the gold tolerance band is on the right end, and this is generally the configuration we use when reading the color bands. To evaluate the resistance, we read the bands from left to right. Because the resistor in Figure 17.5 is only a 4-band resistor, the first two bands represent resistance magnitudes and the third band represents a multiplying factor. If we are reading a 5-band resistor, the first three bands would be resistance magnitudes and the fourth band would be the multiplier.

The sample resistor at the top of Figure 17.5 has color bands showing Red, Blue, and Orange. Using these three bands together we can see that the colors correspond to values of 2, 6, and 3. Based on these values, we can put the 2 and 6 together in sequence as 26 and then use the 3 as an order of magnitude multiplier. In short, the third bar tells us how many zeros to add to the initial 2-digit combination. As a result, we can multiply 26 by 1,000. This means our resistor measures 26,000 ohms. Also, remember that resistors operate within a limited range of acceptable values so our readings may vary slightly from one resistor to the next even if the color bands are the same. Figure 17.6 shows the readout for a 4-band resistor with a color code of Yellow, Violet, and Brown. This means we should have a measurement code of 4 and 7 with a multiplier of 10. Again, we put the 4 and 7 together and multiply by 10 giving us a resistance value of 470 ohms.

Figure 17.6: 470-ohm Resistor

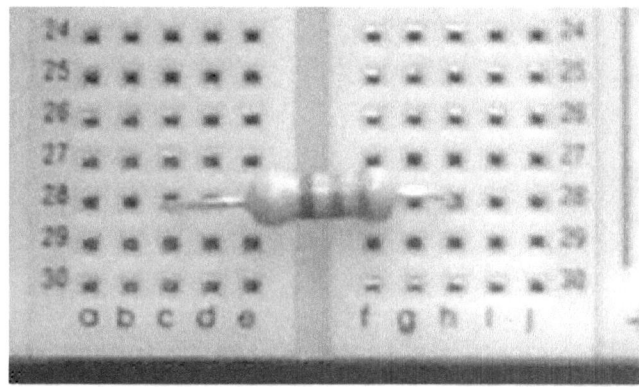

When measuring this resistor with our multi-meter to verify the resistance, we should get something close to 470 ohms, but it may not be exact. To take the measurement, we touch the leads from the meter to the wires on the opposite ends of the resistor, making sure that the contacts are solid. The meter will then slowly settle to its final reading.

An effective way to hold the resistor is by plugging it into a breadboard. As you can see in Figure 17.6, our resistor is plugged into the breadboard in row 28. The resistor wire on the left can be plugged into any one of the sockets on the left hand side, while the wire on the right can go into any of the sockets on the right. The channel in the middle of the breadboard keeps the two sides from being connected, so electricity can only travel from one side of the breadboard to the other through the component we are measuring. Our meter leads can also be inserted into any of the breadboard sockets in row 28. This will allow us to take a reading without even touching the resistor wires. Figure 17.7 shows the measurement of the 470 ohm resistor.

Figure 17.7: Multi-Meter Reading for a 470 Ohm Resistor

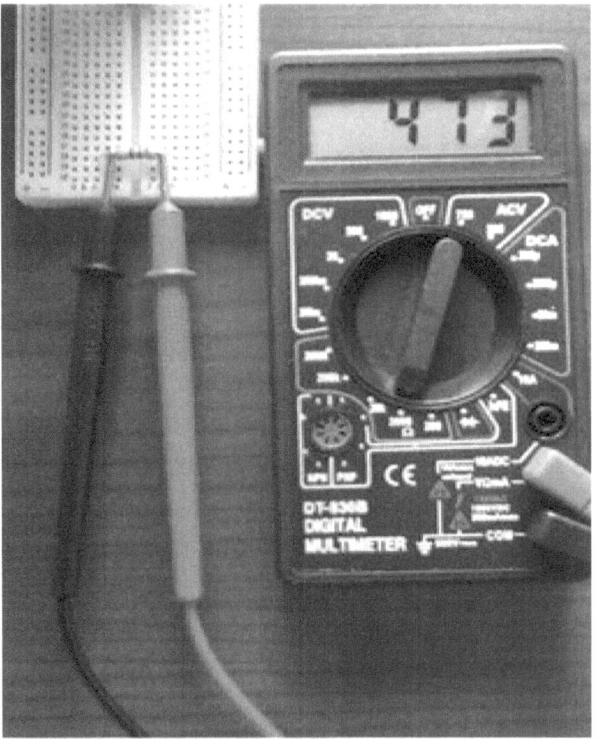

As we can see from the photograph in Figure 17.7, the resistor from Figure 17.6 reads 473 ohms. This is considered an acceptable reading because the value would ordinarily be rounded to 470 ohms based on the first two color bands. The more color bands there are on the resistor, the more precisely the component will function. In this case, our measurement is accurate to within less than ±1% of specifications.

Recall that when we measured voltages, we were able to connect a pair of 9-volt batteries in series. As we know, the voltage shown on our multi-meter represented a sum of the voltages of the two batteries being measured. In our next example, we can see that resistors work in a similar fashion. To demonstrate this fact, let us measure two resistors placed end to end. We will begin by arranging the resistors on the breadboard in an L shaped pattern so we can be certain the resistors are connected in series and there will be no interference from connecting too many components to one row of the breadboard. In this example, we are going to use the 470 ohm resistor from the previous section and connect it in series with resistor having a color code showing Brown, Black, and Red. The resistance measurement on this particular resistor should read approximately 1,000 ohms. If our addition rule holds true, putting the two components together in series should give us a measurement of approximately 1,470 ohms based on the specifications of the components we are using.

As we can see from Figure 17.8, the multi-meter reading is 1450 ohms, which is slightly less than what the combination of color bands indicate. The summing factor of arranging resistors in series does, however, seem to hold true. We can easily explain the differences in measurement and component specifications as falling into acceptable tolerances because we are accurate to within ±1.4% of specifications. Therefore, we can define an equation for total resistance thusly: $R_t = R_1 + R_2 + \cdots R_k$

Figure 17.8: Measurement of Resistors Connected in Series

At first glance, resistor circuits appear to have a rather unique phenomenon when we begin evaluating the outputs. Connecting resistors in series yielded no surprises; however, if we connect resistors side-by-side (parallel) as opposed to end-to-end, we tend to get some unexpected readings.

Most of us would assume that because we are using two resistors rather than one that the total resistance would be greater than either of the individual resistors working alone irrespective of how they are connected. This, however, is not the case. When resistors are connected in parallel, the resistance is shared between the two components in a way similar to how two bridges arranged side-by-side would allow more cars to pass than either bridge would if it were the only path. From this example, it appears that the overall resistance provided by parallel resistors in a circuit could lower the resistance below the specified values of either of the resistors in the circuit.

In the example illustrated in Figure 17.9, we can see that the multi-meter leads are touching both resistor wires at each end. This measurement allows us to see how the two components work together, but the output is counterintuitive as described. We will again use resistors specified at 1000 ohms and 470 ohms and arrange them in parallel. From the photograph, we can see that the resistors are now arranged side-by-side and that the leads of the multi-meter are touching both resistor wires at each end. The meter reading shows 320 ohms of resistance. This is because the parallel arrangement of resistors sums resistance in a reciprocal fashion. To complete our calculation, we will use the following equation based on color code specifications:

$$R_t = \frac{1}{\frac{1}{R_1} + \frac{1}{R_2}} \quad therefore: \quad R_t = \frac{1}{\frac{1}{1000} + \frac{1}{470}} = 319.73$$

Figure 17.9: Meter Reading Parallel Resistance

As we can see, our meter shows a measurement value that is nearly exact based on the specified values coming from our analytic calculation. As you might guess, the parallel resistance rule gives computer and electronics engineers some real leverage in how they design circuits. The appropriate arrangement of components can ultimately create tremendously sensitive systems because the rules governing resistance also apply to other components.

In deriving the formula for parallel resistance, we focus on a comparison of two values. The first is the total resistance in the system. The second is the combined resistance of the two resistors as fractional components of the total resistance. We will define the two resistors as R_1 and R_2. If R_t is the total resistance offered by a parallel circuit using two resistors, then one fraction of the circuit can be defined by R_1 and the other by R_2. Because the resistors are in parallel, the voltage across them must be the same. Knowing this, we can define our system using Ohm's Law:

$$V = I \cdot R_t \quad so \quad V = I_1 \cdot R_1 \quad and \quad V = I_2 \cdot R_2$$

$$I = \frac{V}{R_t} \quad so \quad I_1 = \frac{V}{R_1} \quad and \quad I_2 = \frac{V}{R_2}$$

$$I = I_1 + I_2 \quad so \quad \frac{V}{R_t} = \frac{V}{R_1} + \frac{V}{R_2} \quad and \quad \frac{1}{R_t} = \frac{1}{R_1} + \frac{1}{R_2}$$

$$1 = R_t \left(\frac{1}{R_1} + \frac{1}{R_2}\right) \quad therefore \quad R_t = \frac{1}{\frac{1}{R_1} + \frac{1}{R_2}}$$

With the combination of the *series* rule and the *parallel* rule, we can combine the calculation processes and reverse them to determine the necessary component array for a circuit designed to exact specifications. Mathematically, Ohm's Law defines the underlying structure for many calculations dealing with voltage, current, and resistance, so much of understanding circuits is really about understanding the algebra that governs various components.

Our next step in this process is to look at the linear nature of resistance based on the relationship between the quantity of resisting material and the resistance measurement. We will begin this part of the investigation with a piece of paper and a no. 2 pencil. Our paper and pencil will not be used to take notes or make calculations. Instead, we are going to draw two long, thin rectangles. The dimensions of our rectangles are significant so we will need to be fairly careful as we outline them. The first should be to be at least 21 cm long and 1 cm wide. The second should be at least 21 cm long and 2 cm wide. We will then shade the entire enclosed region of both rectangles with a thick layer of graphite from the pencil. Finally, we will label the long side of both rectangles in centimeters.

In this experiment, we are going to make several resistance measurements on our graphite covered rectangles. What we will discover is that resistance is a near linear measurement based on the amount of graphite separating the leads of the multi-meter. There are, of course, several variables that we cannot control which make our experimental conditions inconsistent (i.e. the graphite layer may vary in thickness because we do not have a way to guarantee exact thickness over the entire length of the rectangle). This will result in measurements that are not exactly linear, but for the most part, we will see resulting measurements that are fairly predictable.

Figures 17.10a-17.10d show the resistance on a 1cm wide graphite shaded line where the meter leads are 5, 10, 15, and 20cm apart.

Figure 17.10a: Meter Readings on a 1cm x 5cm Line

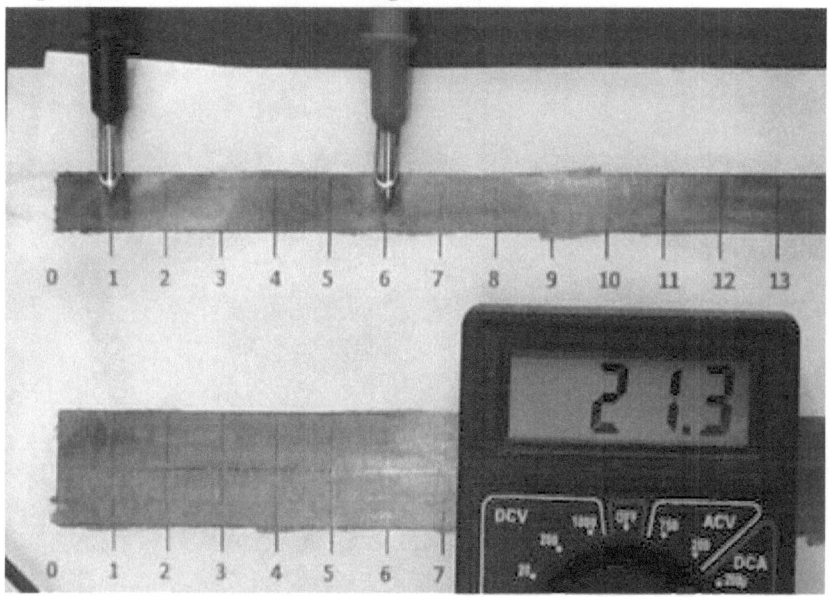

Figure 17.10b: Meter Readings on a 1cm x 10cm Line

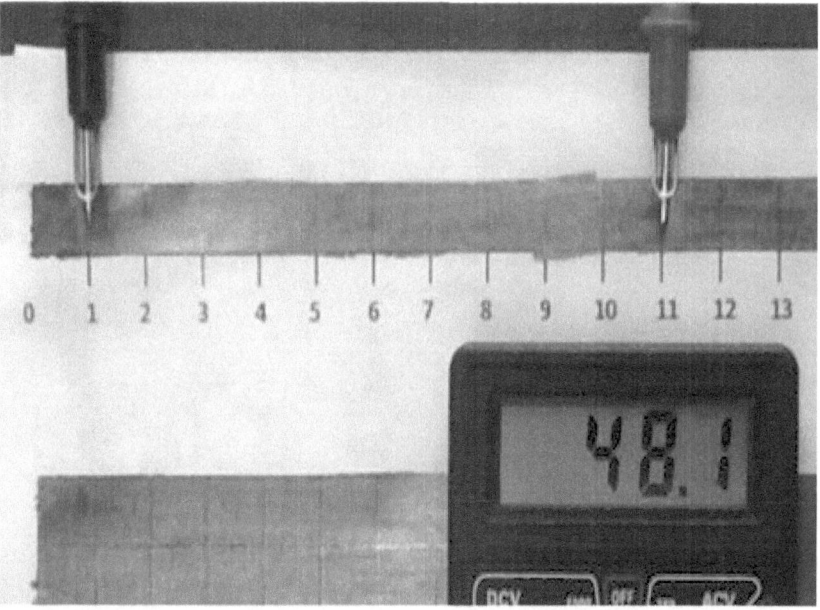

Figure 17.10c: Meter Readings on a 1cm x 15cm Line

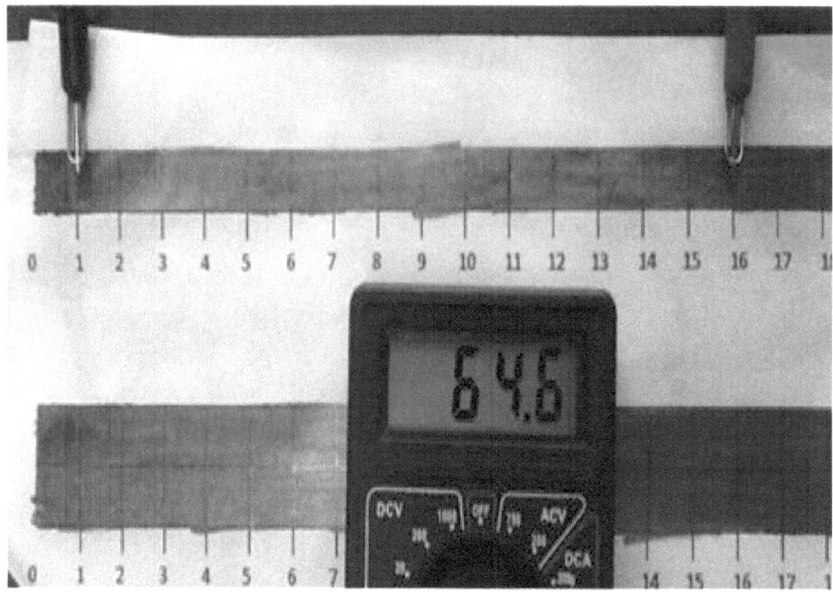

Figure 17.10d: Meter Readings on a 1cm x 20cm Line

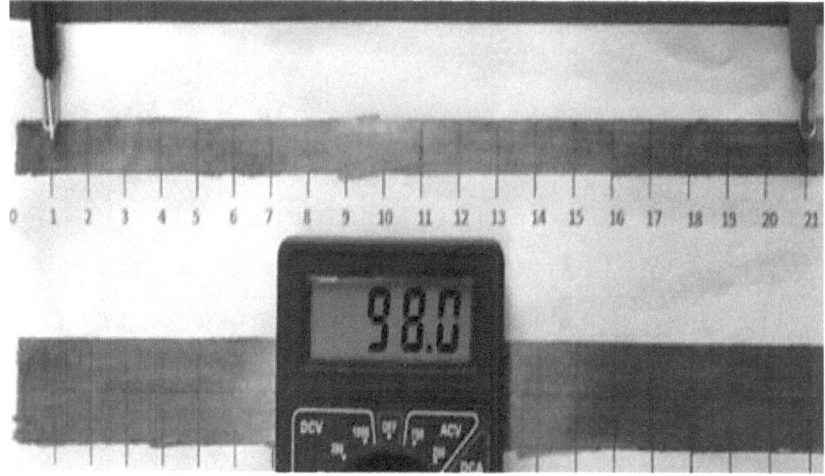

Our resistance measurements of 21.3, 48.1, 64.6, and 98 indicate a fairly linear progression. If we were to define a regression line based on the lowest and highest measurement, we could model the resistance using basic algebra. We begin with a general point/slope form of a line and then define points based on resistance being a function of distance:

point/slope form of a regression line

$$y - y_1 = m(x - x_1)$$

using the points (5, 21.3) and (20, 98)

$$y - 21.3 = \frac{98 - 21.3}{20 - 5}(x - 5)$$

our regression line estimate is

$$y = 5.11x - 4.25$$

testing the equation with the point (3, 48.1)

$$\hat{y} = 5.11(10) - 4.25; \quad \hat{y} = 46.8$$

The error between our measured value and expected value is sufficiently small

$$y - \hat{y} = 1.3$$

As we can see, the regression line is not deterministic based on the measurements we recorded but we do have a fairly reasonable level of prediction given that the error of our test point is relatively small. The same process works for the shaded rectangle that is 2cm in width but we would expect the measurements to be half of what they are on the 1cm wide rectangle.

Our last section of this article is a very brief exposure to circuit diagrams. The language of mathematics has many forms and sometimes it is helpful to see those forms slightly adapted for other uses. In a previous section, we explored *series* and *parallel* resistance; so we are now going to look at those calculations graphically. A circuit diagram is a pictorial representation of circuit. Each component of the circuit has a special symbol. The symbol for a resistor is a short zig-zag line. Within a circuit diagram, the specified operational values are listed next to the components. This means if we have a 220 ohm resistor in our circuit, we can expect to see a 220Ω label by the resistor symbol that carries that value. Figure 17.11 shows a very simple circuit diagram with two resistors, one 220 ohms and the other 100 ohms.

Figure 17.11: Circuit Diagram Showing Resistors in Series

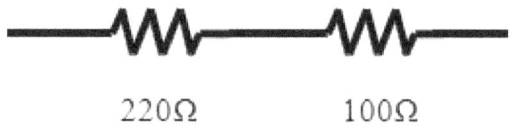

You may recall that resistors connected in series (as they are in Figure 17.11) have a total resistance that is the sum of the resistances in the circuit. In the circuit shown above, the total resistance would be 320 ohms. Circuits can be tremendously complex and can involve a sequence of series and parallel connections that are necessary to allow the other components in a circuit to function as designed. Figure 17.12 illustrates parallel resistance with the same two resistance values.

Figure 17.12: Circuit Diagram Showing Resistors in Parallel

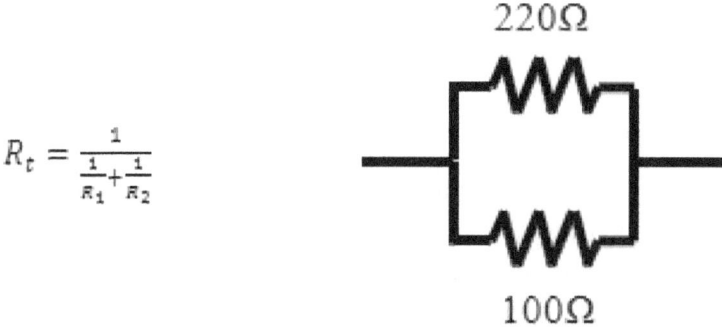

The calculation of total resistance for a parallel circuit such as that in Figure 17.12 is calculated using the formula included in the same Figure. The circuit diagram above represents a total resistance of 68.75 ohms.

Something you may have noticed is that resistance circuits have the same kind of commutative structure as addition itself. In other words, it does not matter in what order we arrange the resistors in our circuit. The total resistance will be the same. Also, remember that we can combine resistors in a sequence of nested parallel and series structures. Figure 17.13 below illustrates an unlabeled diagram of a nested parallel/series circuit.

Figure 17.13: Combination Series/Parallel Resistance Circuit Diagram

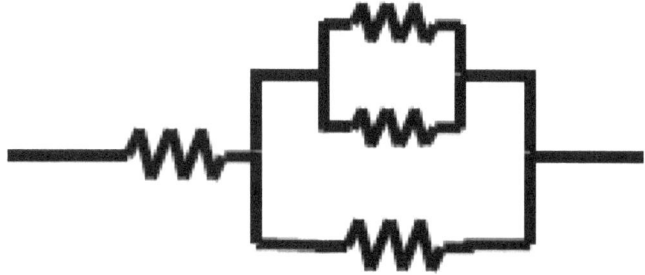

SUMMARY

For the most part, circuits that we find in common household items are much more complex than those illustrated here, but this article is really about connecting the mathematics that is taught in schools in a very deliberate way to computer and electronics engineering technology. Circuitry is in nearly everything with an on/off switch. Measuring the value of scales such as resistance is fundamental to understanding circuits and diagnosing problems. In particular, it is helpful to be able to use measurement devices such as the volt-ohm meter even if you have no interest in electronics. If nothing else, an instrument such as a multi-meter gives us a tool for diagnosing problems that may present safety issues in our homes. Being able to use the multi-meter may even inspire us to look for other measurement devices with a more curious eye.

ADDITIONAL READINGS

Floyd, T.L., & Buchia, D.L. (2009). Electronics Fundamentals: Circuits, Devices & Applications, 8th Ed. Prentice Hall. ISBN: 978-0135072950

McWhorter, G., & Evans, A.J. (2000). Basic Electronics. Master Publishing Inc. RadioShack Series 62-1394.

Mims, F.M. (2003). Getting Started in Electronics. Master Publishing Inc. ISBN: 978-0945053286

Platt, C. (2009). Make: Electronics. O'Reilly Media. ISBN 978-0596153748

ARTICLE 18: OPTICS AND THE GEOMETRY OF LIGHT

ABSTRACT: The article contained hereafter explores *geometrical optics* including reflection and refraction of natural light. Specifically, mathematical elements of reflection and refraction through glass lenses and mirrors are described in the context of geometrical optics. In this context, geometry describes factors of refraction and reflection that allow us to estimate image placement, focal distances, and measuring the speed of light.

INTRODUCTION

Most simply put, optics is a branch of physics that deals with the behavior of portions of the electromagnetic spectrum, including visible light, ultraviolet light, and infrared light. The study of optics is largely about the properties of light, but it also describes how light interacts with matter and how mechanical and electromagnetic instruments can use, detect, or manipulate light. These aspects of science have been significant in the development of energy, space exploration, national defense, and other industries, but let us start this investigation a bit earlier. That is to say, humankind's investigation of light, like so many of the other topics in this book, starts with an interesting history.

The scientific and social writings of many ancient cultures include excerpts on the ideas of reflection and refraction, though, they did not use those terms formally. These ancient civilizations noticed rainbows and even developed what we might roughly refer to as *optical lenses* using polished crystal or quartz as far back as 500 BCE. Early scientists even used transparent containers of water as lenses because they noticed that certain images could be manipulated based on how these containers were positioned with respect to their eyes. Keep in mind that historians believe the properties of rainbows had already been observed and that colored light was under investigation by early scientists, so light was an early source of fascination for many cultures.

One of the more fascinating stories about the early manipulations of light was how Archimedes of Syracuse (c. 212 BCE), destroyed enemy ships with heat from reflected mirrors focused into the paths of approaching ships. Since then, the attempt to use light as a weapon has been a popular notion.

The story of Archimedes' "heat ray" is largely disputed as impossible given the technology of the time. The general conditions necessary to make such a weapon plausible is also a matter of debate simply from a practicality standpoint. Nevertheless, a number of tests of Archimedes heat ray have been carried out in an attempt to replicate the intended results. The most notable was conducted by Greek scientists in the early 1970's. The experiment was done at the Skaramagas naval base outside Athens, Greece. In this experiment, 70 mirrors were used. They were each covered with a copper coating and each about three feet by five feet in dimensions. This was thought to be plausible based on the materials and technology of the time. The mirrors were then aimed at a mock Roman ship constructed of plywood and tar and placed at a distance of approximately 50 meters. When the mirrors were focused, the ship reportedly burst into flames within only a few seconds. Other attempts to replicate the experiment, however, have been largely unsuccessful. Scientists from MIT (2005) and even *MythBusters* (2006 and 2010) have suggested that the weapon probably would have been unsuccessful based on very limited heat production and the extended amount of time it took to generate it.

It was not long after, that the implications of using light to manipulate vision became a popular area of interest for the great scientific philosophers. Though there were earlier historical accounts of the study of light and vision as a part of what we now call optics, one of the most insightful of those accounts came from the Greek mathematician Euclid who wrote a treatise entitled *Optics*. In this manuscript, he connected vision to geometry and in the process define what we generally refer to as *geometrical optics*. Generally, it dealt with the ideas of reflecting light around corners and actually bending light using water.

A number of 17th century mathematicians had a go at describing optics as well. Descartes, Newton, Huygens, and Hooke all published papers and debated over the nature of light and optics. It was Albert Einstein, however, that quantified light itself and paved the way for much of the advancement in theoretical physics related to the properties of light. In fact, it is commonly believed that Einstein received the Nobel Prize for his Special Theory of Relativity when, in fact, it was his writings on the theory of the photoelectric effect. He published the paper in 1905 wherein he explained experimental data that defined the nature of light as being carried in discrete quantized packets. This idea deviated substantially from the wave-effect beliefs about the nature of light. He received the Nobel Prize in physics in 1921 for this work. Since then, the scientific study of light has continued and some creative commercial and industrial products have resulted, such as holographic imaging, laser technology, and ultra-fast optical communication networks.

INVESTIGATION AND NOTES

Our investigation into optics will begin with some basic properties of reflection, but first we need to understand a little bit more about the concept of *geometric optics* versus *physical optics*. Geometric optics differs from physical optics mostly in the way that the properties of light are described. In geometric optics, light is described as a collection of rays that travel in straight lines until they pass through a medium that causes them to bend, or until they strike a reflective surface that causes them to change direction abruptly. In this description, the term *ray* is used somewhat abstractly, particularly in the sense that it is often seen as a vector quantity. In truth, light geometry is much more sophisticated. Physical optics is a much more comprehensive description of the properties of light, but lacks some of the practical aspects of geometric optics that make is useful in the engineering realm.

The optical properties used in this manuscript will focus on geometric optics, starting with the simple idea of *reflection*. Figure 18.1, (on the following page) illustrates the simplest ray-like properties of light using a single ray to describe the most basic understanding of reflection. In this model, light can be treated like a physical object that travels in a straight line, with a constant velocity, toward a surface and then glances off the surface at the same angle at which it strikes the surface. This *reflection* would change the direction, but not the speed of the object. Thus the x and y components of the position of the object are subject to change in direction only; not in speed. We hear this commonly referred to as the angle of incidence equaling the angle of reflection. The glancing surface is called the *incidence line*, the *impact line*, or the *plane of incidence*.

There are a number of methods in which we can mathematically verify the phenomenon of incidence and reflection using component vectors, but the classical approach is simply by inspection. Reflection with mirrors is a concept we have already visited in the article on sextants and astrolabes, but in that article we made assumptions about the reflection properties of light. One of those assumptions was about reflection itself. The angles of incidence and reflection can be looked at in two ways. The most common method is that the angles of incidence and reflection are measured on either side of a Normal Line, which is a line perpendicular to the incidence line. The second and lesser used method is done by measuring the angles of incidence and reflection that are between the rays and the plane of incidence. This second method is often not used in scientific environments because it assumes that the plane of incidence is a real plane. If a reflective medium were to curve on either side of the point of reflection rather than being a plane, the law of reflection as stated would no longer hold.

The inspection approach used here can be supported by looking at vector components of rays as well. In Figure 18.1, the y-component of the light ray impacting the incidence line can be represented by the sine of θ with respect to the normal line (the line perpendicular to the incidence line). Because the magnitude of the unencumbered vector stays constant in the y-direction, we can expect the angle to be equal on each side of the normal line. If the magnitude of the y-component was different after striking the incidence line, then the angle of reflection would have to be different as well. This is illustrated inasmuch as the path of the original vector has the same y-component as the reflected vector at each reflected point across the incidence line.

Figure 18.1: Reflection of a Light Ray

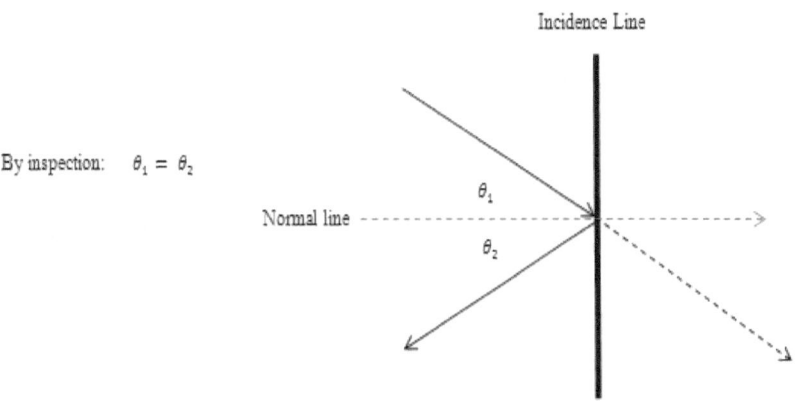

Basic reflection is very simple to understand by inspection, but the physics of optics become more complex very quickly. Reflection is much more complex than simply looking at the behavior of a pair of rays or vectors representing bouncing light. Reflections have two types: *specular reflection* and *diffuse reflection*. Specular reflection is typically what is shown in diagrams where a light ray is bouncing off of some reflective surface. The advantage of specular reflection is that it can be described in geometrically defined spaces such that the images can be associated with a set of ordered triples that represent locations in space. This property allows us to predict the direction of light after any number of reflections, or even manipulate a light ray into reaching an intended location in space by adjusting the angle of the reflected surfaces with respect to one another. Diffuse reflection, on the other hand, describes the behavior of light as it reflects off of opaque surfaces such as grass or snow. Reflections from these types of surfaces are more difficult to describe with geometric properties. Yet they are important in mirror optics because without diffuse reflection, we could not assume that an original image produces light rays that could be reflected in the first place.

In the applied world, light is commonly reflected and refracted simultaneously. For example, if we look into a still body of water, we can see a reflection of the sky or maybe even of ourselves, but we may also be able to see what is in the water. However, as you may have noticed, the location of an object in the water is sometimes difficult to determine because light travels through water at a different speed than it does through the atmosphere. This causes a *bending* effect. In short, when a ray of light hits the boundary between two transparent mediums (such as air and water), it is separated into both reflected and refracted rays. How much the light bends depends on the index of *refraction* that represents the change in mediums through which the light is traveling. The law of refraction states that a refracted ray bends at the point of incidence with respect to a normal line and that the quotient of the sine of the angles on either side of the point of incidence results in a constant, which we call the index of refraction. Figure 18.2 illustrates the basic idea of refraction of a ray of light.

(Diagram can be found on the following page)

Figure 18.2: Refracted Ray of Light

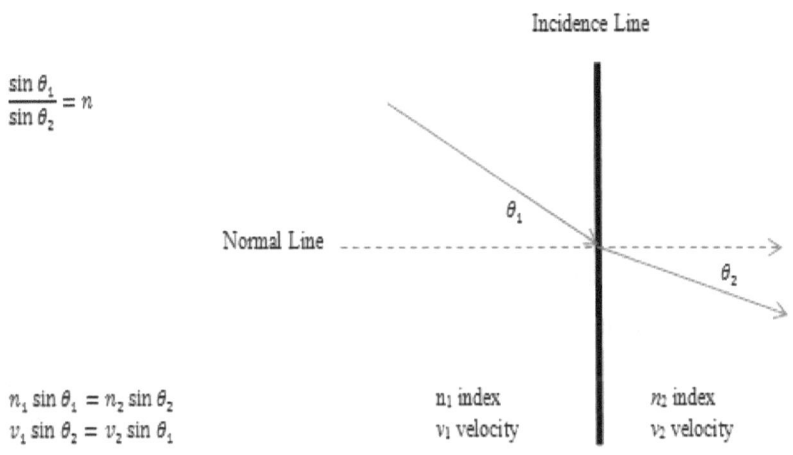

$\dfrac{\sin \theta_1}{\sin \theta_2} = n$

$n_1 \sin \theta_1 = n_2 \sin \theta_2$
$v_1 \sin \theta_2 = v_2 \sin \theta_1$

n_1 index
v_1 velocity

n_2 index
v_2 velocity

The value of a refraction index represented by n depends on how drastically a given material changes the speed of light. The speed of light in a vacuum is approximately 3.0×10^8 meters per second; roughly 186,000 miles per second. The change between light traveling through air and subsequently into water can be extreme, but simple diagrams do not really illustrate what light looks like when it bends from this transition in mediums. Nevertheless, refraction of this nature is what allows optical lenses to work. The two equations in the lower left of Figure 18.2 are versions of Snell's Law where n_1 and n_2 are calculated refraction indices and v_1 and v_2 are known velocities through the mediums on either side of the incidence line. Essentially, changes in the angles of the light ray, with respect to the normal line, gives us information about the refractive indices and the respective velocities of the light through each medium. In fact, the knowledge of the refractive indices of two paired mediums allows us to roughly calculate the speed of light based on measuring where objects appear versus where they are actually placed.

Now, let us look at one of the more curious aspects of reflection and refraction. Have you ever noticed that if you look into a reflective spoon at a certain distance, you may see an inverted image of yourself? This property is true with any regular concave reflector, but you have to be at the proper distance to see the inverted image because the focal distance of a reflector is dependent on the degree of concavity. Highly concave reflectors, for example, have very short focal distances whereas slight concavity results in more extreme focal distances.

If you experiment with your reflection in a spoon, starting very close to your eye, your reflection will be right-side-up but it will also be a bit distorted because of the concavity of the reflective surface. As you slowly move the spoon away from your eye, the image becomes more distorted until it finally comes back into focus, but upside down. Again, the distance at which the image becomes inverted depends on the concavity of the spoon. Slightly concave mirrors invert images at a greater distance because the focal point is farther away, which means for some concave reflection, the point of inversion may be farther away from the reflective surface than the actual image. The reason that images in a concave reflector invert is simply based on the geometric path of the light rays. Figure 18.3 illustrates the basic properties of reflection from a concave mirror.

Figure 18.3: Inverted Image from a Concave Mirror

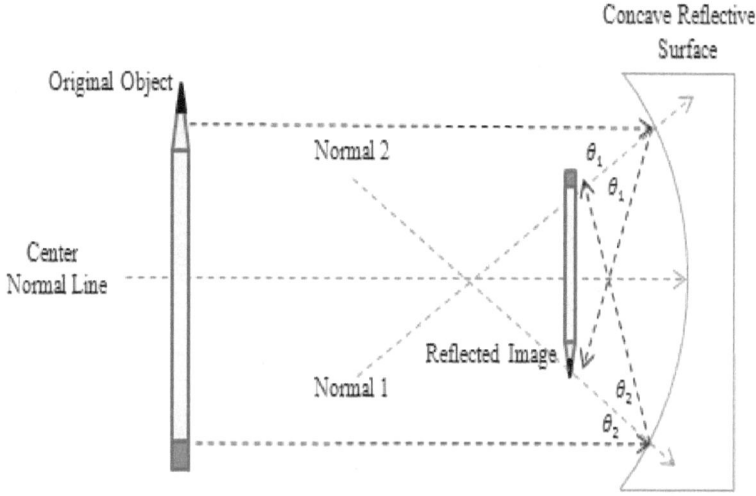

Note that the concavity in the reflective surface represented in Figure 18.3 is fairly pronounced. This means that the focal point is going to be close to the surface. When the image inverts, it does so based on reflective light from the original image of the pencil. When those light rays hit the surface of our mirror, the incidence angle and the reflection angle are the same with respect to the normal line at the point of incidence. However, the angle of the normal line is changing at each point on the mirror because the surface is curved. In our figure above, we can see how the top and bottom of the pencil are inverted based on the reflective angles θ_1 and θ_2.

A question we might ask at this point is what if our surface was transparent instead of reflective? If designed properly, a transparent device that produces converging or diverging light rays based on refractive properties is called a *lens*. For the most part, common forms of lenses include *convex lenses*, which cause light rays to converge at a focal point, and *concave lenses*, which cause light rays to diverge. Predicting how the images from these two types of lenses are formed is similar to how we trace the rays from reflective surfaces such as those shown in Figure 18.3. For example, the two variables of interest in the reflection above are the focal length of the reflective concave mirror and the distance of the original image from the mirror. For our lens equation, we will call the focal length f and the Object distance s_0 and the image distance s_1. Figure 18.4 illustrates a basic ray tracing for a symmetrical bi-convex lens.

Figure 18.4: Ray Tracing for a Basic Lens

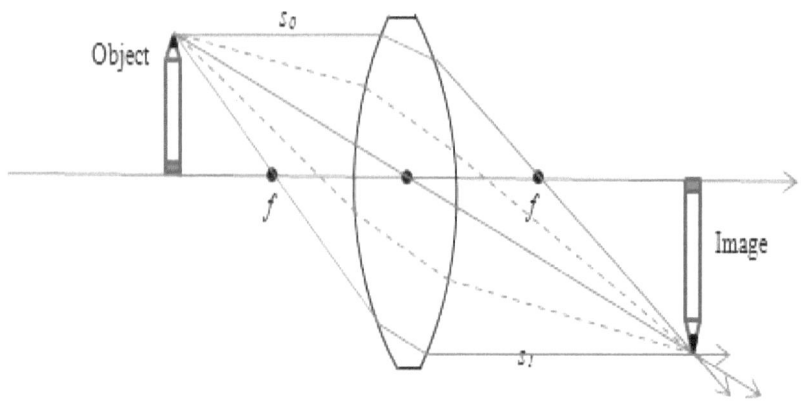

Based on the ray tracing diagram in Figure 18.4, we can determine what is known as the lens maker's equation. $\frac{1}{f} = \frac{1}{s_0} + \frac{1}{s_1}$

This formula can be verified quantitatively by measurement. It is also nice that the same ray tracing technique can be used for different types of lenses and for different locations of the images, objects and focal points. In an extension of this lens maker's equation, we can determine the focal length based on the formula: $\frac{1}{f} = (n-1)\left(\frac{1}{r_1} - \frac{1}{r_2}\right)$ where n is the refractive index and r_1 and r_2 represent the radii of circles use to create the lens. This is a formula for roughly estimating the focal length in air and neglects an important variable, which is the power of the lens.

The focal length formula mentioned the radii of two circles. It turns out that lenses extensively use the geometry of, you guessed it, circles; more specifically, in the Vesica Pisces. Figure 18.5 illustrates how refraction through a lens can be modeled geometrically based on the intersection of two circles that are used to generate the lenses. Note that in some instances, the lenses vary in convexity on each side depending on where the focal point is intended to be.

(Diagram can be found on the following page)

Figure 18.5: Geometrically Modeling the Focal Points and Refraction

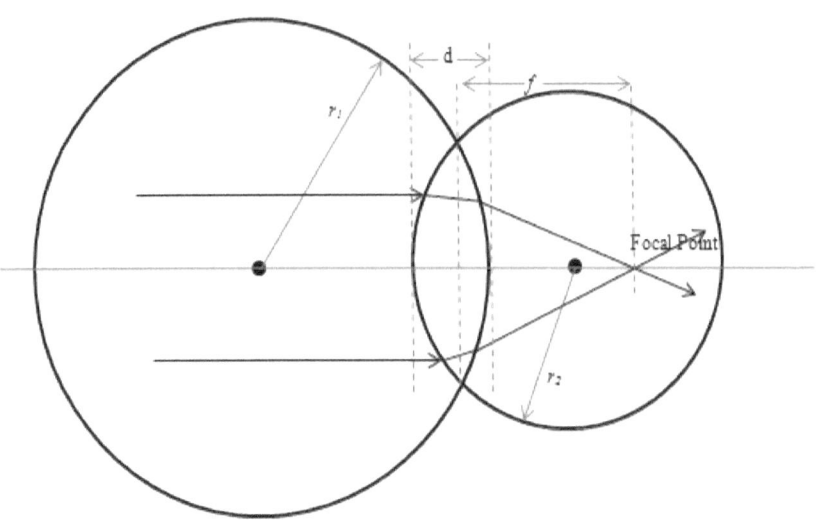

Let us assume that the lens is asymmetrical and represented by the vesica region between the two intersecting circles. The lens has been exaggerated in this figure so we can see all of the critical geometric points. Light rays can be traced through the diagram based on the geometry of circles and calculated thusly for the power of the lens and the focal length (note that the power of the lens and the focal distance are inversely proportional).

$$P = \frac{1}{f} = (n-1)\left[\frac{1}{r_1} - \frac{1}{r_2} + \frac{(n-1)d}{nr_1r_2}\right]$$

If we look back once again at the idea of reflection, we can see that the focal distance is really a critical aspect of optics. For example, parabolic reflectors have a focal point that allow us to channel light rays from the focus point back out in the direction we intend to illuminate. Car headlights use this property by wrapping a parabolic reflector around a light source. The challenge is to create a reflector that optimizes how the light is channeled outward. This means that we need to know the focal distance for a parabola of a given shape and size of a headlight so that the light source is optimized.

Let us suppose for example that we need to create a car headlight that is circular and four inches across at the outside edge of the reflector. The light source is to be inserted through a small hole at the vertex of the parabolic reflector. It must also be inserted at a distance from the vertex such that the center of the illumination is at the focal point based on the cross section of the parabola. Calculating this distance can be achieved by establishing any three desired ordered pairs on a two-dimensional cross section of the parabola. We then use a system of equations to find the quadratic function that produces the shape of the desired reflector. From there, we can find the focal distance as a matter of calculation. Figure 18.6 illustrates how the equation of a parabolic reflector with four inch diameter can be derived.

Figure 18.6: Derivation of a Parabolic Reflector

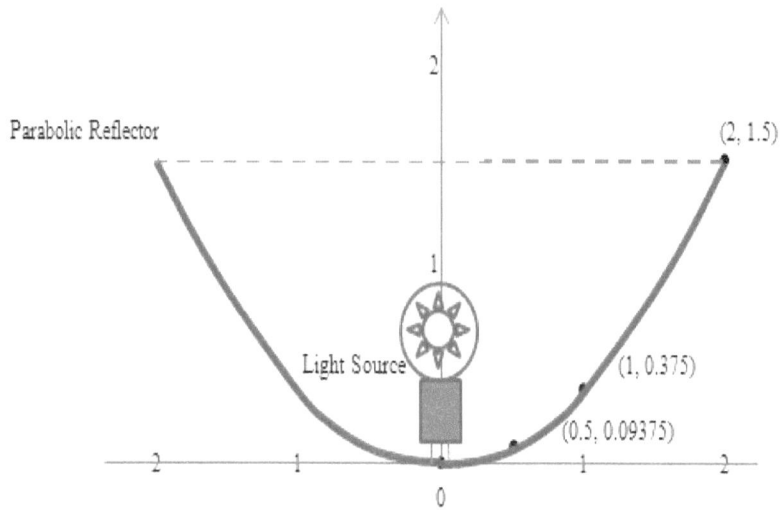

As you can see, we greatly simplify the process by placing the vertex of the parabolic section at the origin of the graph. This allows us to effectively eliminate translational coefficients in our final equation. We will use the points given on the graph based on the dimensions of our parabolic reflector, specifically the points (0.5, 0.09375), (1, 0.375), and (2, 1.5). We can now build a system of equations based on our points. We define the equations by substituting the x-values of each point.

The base function of a quadratic form

$$f(x) = ax^2 + bx + c$$

using the point (0.5, 0.09375)

$$0.09375 = 0.25a + 0.5b + c$$

using the point (1, 0.375)

$$0.375 = 1a + 1b + c$$

using the point (2, 1.5)

$$1.5 = 4a + 2b + c$$

Using an augmented matrix, we will then solve the system of equations to determine the coefficients for our quadratic equation in the resulting linear system. This will, in turn, allow us to calculate the focal distance for the light source in the parabolic reflector.

(-4)Row1 + Row 2 → Row 2

$$\begin{bmatrix} 1 & 1 & 1 & | & 0.37500 \\ 4 & 2 & 1 & | & 1.50000 \\ 0.25 & 0.5 & 1 & | & 0.09375 \end{bmatrix}$$

Row 1/(-4) + Row 3 → Row 3

$$\begin{bmatrix} 1 & 1 & 1 & | & 0.37500 \\ 0 & -2 & -3 & | & 0.00000 \\ 0.25 & 0.5 & 1 & | & 0.09375 \end{bmatrix}$$

Row 2/(-2) → Row 2; (4)Row 3 → Row 3

$$\begin{bmatrix} 1 & 1 & 1 & | & 0.37500 \\ 0 & -2 & -3 & | & 0.00000 \\ 0 & 0.25 & 0.75 & | & 0.00000 \end{bmatrix}$$

Row 2 − Row 3 → Row 3

$$\begin{bmatrix} 1 & 1 & 1 & | & 0.37500 \\ 0 & 1 & 1.5 & | & 0.00000 \\ 0 & 1 & 3 & | & 0.00000 \end{bmatrix}$$

Row 3/(-1.5) → Row 3

$$\begin{bmatrix} 1 & 1 & 1 & | & 0.37500 \\ 0 & 1 & 1.5 & | & 0.00000 \\ 0 & 0 & -1.5 & | & 0.00000 \end{bmatrix}$$

(-1.5)Row 3 + Row 2 → Row 2

$$\begin{bmatrix} 1 & 1 & 1 & | & 0.37500 \\ 0 & 1 & 1.5 & | & 0.00000 \\ 0 & 0 & 1 & | & 0.00000 \end{bmatrix}$$

(-1)Row 3 + Row 1 → Row 1

$$\begin{bmatrix} 1 & 1 & 1 & | & 0.37500 \\ 0 & 1 & 0 & | & 0.00000 \\ 0 & 0 & 1 & | & 0.00000 \end{bmatrix}$$

(-1)Row 2 + Row 1 → Row 1

$$\begin{bmatrix} 1 & 1 & 0 & | & 0.37500 \\ 0 & 1 & 0 & | & 0.00000 \\ 0 & 0 & 1 & | & 0.00000 \end{bmatrix}$$

a = 0.375, b = 0, c = 0

$$\begin{bmatrix} 1 & 0 & 0 & | & 0.37500 \\ 0 & 1 & 0 & | & 0.00000 \\ 0 & 0 & 1 & | & 0.00000 \end{bmatrix}$$

The matrix solution resulting from the row reduction echelon leaves us with the quadratic equation: $f(x) = 0.375x^2$. We can now calculate the focal distance using the formula $c = 1/4a$ where the variable c represents the focal distance and the variable a represents the quadratic coefficient. This gives us a focal distance of 2/3 of an inch, which is suitably represented by the light source in Figure 18.6.

Reflection is central to the study of optics, not simply because it supports the ideas of geometry, or even because it allows for the development of many of the tools we use (such as car headlights); but also because the mathematical concepts of reflection are what laid the groundwork for more advanced physics, including early efforts to measure the speed of light. The speed of light however, varies based on the medium through which it is traveling. The refractive index of a medium varies based on the kind of material, the density of the material, and a few other more advanced variables.

We can determine the refractive index of a material using Snell's law of refraction by experimenting with a mechanism as simple as a fish tank. Suppose we want to determine the refractive index of water. We can begin this experiment by filling a small tank of water to a known height. For our purposes, we are going to use 10 inches for the sake of convenience. Figure 18.7 provides an illustration of the parameters of the experiment.

Figure 18.7: Tank of Water Showing Refraction

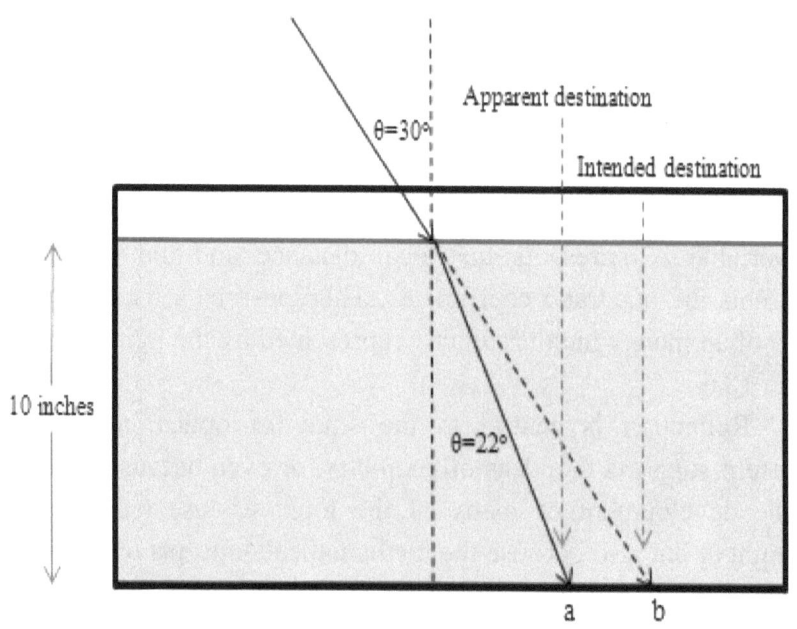

There are several points about this experiment that still need some clarification. First, the tendency of a light ray, as defined in geometrical optics, is to bend toward the perpendicular if it is traveling from a medium with a lower refractive index to a higher one. In Figure 18.7, we can see this tendency as the light ray from a laser pointer is bent toward the dotted perpendicular line during the change in medium from air to water. For our calculation purposes the refractive index of air is 1.000293, which is nearly that of a vacuum. Because we are subject to errors in measurement, however, we will only use the first three decimal digits and call the refractive index of air 1.000. Further, we will assume that the depth of the water in the tank is 10 inches and that the ray of light from our laser pointer is the incidence ray.

We calculate the refractive ray to be bent at 22° from the perpendicular based on the apparent destination of the light hitting the bottom of the tank. This apparent destination is define in Figure 18.7 to occur at *point a,* and is determined by observation from the vantage point of the incidence ray. The intended destination of the light ray on the bottom of the tank is a distance b (defined by point b in the diagram) from the perpendicular line is calculated by b = 10 · tan 30 and should be approximately 5.77 inches. The apparent destination of the light ray is approximately 4 inches. Calculating the arctangent of 0.404 gives us approximately 22°. The intended destination is where the light ray would shine without the interference of the water as an influencing medium. We can now use Snell's law to determine the refractive index of the water. Recall that Snell's Law of Refraction says that $n_1 \sin \theta_1 = n_2 \sin \theta_2$. The n_1 and n_2 variables are the refractive indices. We know that n_1 is the refraction index of air, which we have assigned the value of 1.000. We can then define the refractive index of the water n_2 as the quotient of the sine values of the incidence ray and the refracted ray.

$$n_2 = \frac{\sin \theta_1}{\sin \theta_2} = \frac{\sin 30}{\sin 22}$$

$$n_2 = \frac{0.5}{0.375} = 1.335$$

The calculated value of 1.335 for n_2 is very close to the actual refractive index of water of 1.333. We also not have the ability to calculate the approximately velocity of light through water. Again, we use Snell's Law using the index of refraction of water and the variable c as the speed of light. Our speed of light constant c will be substituted for   Once again we follow Snell's Law using the index of refraction of water and the variable c as the speed of light. Our speed of light constant c will be substituted for v_1 and approximated at 2.9972458 x 108. Again, we use Snell's law using the index of refraction of water and the variable c as the speed of light. Our speed of light constant c will be substituted for v_1 and approximated at 2.9972458×10^8.

$$v_1 \sin \theta_2 = v_2 \sin \theta_1$$

$$v_1 = v_2 \frac{\sin \theta_1}{\sin \theta_2}$$

$$c = v_2 n_2$$

$$v_2 = \frac{c}{n_2}$$

$$v_2 = 2.997245 \times 10^8 / 1.33$$

$$v_2 = 2.253567 \times 10^8$$

SUMMARY

The connection of light and lenses to plane geometry goes well beyond the simple concepts presented in this article. The geometry of light gets so complex, in fact, that two dimensional models can eventually be very difficult to follow. The formulas presented, however, give an effective overview of the basic elements of lenses; those being reflection, refraction, focal length, image position, and lens power. The power of a lens is a geometric function of the refractive index and works somewhat as the last example in bending light to expand or condense an image.

There are other important factors to consider from an engineering standpoint as well, such as the volume of material necessary for manufacturing a lens. This is a rich area of investigation and can also be modeled with circles.

At any rate, the value of lens technology is indisputable whether it be for correcting our vision, communicating through fiber optic links, looking at very small things through a microscope, or indeed, looking out into space with a telescope. It was not so very long ago that contact lenses (named because they are in contact with the eye) did not exist. Telescope technology has continued to improve as well. We can now "see" phenomena in space and gather data that was not available even a decade ago. There are, of course, many applications of reflection and refraction that extend beyond the technology needed for sight and such, but the geometry associated with the many facets of vision is fundamental to understanding the properties of light. From the evolution of Archimedes' ship-burning lenses to advanced telescope technology, we have witnessed a remarkable time in the development of our understanding of light and in the engineering of machines that manipulate light.

ADDITIONAL READINGS

Johnson, B.K. (2011). *Optics and Optical Instruments: An Introduction.* 3rd Edition. Dover Books on Physics, Dover Publications. ISBN: 978-0486606422.

Spero, D. J., & Shipman, G. (1994). Light Reflection and Refraction. Evan-Mohr Educational Publishers. ISBN: 978-1557992949.

Stille, D.R., & Hossain, F. (2005). Manipulating Light: Reflection, Refraction, and Absorption. Compass Point Books. ISBN: 978-0756512581

Waldman, G. (2002). Introduction to Light: The Physics of Light, Vision, and Color. Dover Books on Physics, Dover Publications. ISBN: 978-0486421186.

ARTICLE 19: ENGINEERING MECHANICS (EXPLORATIONS IN STATICS)

ABSTRACT: The following article on engineering mechanics (statics) gives some very basic examples of how vector mathematics and applied linear algebra systems can be used to determine stress points, forces, and static equilibriums in stationary objects such as wall hooks. The statics problems presented herein will also illustrate ways to investigate the real uses of applied engineering mathematics in the design and description of rigid bodies through a process of developing free-body diagrams.

INTRODUCTION

One of the first courses a university-level engineering student will take is in Mechanics - *Statics*. Statics is a substructure of engineering mechanics that deals primarily with forces related to non-moving devices and structures. The subject is often studied through the development of equilibrium problems, which define ways to decompose the various forces acting within a multi-dimensional system so a balance can be analyzed. Statics is highly mathematical, and thus, critical for understanding the discipline that we know is engineering. Nearly all nomenclatures of engineering education require statics as a first course of study because forces are present, in some form, in the design and manipulation of nearly all aspects of the physical world.

As an important part of mechanics, statics is fundamental to understanding the physical forces that influence objects that do not move, but the principles of statics are also foundational to understanding dynamic systems within the broader field of mechanics. In fact, the principles of mechanics are not only critical for research and development processes involving everyday machines, but also for understanding the development of more complex human endeavors that involve vibrations, stability, heat transfer, energy consumption, and even fluid dynamics.

Mechanics (static and dynamic versions) is among the oldest of the physical sciences, and the early history of the physical sciences is recorded largely through engineering endeavors. Some of the earliest recorded writings in what we call mechanics come from Archimedes in his descriptions of the principles of levers. He is often credited with the quote, "Give me a lever long enough and I will move the world." Though the lever could be considered a dynamic tool because it moves, the forces on a lever at any given time can be described through a static equilibrium.

INVESTIGATION AND NOTES

One of the initial steps necessary for understanding statics is to be able to analytically and geometrically quantify and represent forces. We generally know that forces are associated with the colloquial idea of *pressure*. If, for example, we push on something, we are applying a force to the object. What many people do not know, however, is when we apply a force to an object, the object applies a force on us. Knowing this simple fact may help us to conceptualize and answer to the age old question, what happens when an unstoppable force hits an immoveable object? The answer is simple. A static equilibrium happens. The force keeps pushing on the object with a constant magnitude, the object pushes back with an equivalent force magnitude because it is immoveable; and thus, we have our first static equilibrium.

What we do not have yet is a way to quantify the forces succinctly and usefully. We need a short list of rules or conventions for representing forces, so we will create that list heretofore. First however, it is important to note that force expressions in statics have the potential to be defined either analytically or geometrically, which is part of the reason we need some rules for representing them. Both the analytic and the geometric methods of representing forces will use vectors. Finally, because we naturally use x, y, and z axes for graphing in three dimensions, our vectors will be represented with those variables instead of the common i, j, and k components. The following is a list of basic rules for representing vectors. For the most part, the examples illustrated hereafter will focus on the decomposition of forces using these rules.

1) A vector has both magnitude and direction. The magnitude and direction are represented in one equation by using a combination of a scalar quantity and a unit vector indicating the direction of the force, thusly: $\vec{A} = 2\hat{x} + 3\hat{y} - 5\hat{z}$, meaning a vector walking from tail to head is 2 units in the positive x-direction, 3 units in the positive y-direction, and 5 units in the negative z-direction.
2) A vector can (but is not obliged) to move through 3 directions as defined by Euclidean 3-space. For example, a vector moving only in the x direction would have scalar values of zero magnitude for the y and z components.
3) The magnitude and direction of a geometric vector is given by an arrow of given length and direction. The magnitude and direction can be given in either rectangular or polar coordinates.

4) A vector is defined by a symbol with a vector mark such as an arrow over the top of a variable (a vector defined by the variable A would be defined thusly: $\vec{A}$),
5) Vectors can be added or decomposed into parts,
6) Vectors can be *dotted* or *crossed* (meaning a calculation of a dot product or a cross product, each of which defines important values in vector calculations,
7) the magnitude of a vector is given by what looks like absolute value bars (the magnitude of $\vec{A}$ would be defined thusly: $|\vec{A}|$,
8) Vector forces are labeled in pounds or Newtons (named after Isaac Newton and has a label equivalent to kg·m/sec^2). One Newton is about 4.44 pounds.

Although the vector rules listed above may seem like they could be complex, often the most difficult part of statics is accurately defining all of the forces in a *free body diagram* so they can be analyzed and represented by a series of resultant forces. A free body diagram is typically a simple geometric representation that captures the forces and angles acting on a point of interest. We will generally use a method of decomposition to calculate forces such as tensions on cables or springs and directed forces from tools such as levers. Levers, however, also can produce *moments*, which are circular (angular) forces resulting from tools such as wrenches, screwdrivers, and axels.

Recall that any force directed through three dimensions can be decomposed into x, y, and z components, each of which can be written as its own vector. Figure 19.1, however, illustrates the basic decomposition of a vector in two dimensions. Note that the example used in Figure 19.1 is based on a *tension vector*. The force on the string illustrated in this diagram represents a pull in the direction of the arrow. This pull creates measurable forces in the x and y directions, which can be calculated using some basic trigonometry. For our example here, we are ignoring some of the more negligible variables such as the mass and thickness of the string, both of which could have a very small effect on the outcome of the *x* and *y* component calculations, but typically in quantities so small that we tend to ignore them.

Figure 19.1: Decomposition of a Tension Vector

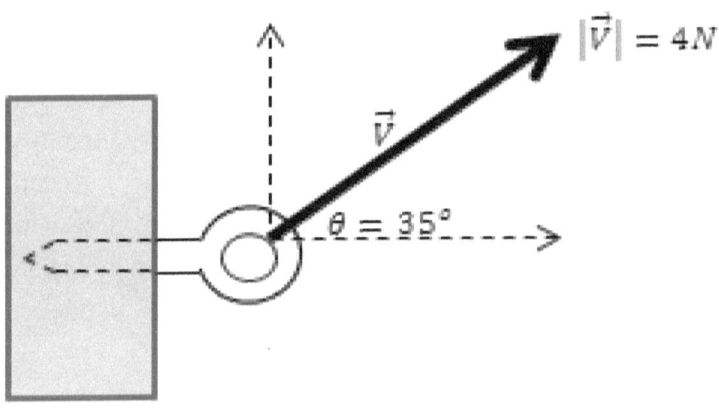

A small eyehook is inserted into a wall bracket. A cable is then attached to the loop and a tension is applied with a magnitude of 4 Newtons at $35°$ with respect to the horizontal. The tension on the cable is represented in Figure 19.1 as a vector, $\vec{V}$. Suppose we want to determine the forces applied to the eyehook in the vertical and horizontal directions. To do this we would decompose the vector using the sine and cosine components of the right triangle created by the string. We label the component vectors with the direction they represent.

$$|\vec{V_x}| = 4 \cdot \cos 35 = 3.277$$

$$|\vec{V_y}| = 4 \cdot \sin 35 = 2.294$$

The magnitude of the tension vector can be checked with the horizontal and vertical components by using the magnitude formula, which is essentially the distance formula used in basic geometry calculations. The same formula can be used when our vectors represent forces applied in three dimensions. Recall that, geometrically, the length of a vector indicates the force it implies. The tension vector itself can also be represented analytically as the component values multiplied by the unit vectors in the x and y directions.

$$|\vec{V}| \approx \sqrt{(3.277)^2 + (2.294)^2}$$

$$\vec{V} = 3.277\hat{x} + 2.294\hat{y}$$

Now that we have a basic example we can use to describe a vector and the resulting decomposition of forces, let us examine a bit more complex arrangement of forces. The following example would represent a simple but fairly authentic statics application.

Suppose we have a mass hanging from a pair of strings suspended between two eye hooks. Our goal is to define the tensions on each string based on the relative position of the mass suspended between them. Figure 19.2 illustrates the arrangement of cables and forces.

Figure 19.2: Mass Hanging between Two Eyehooks

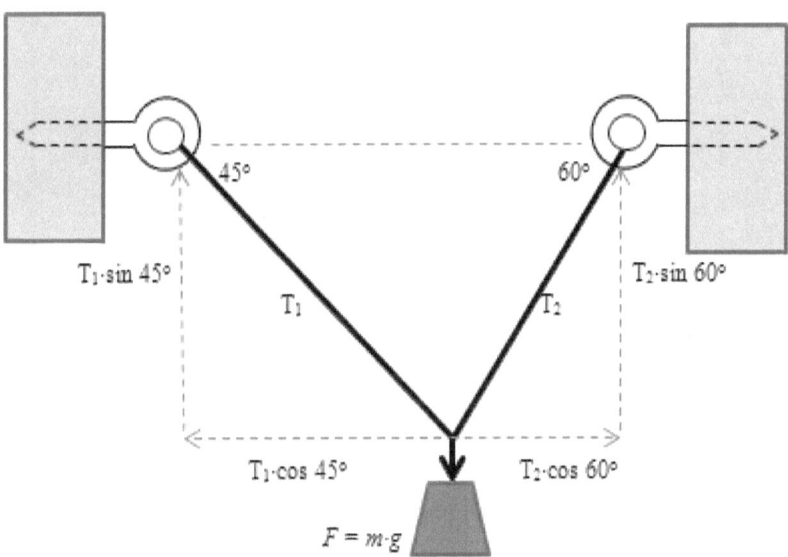

In the scenario proposed in Figure 19.2, the mass hanging from the two eyehooks does not move. Based on this realization, we can call the environment *static* and define a series of forces in the x and y directions that have sum force totals of zero. For example, if string 2 were to be cut, the mass would swing to the left, which means there is a force in the x direction holding it in place. If string 1 were to be cut, the mass would swing to the right for the same reason. Because the mass is not moving, we can conclude that the component forces in the x-direction created by each string are pulling in opposite directions with equivalent magnitudes. The same must be true for the vertical components. Because the mass is not ascending or descending, we can conclude that the y-components that are pulling upward must be equivalent to the magnitude of downward force created by the mass multiplied by the gravitational acceleration. Therefore, our static system is currently in equilibrium and must adhere to the following:

$$\Sigma \vec{F_x} = 0, \text{therefore: } T_1 \cdot \cos 45 - T_2 \cdot \cos 60 = 0$$

$$\frac{\sqrt{2}}{2}T_1 - \frac{1}{2}T_2 = 0 \text{ or } T_1 = T_2/\sqrt{2}$$

$$\Sigma \vec{F_y} = 0, \text{therefore: } T_1 \cdot \sin 45 + T_2 \cdot \sin 60 - m \cdot g = 0$$

$$\frac{\sqrt{2}}{2}T_1 + \frac{\sqrt{3}}{2}T_2 - m \cdot g = 0$$

$$\frac{\sqrt{2}}{2} \cdot \frac{1}{\sqrt{2}}T_2 + \frac{\sqrt{3}}{2}T_2 - m \cdot g = 0$$

$$T_2 = \frac{2mg}{1+\sqrt{3}} \text{ and } T_1 = \frac{T_2}{\sqrt{2}}$$

We have now described a system for a weightless mass for the two string tensions. If we apply a specific force for our system we can easily calculate the tension on each string. Suppose we have a 10kg mass hanging at the end of our system. The tension in string 2 would be approximately 71.81N. The tension in string 1 would be approximately 50.78N.

Now that we have explored two examples of decomposing vectors to examine forces, let us look at another type of force known as a *moment*. A moment, also known as *torque*, is the force that tends to rotate a body around an axis. A familiar application associated with the concept of a moment or torque is a wrench or plier used to turn a bolt. A *moment* can be easily calculated by multiplying the length of the lever arm by the force being applied at a perpendicular. The moment is represented as a vector that is perpendicular to the plane of rotation.

Let us return to our eyehook example. In Figures 19.1 and 19.2, the eyehook had already been screwed into the wall bracket. But what kind of force was necessary to do this? Clearly the problem is somewhat dynamic because the force needed to turn the eyehook increases with the depth of the screw. To a large extent, it is a dynamic friction problem. Let us consider a static problem where we want to calculate the moment about the axis of the eyehook at a given depth. If we were to apply a force of 10N perpendicular to a lever arm of 30cm, we would multiply the force and the lever arm length and conclude that $M_o = 10N(0.3m) = 3N \cdot m$.

In a similar example, Figure 19.4 illustrates the forces being applied to a hexbolt at an angle of $30°$. Note that the force being applied is not perpendicular to the lever arm so the torque cannot be calculated directly. Instead, the force is applied downward in a vertical direction and we must translate the force to a perpendicular component. The length of the wrench is 35cm and a 20N force is being applied in the negative y direction.

Figure 19.4: Torque Calculation on a Hexbolt at an Angle:

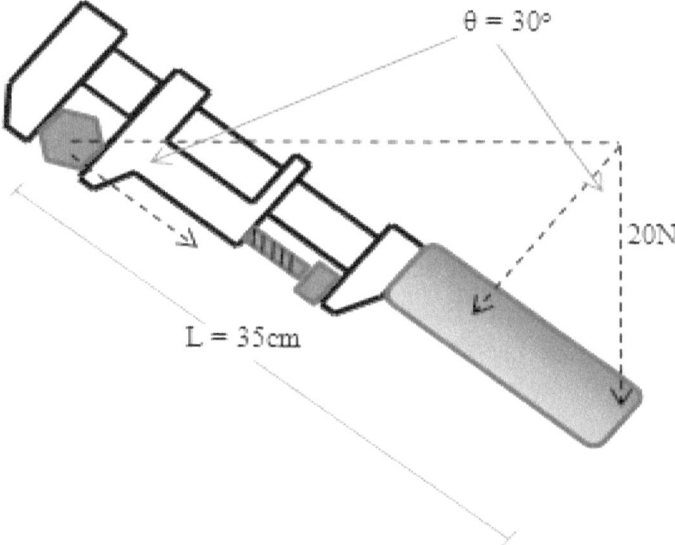

As we can see, the force is being applied to the wrench in the negative y direction but the normal force must be calculated to determine the moment on the hexbolt. With some basic triangle geometry, we can determine that the angle between the applied force and the normal force is also 30°. We can then calculate the force perpendicular to the wrench to be 20·cos30°. Our moment calculation is then our perpendicular force multiplied by the length of the wrench. M_h = 20·cos 30 (0.35m). The result is 6.06N in the negative z-direction.

As far as the direction of the resultant moment vector is concerned, recall that the direction of the resulting moment must be perpendicular to the plane of rotation. You may have noticed, however, that there is one additional consideration. Does the resulting vector go in the positive or negative z direction? This question can be answered with a basic property of torque called the *Right Hand Rule*. If you were to grasp a vertical pole with your right hand, your fingers would follow a counterclockwise direction in the x-y plane as you look down from above your hand. From this orientation, your thumb points in the positive z direction. The resulting vector of a moment always points in the direction of your thumb. If we were to grasp the same pole so that our fingers gripped the pole in a clockwise direction, our thumb would point in the negative z direction. We can then see from our diagram that because the wrench is being forced in the clockwise direction that our resultant vector must be in the negative z direction. To some extent this is what is responsible for the old saying "lefty loosey, righty tighty." As we turn a bolt clockwise, the bolt goes into the plane, which represents the negative direction. Alternately, if we rotate the same bolt counterclockwise, the bolt raises up out of the plane, which represents the positive direction.

SUMMARY

For the most part, many engineering statics applications can be resolved by decomposing vectors into their horizontal and vertical components. The goal of these kinds of calculations is to help determine the forces within a rigid body structure so that the devices they represent will function properly and safely. There is, of course, virtually no end to the complexity that exists with mechanical systems. Statics alone represents a number of challenges, and historically effective designs are complicated by various design constraints and other factors such as aesthetics. Engineers must be thoughtful in their designs so that solutions to complex problems can be described mathematically in comprehensive and convincing ways. In some sense, the design cycle of engineering follows the elements of Science, Technology, Engineering, and Mathematics learning cycle. That is to say that mathematics is the foundation for the description of all physical phenomena.

ADDITIONAL READINGS

McMahon, D. (2006). Statics and Dynamics Demystified. McGraw Hill Professional, 1st Ed. ISBN: 978-0071478830.

Meriam, J.L., & Kraige, L.G. (2010). Engineering Mechanics: Statics. John Wiley & Sons, Inc. ISBN: 978-0-470-49977-1

ARTICLE 20: USING CALCULUS IN PRODUCT DESIGN

ABSTRACT: The following article on the uses of calculus in the engineering design process demonstrates how advanced mathematical computation methods using calculus are necessary in defining the parameters for solving materials and methods problems. The premise is that many of the algebraic and geometric procedures used to illustrate previous examples are insufficient for sensitive calculations where certain amounts of precision are needed. Specifically, this article defines a model for calculating and optimizing the amount of a composite needed to manufacture a simple drinking cup.

INTRODUCTION

Materials selection in purchasing is one of the most basic factors necessary in creating successful manufacturing environments. Certainly, engineers design product solutions to problems and define those solutions mathematically to create a framework whereby the product can be created or reproduced. But design processes include properties other than those that can be represented using free body diagrams or dynamic geometric structures of the products themselves. In fact, efficiency and optimization are important elements of fabrication so that both materials and methods can be optimized. To engage in this kind of optimization, we need special mathematical tools that go well beyond the traditional mathematical structures we experience in secondary schools. One such mathematical tool I believe needs special attention is calculus.

The importance of calculus cannot be overstated in aspects of product development, particularly in the way it helps us examine important computational values as machines move, and movement patterns of parts change relative to one another. We rely on graphs for much of our engineering analysis, but we also have traditionally needed formulas to explain the mathematical behavior of machines. Unfortunately, we have been led to believe that these formulas have magically existed, in and of themselves, since the dawn of mathematical thinking. But, in fact, many of the algebraic and geometric formulas upon which we rely are *products* of mathematical engineering. In other words, we have defined formulas as the manufactured products of ideas when we have needed to complete some specific kind of calculation. In order to *manufacture* these formulas, we need to be able to establish constraints that sometimes take us beyond the computational capacity of traditional algebra and geometry.

Calculus is probably one of the greatest conceptions of humankind. Though Isaac Newton and Gottfried Leibniz are generally credited with the conception and early notation of calculus, the ability to examine very tiny parts of mathematical behavior patterns has given us great power to advance industry, and the methods can be understood by those with much less natural aptitude than Newton and Leibniz. The concepts of calculus and the resulting differential equations have been critical in the advancement of engineering in the modern world. Without the mathematics of calculus, we would likely still live with the technology of the 19th century.

INVESTIGATION AND NOTES

As you may know, calculus deals with rates of change, but the underpinnings of calculus have given us methods by which we can derive formulas and make calculations on changing processes too. With this in mind, we are going to establish the parameters for a very simple drinking cup design using the fundamentals of calculus. The idea here is to model production strategies, to some extent, by defining the parameters of our cup. Let us suppose that we are interested in using a 3D printer to create our own cup design. We need to be able to tell the computer that controls the printer what to do.

A good place to start in this process is to create dimensions for our cup. Knowing what a standard cup looks like helps, but we need to be thorough in our dimensional description. For example, a description of the measurement of base and height are not enough. We need to describe it as a circular cross section where the base and sides of the cup have a given thickness. We also need to define the extent to which the cup's diameter may change from top to bottom. We need to know if the cup is going to have a completely flat bottom or if it is going to set on a rim for added strength. Finally, we need to label a diagram that represents our measurements. An example diagram with dimensions is given in Figure 20.2. However, before we look at the illustration, it is worth deciding if we want our cup to hold a given amount of fluid because the amount of material used to create the cup can vary substantially around a constant amount of volume.

Let us assume that for our cup, we intend for the container to comfortably hold 12 fluid ounces. We would also like for our cup to be shaped like a circular *frustum*, which is like a cone with the pointed end removed. In order to calculate our dimensions, we need to make a number of arbitrary decisions. The reason is that many different variations of top and bottom radii and height will result in a 12 oz. quantity.

For our cup, we are going to arbitrarily decide that we want a frustum shaped cup of a circular cross section with the height at 12cm and the top and bottom diameters only differing by 2 cm.

With these as our initial parameters, we can calculate the radii using the formula for the volume of a circular frustum. These parameters were chosen based on the relative size of a 12 oz. soda can. Figure 20.1 defines the method of calculating the radius parameters based on the known values for height and volume. Note that we will be using h = 12 cm and V = 355 cm³. Further, because we are defining the top and bottom diameters as being only 2 cm difference, we are going to use *R* as the radius of the top of the cup and *r = R – 1* as the radius of the bottom of the cup.

Figure 20.1: Calculation of Radii Given the Height and Capacity

$$V = \frac{\pi \cdot h}{3}(R^2 + Rr + r^2)$$

$$355 \leq \frac{3.14 \cdot 12}{3}(R^2 + R(R-1) + (R-1)^2)$$

$$355 \leq 12.56(R^2 + R^2 - R + R^2 - 2R + 1)$$

$$355 \leq (3R^2 - 3R + 1)$$

$$28.26 \leq 3R^2 - 3R + 1$$

$$0 \leq 3R^2 - 3R - 27.26$$

$$R \approx 3.55, \quad r \approx 2.55$$

The resulting quadratic equation gives us a positive quantity of R = 3.55, which would be the radius of the top of the cup. We do not need to consider the opposing negative value because it is a non-physical quantity. This gives us an inside diameter of approximately 7.1 cm at the rim of the cup, which is slightly larger than the widest section of a soda can. The inside diameter of the bottom of the cup would be approximately 5.1 cm, which is slightly smaller than the narrowest section of a soda can. The height of the cup was defined to be the same as the soda can so our radius solution seems reasonable. We can now construct our diagram with a few additional parameters such as the thickness of the cup at different locations. Figure 20.2 illustrates the design parameters of the cup.

Figure 20.2: Design Parameters for a 12 Fl. Oz. Cup

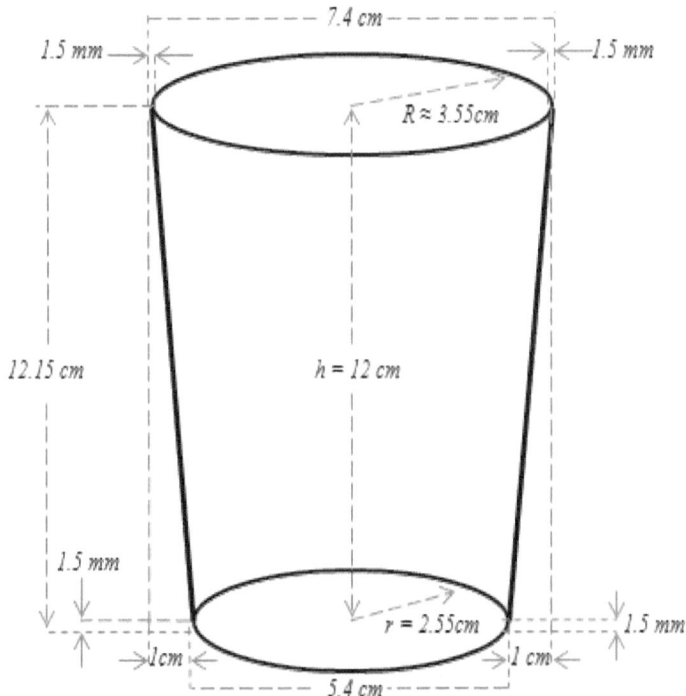

Our diagram, with the given measurements, is now fairly complete. Note, specifically, that both inside and outside dimensions are given so that the measurements account for the thickness of the composite material used to make the cup. Note also that the initial volume calculation was completed with the measurements given for the inside of the cup; that which represents the actual capacity of fluid it will hold.

Because we are dealing with a shape that is the frustum of a circular cone, for which the formula is already defined, the task of calculating the quantity of production material in cubic centimeters is not terribly difficult. All we will really need to do to find the quantity of material is calculate the difference between the larger frustum, represented by the outside measurements and the smaller frustum represented by the inside measurements.

$$V_c = V_O - V_I$$

$$V_c = \frac{\pi \cdot 12.15}{3}(3.7^2 + 3.7 \cdot 2.7 + 2.7^2)$$
$$- \frac{\pi \cdot 12}{3}(3.55^2 + 3.55 \cdot 2.55 + 2.55^2)$$

$$\approx 40.2 \; cm^3$$

Our resulting value of 40.2 cubic centimeters appears to be a reasonable solution. If we were to envision an equivalent amount in the shape of a cube, it would measure approximately 3.43 cm per side. If we were to then manufacture this cup on our 3D printer, we would need to create a program code that would follow the exact specifications given in Figure 20.2. If this were carefully done, we could accurately predict the amount of material used for each cup.

So far, we have not used calculus to complete any of the design parameters, but that is about to change. Let us suppose that we want to redesign our cup so that the lateral surface was curved from the bottom to the top. The simplest way to describe this mathematically would be to have the figure follow a known function. The diagram, with measurements, would be fairly difficult to produce because the amount of tapering from the top of the cup to the bottom would be meaningless without knowing how it was curving between those two dimensions.

We will approach this problem slightly differently than the last in that the cup is going to be oriented sideways with different design parameters, and follow a root function within a given domain. Figure 20.3 illustrates the design parameters of the new cup design.

Figure 20.3: Design Parameters for a Cup with a Curved Surface

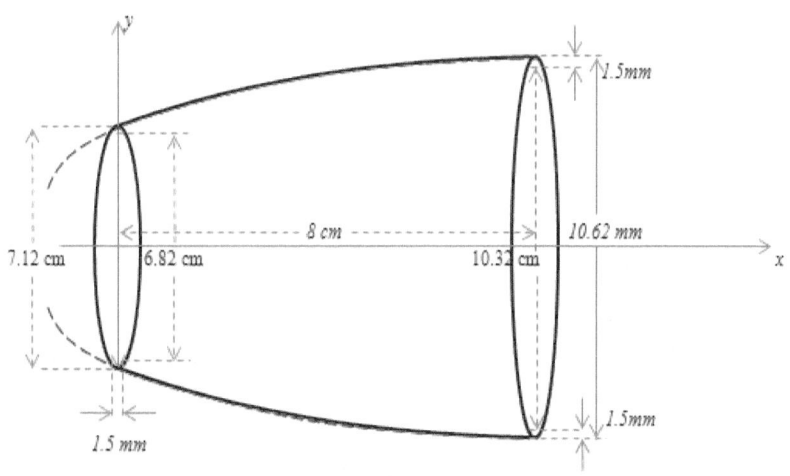

Inside dimensions determined by the function: $f(x) = \sqrt{x+2} + 2$ rotated about the x-axis

Outside dimensions determined by the function: $f(x) = \sqrt{x+2} + 2.15$ rotated about the x-axis

    The design parameters for our new cup do not look too much different than the original cup other than that the measurements themselves are different. We are still using the 1.5mm thickness but our cup is much broader and only 8 cm high in this model. The question is, will it still hold 355 cm^3 of fluid? Our calculation becomes a bit more difficult because we now are dealing with a lateral surface that is curved, which makes the calculations more cumbersome from an algebra standpoint. In fact, we do not have a formula to calculate the volume for this slightly odd shape in the way we did for the frustum. The technique we are going to use to calculate the volume of composite needed for the cup will once again be the volume of the inside measurements subtracted from the volume of the outside measurements. To do this, we will use an integration model that will calculate the area under the function we have defined, but then rotate that curve about the x-axis. By rotating a single point along the curve around the x-axis, we would essentially trace out the path of a circle. That circle would have a radius that is the distance of the point from the x-axis, namely $f(x)$ at the point x. The circular areas swept out by all of the individual points will be summed to find the volume. Finally, the inner volume will be subtracted from the outer volume. Note also that the inner function will be integrated starting at 0.15 cm as opposed to 0 to account for the thickness of the bottom.

We need to calculate the following where VC is the volume of the cup, V_O is the outside volume and V_I is the inside volume:

$$V_C = V_O - V_I$$

Recall that rotation around an axis calculated thusly:

$$V_T = \int_a^b \pi [f(x)]^2 \, dx$$

Therefore our calculation is completed as follows:

$$V_O = \int_0^8 \pi \left(\sqrt{x + 2.15} + 2.15\right)^2 dx$$

$$V_I = \int_{0.15}^8 \pi \left(\sqrt{x + 2} + 2\right)^2 dx$$

$$V_C = \int_0^8 \pi \left(\sqrt{x + 2.15} + 2.15\right)^2 dx - \int_{0.15}^8 \pi \left(\sqrt{x + 2} + 2\right)^2 dx$$

$$V_C = \pi \int_0^8 (x + 2.15) + 4.3\sqrt{x + 2.15} + 4.6225 \, dx$$

$$- \pi \int_{0.15}^8 x + 2 + 4\sqrt{x + 2} + 4 \, dx$$

$$V_C = \pi \int_0^8 x + 4.3\sqrt{x + 2.15} + 6.7725 \, dx - \pi \int_{0.15}^8 x + 4\sqrt{x + 2} + 4 \, dx$$

$$V_C = \pi \int_0^8 x + 4.3(x + 2.15)^{1/2} + 6.7725 \, dx$$

$$- \pi \int_{0.15}^8 x + 4(x + 2)^{1/2} + 4 \, dx$$

$$V_C = \pi \left[\frac{x^2}{2} + \frac{8.6(x + 2.15)^{3/2}}{3} + 6.7725x \right]_0^8$$

$$- \pi \left[\frac{x^2}{2} + \frac{8(x + 2)^{3/2}}{3} + 4x \right]_{0.15}^8$$

$$V_O = \pi \left[\frac{8^2}{2} + \frac{8.6(10.15)^{3/2}}{3} + 6.7725(8) \right]$$

$$- \pi \left[\frac{0^2}{2} + \frac{8.6(2.15)^{3/2}}{3} + 6.7725(0) \right]$$

$$= 533.58 \, cm^3$$

$$V_I = \pi \left[\frac{8^2}{2} + \frac{8(10)^{3/2}}{3} + 4(8) \right]$$

$$- \pi \left[\frac{0.15^2}{2} + \frac{8(2.15)^{3/2}}{3} + 4(0.15) \right] = 437.65 \, cm^3$$

$$V_T = 533.58 \, cm^3 - 437.65 \, cm^3 = 95.93 \, cm^3$$

As we can see from our calculation, the curved outer surface of the cup, even though shorter by a third, requires over twice the production material. Granted, it does hold nearly 100 cm^3 more volume, but it is still quite a lot more inefficient than the other style of cup. This phenomenon is logical when you think about it. A curved line is longer between to fixed points and therefore requires more material. But, there are ways in which a little more material can result in a lot more volume, which brings us to our next point.

The calculation for the curved cup was fairly complex compared to that of the frustum shaped cup. How would we go about changing the parameters of our curved cup and optimizing our solution without having to individually test all of the potentially changing values with a cumbersome formula? The solution relies on a series of partial differential equations, which is beyond the scope of this book; nevertheless, we do have some efficient avenues for finding a solution in a part of STEM that has been largely unrepresented in this book and that is *technology*. By setting up a series of spreadsheet tables, for example, we could simulate a more complex process and analyze the patterns in each of the tables that are responsible for the largest growth in volume compared to the smallest growth in material used.

We would also want to consider the advantages of certain shapes of cups depending on how they might be used. For example, cylindrical cups have a distinct disadvantage simply because they do not stack easily. Frustum shaped containers stack naturally and, as a result are much easier to transport and store. On the other hand, our frustum shaped cup has a centroid that is fairly high so it would be much more susceptible to spilling.

SUMMARY

What we are really exploring here is the concept of mathematical modeling within the STEM learning cycle. If we look carefully at how engineering tasks are approached, we find that the problems are commonly modeled mathematically before any mock-ups are created. This modeling includes analytical descriptions of our problem, and often diagrams as we did here with our cup problem. The STEM cycle is really one of efficiency that is a bit broader than the scientific method or an engineering heuristic, but it relies on the natural relationships between the STEM disciplines. That is to say, Science is applied Mathematics, Engineering is applied Science, Technology is applied Engineering. When we want to improve the technology, we model the improvements with new mathematical descriptions and the cycle starts again. The entire cycle of STEM learning can be approached as a careful integration of ideas from each of the disciplines.

Irrespective of the problem, calculus remains perhaps the single most useful mathematical tool in the history of engineering production. And though it may seem that all that can be invented has been invented, we are faced with a world that needs efficiency. There are many problems that will benefit from thoughtful reconsideration using the language of mathematics. For that reason, it is important to look at mathematics as a descriptive language rather than as a series of ambiguous textbook problems. Perhaps that is the first thing that needs careful reconsideration.

ADDITIONAL READINGS

Kamien, M. L., & Schwartz, N. L. (2012). Dynamic Optimization: The Calculus of Variations and Optimal Control in Economics and Management. 2nd Ed. Dover Books on Mathematics. ISBN: 978-0486488561

Polak, E. (1997). Optimization: Algorithms and Consistent Approximations (Applied Mathematical Sciences). Springer. ISBN: 978-03879497

INDEX OF ARTICLE TERMS & AUTHORITIES

amperes, 310
anchor escapement, 278
Antikythera, 219
apothem, 24, 87
Archimedes of Syracuse, 37,45,46,54,55,78,103,336,356,359
armillary, 193, 194
Astrolabe, 9,200,201,202,203,212-215,219, 220,338
Basel problem, 79-81
Bernoulli
   jacob, 46, 55
Brachistochrone, 11, 45,46,55,59,60,66, 103, 263
Buffon's needle problem, 83
Chebyshev, 238, 244, 245
Chord-Chord Power Theorem, 12, 18-24
concave lenses, 345
convex lenses, 345
current, 306-314,327
curves of uniform width, 223
Cycloid, 55-26, 66,69-75,234
d'Ocagne, 111
Diffuse reflection, 340
draftsman's method, 38
Elements (The), 92,93
Ellipse, 36-44,64,213,215,216,222,231,232-234
Epicycloid, 61,62,74,75.234
Escapement, 266-270,275,277,278
Euclid, 45, 92, 337,360
Euler, 77,79, 80, 236
free body diagram, 361,370
Frustum, 372-380
Galileo, 47
gelosia multiplication, 152

INDEX OF ARTICLE TERMS & AUTHORITIES

geometric centroid, 231,232
Geometric Mean, 22,23
geometric optics, 338
Gnomon, 179-191,194,197
Goodwin, 88, 89
Guilloche patterns, 61-69, 73,75,76
Hart, 258
Herodotus, 85
Hoekens, 238, 283, 284,286,287,290,293-298
Huygens, 263, 337
Hypocycloid, 61,62,66,70,73-75,234
inscribed angle, 15,18,19
Inversor, 246
Jansen, 283, 290-301
Kepler, 31, 43
L'Hopital, 55
Law of Cosines, 97,98
Lens, 43,335,336,342,344-47,356
Lever, 239-242,256,269,272,273,300,359,361,366
Logarithms, 117,118,120,125,148,150,151,174,176
Macadie, 307
Mater, 213
Mechanics, 31,238-242,304,305,358,359,369
Meridian Mark, 183, 184
Napier, 109,151,152,159,160,162,163,165-168
Newton, 7, 31, 55, 60, 202, 265, 305, 337, 361, 362,371
Nilakantha, 79
Nomograph, 109-120,122-125,174
Ohm, 306-312,319,322,324,326,331-333
Pantograph, 256, 257
Peaucellier, 238,246,248,250,251
Pelekinon, 197, 198

INDEX OF ARTICLE TERMS & AUTHORITIES

Pendulum, 179,200,203,260-268,275,277,278
Pythagoras, 91
Pythagorean Identities, 27,96
Reflection, 193,202-209,211,212,335,337-341,343-345,348,352,356,357
Refraction, 335,341-343,346,347,353-357
Reitwiesner, 79
Resistance, 306-314, 317-320,322327,330-333
Reuleaux triangle, 221-236
Riemann
   bernhard, 80
Riemann Zeta Function, 80
Right Hand Rule, 368
Roberts, 258, 304
Sagitta, 12, 24
Sarrus, 258
Scheiner, 256, 257
Sliderule, 112,119, 124,131,132,134
Solution Shark, 109, 126-131
Specular reflection, 340
Statics, 305, 358-361,363,368,369
Stereographic Projection, 12,200,201,213-217
Sundial, 109,124,178-190,193-199,260,261
Tension Vector, 361-363
Thompson, 258
Torque, 31,269,271,273,274,294,297,366-368,372
Trammel method, 30,33-35,37
Venetian Squares, 152
Venn, 13
Versine, 26
Vesica Piscis, 12- 15, 111, 224,226
Voltage, 306,307,309-317,322,326

INDEX OF ARTICLE TERMS & AUTHORITIES

Watt, 223,224,230,238,239,242-244,258,259,310
White, 258

www.ingramcontent.com/pod-product-compliance
Lightning Source LLC
Chambersburg PA
CBHW021958160426
43197CB00007B/175